Historic Buildings of Waco, Texas

Funding for publication of this book
was generously provided by
Summerlee Foundation

Historic Buildings of Waco, Texas

Kenneth Hafertepe

Texas A&M University Press
College Station

♾ This paper meets the requirements of ANSI/NISO Z39.48–1992
(Permanence of Paper).
Binding materials have been chosen for durability.
Manufactured in China through Martin Book Management

Library of Congress Cataloging-in-Publication Data

Names: Hafertepe, Kenneth, 1955– author.
Title: Historic buildings of Waco, Texas / Kenneth Hafertepe.
Description: First edition. | College Station: Texas A&M University Press,
    [2022] | Includes bibliographical references and index.
Identifiers: LCCN 2022048664 (print) | LCCN 2022048665 (ebook) | ISBN
    9781648430831 (cloth) | ISBN 9781648430848 (ebook)
Subjects: LCSH: Historic buildings—Texas—Waco. | Waco (Tex.)—Buildings,
    structures, etc.
Classification: LCC F394.W12 H23 2022 (print) | LCC F394.W12 (ebook) |
    DDC 976.4/284—dc23/eng/20221007
LC record available at https://lccn.loc.gov/2022048664
LC ebook record available at https://lccn.loc.gov/2022048665

Unless otherwise indicated, all photographs are provided by the author.

CONTENTS

My recent book about historic homes in Waco was dependent on the many homeowners who have taken on the task of caring for an old house; a book about all other sort of historic buildings in Waco is somewhat different, as churches, commercial buildings, schools, and other such buildings are more often open to the public and almost always a shared responsibility. Because the relationship between many historic buildings and their owners is not as intimate as that between owners and their houses, it has often been easier to access the building but not as easy to hear how modern-day owners live and care for an old building.

The features of one historic building were particularly easy to recall because I have sat in its pews for more than twenty years: St. Paul's Episcopal Church. Similarly, I have been able to experience the historic buildings of Baylor University for a similar amount of time, as I have been on the faculty for that long.

As I mentioned in *Historic Homes of Waco, Texas*, I am indebted to many libraries, especially to the Texas Collection, which is housed in the old Carroll Library, discussed in this book. Amie Oliver, Paul Fisher, Brian Simmons, Benna Vaughan, Geoff Hunt, and many others at the Texas Collection have been a tremendous help over the years. I have been very fortunate to have such an outstanding resource just a short walk from my office. And in recent years it has been made even more accessible via the internet; at the Baylor University Library web page one can peruse the Baylor Digital Collections, including Waco city directories, Waco newspapers, and a collection of blueprints of Baylor buildings. The Armstrong Browning Library is an architectural gem as well as a treasure trove for research; early in my time at Baylor Kathryn L. Brogdon provided photocopies of obscure but helpful articles about the ABL that it has taken me years to use. The Waco-McLennan County Library also has an excellent local history room, and Sean Sucliffe provided me with important information for this book.

Beyond Waco I have been able to access the collection of the Alexander Architectural Archive at the University of Texas (named for my one of my old UT professors, Drury Blakeley Alexander), which contains such treasures as the drawings for the Amicable Life Insurance Building (the ALICO), for the spire of the post-tornado Fifth Street Methodist Church, and for the new plans for First Methodist Church. It is always a good day to visit with Nancy Sparrow and see what treasures she has found for me.

I have also benefited from the kindness of institutions that have shared architectural drawings of their building, notably the Dr Pepper Museum and Free Enterprise Institute (thanks to Chris Dyer, Joy Summar-Smith, and Rachael Nadeau Johnson) and Temple Rodef Sholom, which shared blueprints, specifications, and a wealth of other information.

The internet has made possible the Portal to Texas History, which has opened the door (sorry) to many precise internet searches of newspapers, books, and even applications for historical markers. The Perry-Castañeda Library Map Collection at the University of Texas has been a crucial source of Sanborn Fire Insurance Maps before 1925; and the Library of Congress, for such maps before and after 1925. The website Newspapers.com also allowed for excellent searches by words or phrases; I have also used HeritageQuest to utilize the US Census to find people who had Waco in their past, present, or future. I am grateful for all of these wonderful tools.

I have also been the beneficiary of good old-fashioned human kindness. I am thankful for the friendly welcome and the tours I received at many houses of worship, such as the Austin Avenue Methodist Church (now the downtown branch of First Methodist Church), New Hope Baptist Church, First Presbyterian Church, Temple Rodef Sholom, St. James Methodist Episcopal Church, Mighty Wind Worship Center (originally Central Christian Church), and Greater Light New Missionary Baptist Church (originally St. John's Methodist Church). I experienced St. Mary of the Assumption Catholic Church and St. Louis Catholic Church several times because my father, Charles Hafertepe, was not going to miss Sunday Mass just because he came down to repair plumbing or to paint walls or to do anything that needed doing around my house.

I am also grateful for the many discussions I have had with other historians of Waco, especially Eric Ames, Willis T. Bradford, Don Davis, and B. J. Greaves. Although I sometimes feel like a historic building prophet crying in the wilderness, it is reassuring to know that there are actually several colleagues with deep knowledge who also have been leaders in preserving the heritage of Waco.

I probably should not put this into print because it might cause whatever reputation I have as a highly productive author and photographer to evaporate, but several of my most recent books, and the many, many color illustrations, have been made possible by the Summerlee Foundation of Dallas. John Crain, Ron Tyler, and Gary Smith—you guys have made possible many of my crazy dreams. Thank you!

And speaking of grants and grant applications, I must thank Joanne Spitz, former senior director of Grant Initiatives in University Advancement at Baylor, who shepherded the Summerlee money through the appropriate Baylor channels.

And, of course, another essential part of the enterprise is Texas A&M University Press. This is my fourth book with Team TAMU, and this one produced in spite of a worldwide pandemic. Thanks as always to Jay Dew, Thom Lemmons, Katie Duelm, copyeditor Cynthia Lindlof, and the whole team. And I am very appreciative of the two anonymous reviewers, whose comments were critical in the best possible way.

Historic Buildings
of Waco, Texas

Waco's Historic Buildings

THE CITY OF WACO prides itself as the "Heart of Texas" and in the second half of the nineteenth century grew to become one of the most important towns, if not the most important Texas town, between Austin and Dallas. Like many small towns it can be accused of provincialism, though that idea could be rebutted with the observation that provincialism can simply be independence and self-sufficiency. Whatever one chooses to call it, the little we know of Waco in its early years reminds us that it was a frontier town built to remind its settlers of the places from which they came. Its origins were largely Southern—the Deep South but also the Upland South—but from an early date its population was refreshed with new citizens from all over the United States, including newly freed African Americans, and with immigrants from a variety of European countries.

For its first quarter century Waco was built by carpenters, brick masons, and others in the building trades. The first two architects to settle permanently in Waco were Wesley Clark Dodson, who arrived in 1875, and W. W. Larmour, who arrived some four years later. Dodson was a native of Morgan County in northern Alabama, while Larmour was from Hackensack, New Jersey; though from different regions they both received their training on construction sites. Dodson designed the Gothic Revival Fifth Street Methodist Church and the McLennan County Courthouse, the first of Dodson's many Second Empire Texas courthouses. Larmour designed Waco's City Hall, the First Baptist Church and Temple Rodef Sholom, and the two earliest buildings for Baylor University after the college moved from Independence, Texas.

In the early twentieth century a new generation of architects moved to Waco. Other than Roy E. Lane, who studied at the University of Minnesota, these were men whose training was practical rather than academic. Milton W. Scott served as chief draftsman for W. W. Larmour for a decade before partnering with Glen Allen, then T. Brooks Pearson, and finally opening his own firm. Scott's drafting room became the training ground for future Waco architects, including E. McIver Ross and Herman F. Cason (who later worked sometimes together, sometimes separately), and Birch D. Easterwood. James P. Baugh was a draftsman for Easterwood before striking out on his own, and Harry L. Spicer worked for Roy E. Lane before opening his own practice of architecture and engineering. In 1945 Spicer hired John William "Bill" Bush, who had an architecture degree from Rice University. With Spicer's retirement in 1953, the firm became Bush and Witt.

The first architect to design a Waco building who was not a Waco architect or builder was William Pitt Wentworth of Boston, who designed St. Paul's Episcopal Church in 1878. An Episcopalian himself, Wentworth designed Episcopal churches in New England, Upstate New York, and Virginia. St. Paul's was the farthest of Wentworth's churches from Boston, and St. Paul's is the Waco historic building designed farthest from Waco. (Coming in second was the Coca-Cola Bottling Plant, designed in Los Angeles by Robert Derrah.)

Seventy percent of the churches in this book were designed by local architects. Larmour's building for First Baptist was in a sober Victorian Gothic style, while Temple Rodef Sholom was in a picturesque style with Gothic arches and onion domes, which was thought appropriate for synagogues. Milton W. Scott designed neoclassical replacements for both of these congregations: a somewhat freewheeling and ornamental building for the Baptists and a more straightforward version of the style for the Jewish community. In the 1940s and 1950s Walter Cocke, a Waco native, designed St. Mary of the Assumption Catholic Church for Waco's Catholics and St. Alban's for Episcopalians and masterminded a remarkable Colonial Revival remodeling of Columbus Avenue Baptist. (Cocke also designed the earliest education building for First Baptist, running along Fifth Street.)

Though out-of-town architects were fewer in number, they left Waco with some remarkable buildings. Besides Wentworth, Frederick M. Mann, a graduate of the School of Architecture at the Massachusetts Institute of Technology, designed the First Presbyterian Church in Waco, while R. H. Hunt of Chattanooga, Tennessee, a graduate of the school of hard knocks, designed the Austin Avenue Methodist Church. Both of these churches were in the Gothic Revival style, though remarkably different takes on the style. Mann's church for Presbyterians was a study in asymmetry, with a three-story tower at the corner of Austin and Eleventh, while the interior was graced with a hammer beam ceiling. The Methodist Church took a very different approach, with formal symmetry and the main floor atop a very high basement. It, too, featured a tall tower, but this was placed toward the rear facing Thirteenth Street.

Although the 1910s and 1920s were a time of racial tension in Waco, with a horrific lynching and Ku Klux Klan parades, three African American congregations built impressive new sanctuaries, almost as if they were asserting through brick and mortar their right to worship and their right to full citizenship. Each one was in a different style. St. Paul's African Methodist Episcopal Church was in the Mission style; alas, this was demolished to make room for a hotel. The architect of New Hope Baptist Church (1921–23) is unknown, but it was a handsome essay in the Neoclassical style. The congregation of St. James Methodist Episcopal Church hired a white architect, Carleton W. Adams of San Antonio, to design a new building in the Tudor Gothic style in 1924. (Adams had recently designed a similar church in San Antonio: St. Paul's Methodist Church, also an African American congregation.)

Two of the most modern church buildings in Waco were designed by architects from elsewhere in Texas: Temple Rodef Sholom by MacKie and Kamrath of Houston, and First Methodist Church by Henry J. Steinbomer of San Antonio. By the 1960s architects were expected to have college degrees. Fred MacKie and Karl Kamrath attended Rice University in Houston, though their Waco clients would have been more interested in their 1949 design for Temple Emanu El in Houston, a sophisticated essay in the style of Frank Lloyd Wright—Rodef Sholom was also very Wrightian. Steinbomer attended the University of Texas, then began his career as an architectural traditionalist; after World War II, he began to search for modern expressions of faith. First Methodist in Waco was his last church before he passed away. As the congregation continued to grow, many additions designed by other architects were made, and their work has basically swallowed up the original building.

Commercial buildings and buildings for wholesale commerce and manufacturing were among those most likely to have been designed by local architects. Milton W. Scott designed at least two buildings as early automobile showrooms, for Central Motor Company (Dodge) and the McDermott Motor Company (Buick). Early gas stations, of which there are quite a few in Waco, tended to be based on one of a small number of designs that came from corporate headquarters. Harry L. Spicer designed basic commercial buildings such as the Clemens Building at Austin and Seventh, but also Citizens National Bank, a middle-of-the-block neoclassical temple, and the one-story store at 1018 Austin, which would bring in enough rent to pay the property taxes; such buildings were thus nicknamed "taxpayers." Another taxpayer, just across the street at 1023 Austin, was designed by Herman F. Cason.

The designers of two of Waco's most iconic commercial buildings have been virtually forgotten until now. The Elite Café at the Circle, a Spanish Colonial Revival coffee shop that is now known as Magnolia Table, was another design of Herman F. Cason. Another Waco icon was the small shopping center known as Sachs Austin Avenue, built in 1954, which has been known for many years as Sironia. It was designed by a recent arrival to Waco, Harris H. Roberts. Just across Austin from Sironia is a charming art deco building that was originally Losavio's Grocery Store. A drawing of the design was signed by J. Scribner Dunne, who worked for the Mailander furniture company in Waco; though Dunne sometimes did presentation drawings for other Waco architects, he may well have designed the building himself.

My research has uncovered only two architects of commercial buildings from out of town. One was Robert V. Derrah of Los Angeles, who designed the Coca-Cola Bottling Plant on Austin Avenue and had previously designed the Coke plant in Los Angeles. The other was A. C. Lenander of Columbus, Ohio, who built up a firm specializing in the design of banking houses and savings and loan buildings; he designed the First Federal Savings and Loan Building, which, ironically, stands across Austin Avenue from Derrah's building for Coke. The two make for an interesting contrast: the minimalist Art Deco style of the bottling plant and the ornate Colonial Revival of the savings and loan.

In the 1910s the design of skyscrapers was highly specialized, and the earliest tall buildings in Waco were designed in Fort Worth or Dallas. The Amicable Life Insurance Company Building, now better known as the ALICO, was designed by Sanguinet and Staats of Fort Worth. This firm designed many important skyscrapers in the 1910s, including the Burk Burnett Building in Fort Worth, the Carter Building in Houston, the Scarbrough Building in Austin, and the Rand Building in San Antonio. Unknown until now, Sanguinet and Staats also designed the Bankers Trust Building on Austin at Sixth. As was often the case with out-of-town architects, Sanguinet and Staats contracted with a local architect, Roy E. Lane, who would keep watch on the progress of the building. Often in Waco the design of the building is attributed to Lane, but all twenty-two drawings were done in Fort Worth by Sanguinet and Staats draftsmen. When the ALICO was built, the Carter Building in Houston was one story taller, though the ALICO was the second-tallest building in Texas for nearly two decades.

The terra-cotta classicism of the ALICO contrasted with the more progressive Prairie stylings of the Riggins Hotel, later known as the Raleigh Hotel, and now an unnamed and unloved office building. The architects were Lang and Witchell of Dallas, with Roy E. Lane once again as local associate. When this building was designed, the chief draftsman for Lang and Witchell was Charles Erwin Barglebaugh, an Arkansas native who had worked for Frank Lloyd Wright in Chicago for a year or so. The Waco building featured ornament of a type associated with Wright's master, Louis H. Sullivan, as did the original Hippodrome Theater just across Austin Avenue, though the Prairie style facade of the theater was obliterated when the theater was given an extreme makeover and adapted for talkies in the late 1920s.

Lang and Witchell continued in business for many years, though Barglebaugh left the firm in 1914. When they designed the Hilton Hotel (later the Roosevelt Hotel) in 1927, the style was closer to the Classical style of the ALICO than to the Prairie style of their own earlier design for the Riggins/Raleigh. For the Hilton the local associate was Milton W. Scott, and when the hotel proved such a success that Conrad Hilton wanted to double the size of the building, he hired not Lang and Witchell but Scott. The Waco architect was already intimately familiar with the original design because he had overseen its construction. A final Lang and Witchell building in town was Waco Hall on the Baylor University campus; Dudley S. Green, a native of England who lived in Waco at the beginning of the century, was the chief designer for the art deco building. Another Dallas firm working in Waco was C. W. Bulger and Son, which had designed the Praetorian Building in Dallas and produced a smaller version for Waco. Its extensive use of terra-cotta, mainly white but with accents in many colors, gave it a very distinctive appearance.

In the 1920s local architects began to venture into the design of tall buildings. Harry T. Spicer designed the Stratton Building, built to house a furniture store with offices above. It was a no-nonsense building, with a minimum of money spent on traditional ornament and with ample light from modern metal-frame windows. Spicer developed a reputation for designing buildings that were completed on-budget and on-schedule.

Birch D. Easterwood designed the Liberty National Bank Building located a few blocks down Austin Avenue, the tall-building equivalent of his many period houses of the 1920s and 1930s.

After World War II the 800 block of Washington Avenue, formerly the home of St. Mary's Catholic Church and the Academy of the Sacred Heart, became the heart of Waco's financial district. When the Catholics decamped to the west, this became the home of Pioneer Savings Association and of the First National Bank. The latter hired Wyatt C. Hedrick of Fort Worth, who had recently designed the Armstrong Browning Library at Baylor in conjunction with Eggers and Higgins of New York. For the First National Bank Hedrick proposed a low-slung three-story building that would have a tower rising out of the middle, with stone facades north and south and modern curtain walls—glass held in place by an inner frame of steel. It was to be built in two phases, first the western unit of three stories, then the tower and the eastern unit at Washington and Eighth. The scheme would echo the design of the United Nations Secretariat Building in New York City in some respects and of Lever House, the New York headquarters of Lever Brothers, in others. The western unit was built first, and the rest was never constructed. Instead, in 1964 a larger, boxier tower was built on the rest of the block to the designs of local architects Walter Cocke and Robert Bennett.

Waco once had a Victorian-era city hall and a county courthouse, the former by W. W. Larmour, the latter by Wesley C. Dodson, but both were later replaced. Those replacements have become historic in their own right: J. Riely Gordon designed the neoclassical county courthouse, which was built 1900–1902; and Harry L. Spicer designed the art deco City Hall, which was built 1929–30. In local lore Wesley C. Dodson "really" designed the 1902 courthouse because he helped choose the winning competition plan and supervised the construction. In reality Gordon had become the leading architect of Texas courthouses, and the McLennan County Courthouse reflected his transition from Richardsonian Romanesque to the Beaux-Arts classicism that become popular across the United States after the Columbian Exposition of 1892–93.

Spicer's City Hall was a relatively low-key example of the Art Deco style, appropriate given that the Great Depression had just begun. His use of ornament was so limited that the term "stripped classicism" would certainly apply to this building. The earlier city hall had served as the backdrop for the horrific lynching of Jesse Washington in 1916. That memory may have increased the desire for a new building, one that was not associated with the "Waco Horror" but that looked instead to Waco's future.

A new US Courthouse and Post Office was built on Franklin Avenue in 1936. Though local architects such as Milton W. Scott and Harry L. Spicer hoped to win the prize, it was designed in the office of the supervising architect of the Treasury. It was designed in Washington, but the actual architect was a native Texan, William H. Schimmelpfennig. As occurred with the new Waco City Hall, the Great Depression limited the amount that could be spent on ornament, which might be considered a frill. The courthouse had just enough Spanish Colonial trim to make the building presentable. A smaller building in the same style had just been built in 1931–32 a few blocks away. This was the new Central Fire

Station and Drill Tower, to the designs of T. Brooks Pearson, former partner of Milton W. Scott and another longtime Waco architect; the fire station was a much more successful exploration of the Spanish Colonial Revival style.

Waco's embrace of modern architecture was quite tentative, as is seen with the design for the Waco-McLennan County Library (1961) by Bush and Witt. Large panels of Alabama marble alternated with windows of plate glass. Another attempt at a definitively modern building was Bush and Dudley's Bledsoe-Miller Recreation Community Center in East Waco facing the Brazos River (1971–72). This building combined concrete, glazed red brick, and plate glass in a way that had not been done locally.

One of the grandest early twentieth-century buildings in town is Waco High School. Although the cornerstone states that it was designed by Waller and Field of Fort Worth, with Scott and Pearson associated, locals often cite it as a Scott and Pearson building. However, Marion L. Waller had recently designed eleven school buildings in Fort Worth, including a new high school that was a clear precedent for the Waco building. Scott was responsible for the east and west wings, and Pearson for the north wing, all following the style set by the original unit facing Columbus Avenue.

Waco High was built in an era of strict segregation, and its opulence makes an almost shocking contrast with the First District School for what were then termed "Colored" students. The two-story brick building had classrooms lit by large windows, but no restrooms and no lunchroom. It was separate but by no means equal. Despite many obstacles, Paul Quinn College in East Waco continued to grow. After a fire destroyed the main building in 1901, a new one was built, and the next major project was Johnson Hall built in 1921–23. Forgotten until now, the architect was William Sidney Pittman, son-in-law of Booker T. Washington and the most prominent African American architect in Texas in the first half of the twentieth century. It had little ornament but was spacious, fireproof, and built with steel-reinforced concrete. At this writing it is still standing despite years of neglect.

Baylor University tended to hire local architects as the campus was built, though there were some notable exceptions. The earliest buildings came from W. W. Larmour and his young partner, Samuel P. Herbert; Old Main and Georgia Burleson Hall, in a Victorian-style drawing much from the French Second Empire, remain campus icons. For the neoclassical Carroll Science Hall and Carroll Library, the university hired the Fort Worth firm of Messer and Smith. Both Howard Messer and S. Wemyss-Smith were natives of England, but their building reflected the impact of French Beaux-Arts classicism as had been promoted by the 1893 World's Fair in Chicago. Just a few years later Smith moved to Oklahoma City and joined forces with Solomon A. Layton to design the Oklahoma State Capitol (1914–17).

Starting with Brooks Dormitory (1919–21), the university, guided by President Samuel Palmer Brooks, settled on one architectural style and one architect: the Colonial Revival style as interpreted by local architect Birch D. Easterwood. The Colonial Revival was popular on college campuses across the country in the 1920s, but Baylor built in the style well into the 1930s, when other universities began to dabble with other revivals or with a variety of modernism. Red bricks, classical ornament, and slate roofs became the Baylor style.

Introduction

Easterwood, who was simultaneously designing houses in a variety of period styles all over Waco, designed Brooks for men, then Women's Memorial and Catherine Alexander Hall, culminating with Pat Neff Hall. Pat Neff was the largest and grandest of the Easterwood buildings; Governor Neff's favorite part of the building was the thing that was least colonial: a dome of stainless steel.

A few Baylor commissions did not go Easterwood's way. Waco Hall, which was to be an auditorium that could also serve as the university's chapel, was built with a large donation from the citizens of Waco, which may explain why the commission went to Lang and Witchell of Dallas, who had designed the Raleigh Hotel and then the Hilton Hotel. The Raleigh had reflected progressive tendencies of the Chicago school, and the Hilton, a more traditional Neoclassical style, but Waco Hall was a sophisticated art deco building, showing the influence of recent works such as the Nebraska State Capitol and the Los Angeles Public Library, both by Bertram Grosvenor Goodhue.

A. J. Armstrong, chair of the Baylor English Department and creator and curator of a large collection pertaining to Robert Browning and Elizabeth Barrett Browning, aspired to build a library to house this collection. He consulted with John Russell Pope, the architect of the National Archives building, the National Gallery of Art, and the Jefferson Memorial, but Pope died in 1937, leaving only a sketch of a facade. After World War II Armstrong was able to hire Eggers and Higgins, longtime associates of Pope, to collaborate with Texan Wyatt C. Hedrick, who had joined the firm of Sanguinet and Staats and eventually became the firm's sole proprietor. Hedrick is perhaps best remembered for his design work on the campus of Texas Tech University. The Armstrong Browning Library had an exterior that was as dry as a West Texas wind but an interior rich with allusions to England and Italy.

Another specialized building was to be erected for the Department of Religion. Josiah Blake Tidwell hoped to build Tidwell Bible Building to house classrooms, a chapel, and a large collection of Bibles. His son-in-law, Guy Carlander of Amarillo, was retained to design the building. Carlander's proposal for a high-rise building that far exceeded the university's budget led to the architect's dismissal, followed by a lawsuit. Birch Easterwood and his son Kenneth were still working on Baylor buildings, notably Herbert Lee Kokernot Hall and Marrs-McLean Gymnasium, and were tasked with designing a building for the amount the university was willing to spend. Their Tidwell Bible Building seemed to absorb some of the art deco spirit of adjacent Waco Hall but was draped with a great deal of neoclassical ornament.

Waco also has a long-standing connection with Freemasonry. The Grand Temple—the state headquarters—moved from Houston to Waco in 1904. The new temple was designed by James E. Flanders of Dallas. Little more than a decade later, Waco's local Lodge #92, chartered in 1852, decided to build a temple for its own use at Washington Avenue and Eighth. Milton W. Scott designed the new building, with the lodge on the upper floors and rentable space on the ground floor to generate income. Scott was the only local architect to work with the Masons. In 1927 the Scottish Rite Masons hired Herbert M. Greene of Dallas, who had designed several Masonic temples in Texas and was a Mason himself, to design their new temple at Seventh Street and Washington Avenue.

After World War II a new Grand Masonic Lodge was built on Columbus Avenue to replace the one on Franklin. Again, the Masons turned to Dallas architects Broad and Nelson, with Robert Leon White of Austin consulting. In addition to an auditorium seating more than thirty-seven hundred, there were offices, a museum, and a library. Apparently this building inspired the members of the Scottish Rite to build their own auditorium, museum, and library on Waco Drive, which Donald Nelson of Broad and Nelson also designed.

Waco was thus a typical small American city, albeit with an overlay of segregation as practiced in most Southern American cities. As the regional hub for processing, selling, and shipping cotton and other agricultural products, it grew slowly but consistently over time. The taste of Wacoans leaned toward the traditional—only here and there did locals embrace Prairie progressivism or avant-garde modernism. Yet Wacoans were concerned about quality and erected many fine buildings, although usually within the parameters of tried-and-true style. Many of these were designed by local architects, but often churches, skyscrapers, government buildings, and school buildings were designed in Dallas or Fort Worth or even farther away.

Within the city limits of Waco can be found many fine buildings in Victorian, Neoclassical, and other revival styles, and even occasionally in the Art Deco or Modern styles. At the same time, the segregated schools of Waco spoke to drastically different standards for white and black schools and the fatal fallacy of "separate but equal." In spite of its failings, which were similar to failings in many Southern cities and even in American cities farther afield that were supposedly built on a more fair foundation, Wacoans have built a city with many buildings worth preserving, a city that one can reasonably hope will be the starting point for an even better Waco.

A Note on Numbering

I began my study of Waco landmarks with my book *Historic Homes of Waco, Texas*, which was published in 2019. In that book the 120 houses were arranged in roughly chronological order, while trying to cluster houses by style as well. To avoid confusion with the houses discussed in that book, the numbers in *More Historic Homes of Waco, Texas*, which was still in preparation at that time, pick up with 121, while following a similar chronology and grouping. This separate volume, *Historic Buildings of Waco, Texas*, considers the subject by building type—churches, commercial and industrial buildings, skyscrapers, public buildings, educational buildings, and Masonic buildings and museums—and within each chapter the structures are arranged chronologically, in the hope of showing the evolution of each type. These later two volumes are cross-listed to each other and to *Historic Homes of Waco, Texas*, in the hope that this will inspire readers to think about the relation between people's houses, the places they worked, and other buildings that played a role in their lives and also to think about how class, race, and gender influence the places where we live.

St. Paul's Episcopal Church

Houses of Worship

1. St. Paul's Episcopal Church

515 Columbus Avenue / 1878–79
William Pitt Wentworth (Boston), architect

Waco's Episcopal church is not the oldest congregation in town, but it has the oldest surviving church building. Founded in 1863, the congregation worshipped from 1869 to 1879 in a small frame structure at South Fourth Street and Webster Avenue, catty-corner from the Fort House. The growth of the congregation led to plans for a larger and more permanent building. Land was acquired on the north side of downtown, backing up to Barron's Creek. The neighborhood was decidedly mixed: one block to the east was the home of Champe and Emma McCulloch, who were leading members of the congregation; at the other end of the property, facing Sixth Street, were six scraggly wooden houses, marked on the 1889 Sanborn Map as "Negro Tenements."

The congregation commissioned plans from William Pitt Wentworth, a Boston architect in his late thirties. A native of Bellows Falls, Vermont, Wentworth worked and studied with English-born architect Henry C. Dudley in New York City. With his partner, Frank Wills, and on his own Dudley had designed many Episcopal churches in New York but also churches as far away as Huntsville, Alabama, and Nashville, Tennessee. After the Civil War Wentworth moved to Boston and opened his own practice. An Episcopalian himself, Wentworth would go on to design numerous Episcopal churches, including ones in Woods Hole, Massachusetts; Jamestown, New York; and Norfolk, Virginia. There is no evidence that Wentworth ever visited Waco; presumably the builders of the church had to rely on the drawings and materials sent from the northeast, mainly the windows and altar fittings.

The cornerstone of St. Paul's was laid on August 15, 1878, and the first service was held June 15, 1879. The building was wood-framed with a shingled roof and an eighty-five-foot belfry at the southeast corner. The prominent chancel was a clear expression of the importance to the congregation of the Holy Eucharist—the sharing of the body and blood of Jesus in communion. Buttresses alternated with diamond-paned stained-glass windows with pointed tops, hinged on the side so that they could swing inward at the top. On the roof were diminutive dormer windows, which could open to provide ventilation.

In the interior the structural posts were set within the wall; the exposed rafters landed on these posts. However, another vertical member was attached to the upper part of each post by a metal plate and large metal bolts. At the upper part of these posts were short horizontal beams that projected out about four feet; they were supported by angled struts below (known as hammer braces) and in turn supported curving timbers known as collar braces. Closer to the ridge tie beams ran across the entire space between rafters. This elaborate hammer beam ceiling, which allowed a wider interior without the use of interior columns, must have been a very impressive statement in a new town like Waco.

Halfway between each post was a stained-glass window with a pointed Gothic arch. The walls were covered with wooden wainscoting up to the tops of the trefoil pew ends; the sills of the stained-glass windows rested on the wainscot. The plaster walls were stenciled above the wainscoting, around the windows, and above and beneath the exposed wooden beam (the plate), which ran from the front to the back of the church. (This stenciling has been covered over in later repaintings.)

His years in New York allowed Wentworth to suggest that the congregation order stained glass and other church furnishings from J & R Lamb, Church Furnishers, of New York, a firm founded in 1857. Indeed, given that Wentworth worked for an architect who specialized in designing churches, it seems highly likely that he knew Joseph and Richard Lamb personally. J & R Lamb designed seven windows for the chancel and the west wall. The chancel glass focused on Christ as the Good Shepherd, flanked by windows devoted to St. John and St. Paul. On the west wall were four windows representing the Evangelists, above which was a rose window centered on a pelican feeding her young, surrounded by eight smaller windows symbolizing aspects of faith. All the windows on the side walls were cathedral glass—a lovely euphemism for cheaper, diamond-shaped pieces of stained glass that were non-pictorial. In addition to the ancient tradition of stained glass, the church was lit by thoroughly modern gas. In the middle of every third pew was a vertical pipe feeding three lamps. Even before plans for this building were begun, a bell had been ordered from the Meneely Bell Foundry in West Troy, New York (established 1826).

A two-story rectory was built in 1891, next to the tenement houses. The rectory did not face west toward Sixth Street but east toward the church building. It was designed by W. W. Larmour of Waco, who designed many fine Waco homes in the Victorian era as well as the original buildings of Baylor's campus in Waco. In 1897 the rectory burned, but it was immediately rebuilt. It was reoriented to face Columbus Avenue, which used to run where the St. Paul's parking lot is now located (only for that one block).

Also in 1897 the church was enlarged, with the addition of forty-seven feet at the west end. This increased the number of pews but also allowed for a much larger chancel. The floor of the sanctuary had always been elevated; now the floor in front of this was raised to provide room for the organ, choir, lectern, and pulpit.

Another addition happened in 1906, with the erection of the Parish House, a T-shaped building that just touched the church at its northwest corner. By 1926 a gymnasium had been built west and northwest of the rectory, a project that seems to have finally removed the tenement houses.

In the 1930s the church embarked on an ambitious new program of adding stained-glass windows under the leadership of rector Everett Holland Jones and parishioner Julia Sarratt Sinclair. Many of the new windows were made by Franz Mayer of Munich, Germany. The Mayer firm had been established in 1847 and opened a New York branch in 1888. The family was Catholic, and most of the prominent Mayer commissions were for Catholic cathedrals and churches, though the firm did receive some commissions for Episcopal churches. Stained glass from Mayer and other studios filled all the windows on the side walls of the nave. In 1938 the impressive new reredos (the altar and screen covering much of the back wall of the chancel) was installed, thanks to the Hamilton Memorial Fund. This required the removal of the bottom part of each stained-glass window, and each is now displayed elsewhere in the church. At about this time the wooden exterior was stuccoed over to make it look more stone-like.

The rectory and gymnasium were demolished in 1955 to make way for a larger parish hall and a school building. Also in the 1950s Columbus Avenue was moved several yards south to align with the rest of the avenue. This required demolition of the old Knights of Columbus Hall, the Elks Lodge, and an automobile showroom; as a result, St. Paul's suddenly had a spacious parking lot. In 1988 a narthex was built just to the west of the church, allowing for a sheltered space to meet and greet before and after services. ▪

500 Webster Avenue / 1906
Glen Allen and Milton W. Scott, architects

From 1857 to 1877 Waco Baptists had worshipped in a simple brick church at the northwest corner of South Fourth and Mary. A fire in 1877 destroyed that church, and Pastor B. H. Carroll began to plan a new building. W. W. Larmour designed it in true polychromatic High Victorian style. At 120 feet the spire was far taller than the 85-foot tower at St. Paul's Episcopal. The church seated a much larger congregation and had ground floor rooms dedicated to the different levels of Sunday school students. Apparently the leaders of the church were pleased with Larmour's work, because a few years later he was hired to design the new campus of Baylor University.

By the early twentieth century, as downtown expanded west and south, the congregation decided to move a few blocks in each direction while maintaining their central location. The cornerstone of the new building was laid on February 3, 1906, and the building was completed in May 1908. The architects, Glenn Allen and Milton W. Scott, were partners only briefly but managed to design three iconic Waco buildings: the Artesian Manufacturing and Bottling Company (now the Dr Pepper Museum), the Madison and Mattie Cooper house (now the Cooper Foundation headquarters), and this building. Allen was born in Pennsylvania and Scott in Louisiana, but they both grew up in families of practical builders, and neither had a formal architectural education. As a result, they had a more innovative—one might say freewheeling—attitude about style and ornament, which showed in each of these buildings. Allen seems to have been the lead designer on this church and the Cooper house, and Scott on the Artesian building.

From external appearances, the building suggested that the interior was centrally planned, an allusion to the early church (that is, the church for the first few centuries after Christ) that would be appealing to a Baptist congregation. It was centered on a classical dome, from which roofed pavilions projected out on three sides; on the fourth side was a semicircular projection. Each of the corners between these projections was filled in with a portico (the one on the southwest has been enclosed by later additions). Here Allen and Scott threw in a cornucopia of classical ornament. The columns and pilasters were in the Composite order—the blending of the Ionic and the Corinthian—which was the most ornate Roman order. On three sides were large round-arched windows with stained-glass windows. Between the upper and lower part of each window was a row of panels that obscured the fact that a gallery was just inside. The row of pointed-arch windows just above this were originally hinged on the sides so that the tops of the windows could open inward. (This is a reminder that air-conditioning was not introduced in Texas until the 1930s and did not become common in public buildings until the 1950s or later.)

The church was built of buff pressed brick, with a yellow color similar to those used for the Artesian Manufacturing and Bottling Company. The bricks for that building are known to have come from the Elgin Press Brick Company, northeast of Austin, and the

First Baptist Church

bricks for the church probably came from the same source. As it was on the Artesian building, the roof was covered with traditional red tiles, which were affixed to a modern steel
frame.

An old postcard of a colored drawing of the church, presumably by the architects themselves, suggested that they proposed that the building would have a raised base of stone;
both the walls of brick and the windows of stained glass would rest on this base. However, historic photos show that the base was of brick, with five horizontal rows of set-back
bricks, giving the impression that in between were courses of stone. The dome originally
had a metal crest, but that may have seemed to be a bit too ornamental for this particular congregation and it was later removed. The building also had the latest technologies,
being lit by electricity and heated by steam.

The interior made it clear that the sanctuary was centrally planned, but with a twist.
The main group of curving pews were in the center of the space under the dome, with

wings to the north and south and space for the ministers and choir on the east. However, on the west side the pews expanded into the semicircular projection, giving the church more seating and depth, even if it undermined the notion of early Christian central planning. In addition to that on the main floor, galleries on the north, south, and west provided more seating. After the exuberant use of ornament on the exterior, the classical decoration of the interior almost seems sedate. However, its sober dignity has served the congregation well for more than a century.

In 1907 Glen Allen left Waco for California, settling in Stockton, but Milton W. Scott remained and solidified his position as a leading Waco architect, a position he held into the early 1930s. The chairman of the building committee was the local lumberman Elihu R. Nash, and as the construction process drew to a close, he wrote an endorsement of Scott as "an architect of ability and reliability." (For Nash's Victorian-style house, see *Historic Homes*, 15.) Many years later, Reverend A. J. Barton, who had been pastor at the time of its construction, had words of praise for both "the large and handsome church building" and architect Scott as "an agreeable and efficient man."

By 1926 the congregation had grown to such an extent that Sunday school classes were held in three small houses at the western end of the block and in two larger frame structures just south of those. Unlike the church building, which was heated by steam, these structures were heated by gas stoves. By 1950 the three small houses were replaced by a new building, and three additional Sunday school buildings had been erected, one adjoining the western end of the church building.

The rest of the block along South Fifth Street, now part of the First Baptist complex, previously held the buildings that Baylor University occupied when the school moved to Waco from Independence. This group of brick buildings had been built in 1859–60 for the Trinity River Classical School, then Waco Classical School, and finally Waco University, which was under the direction of former Baylor president Rufus Burleson. When the female students of Baylor University moved to Belton (which eventually became Mary Hardin-Baylor College, now the University of Mary Hardin-Baylor), the male students merged with those of Waco University and Burleson once again became president of Baylor. The brick buildings, one of which sat where Clay Street is today, continued to be used as dorms even after the new Main Building farther down Fifth Street was occupied. The present two-story educational building and chapel (at the corner of Clay) were designed by Walter Cocke Jr. and built in 1950–51. The complex now covers the entire block. ◼

    Chapter 1

3. First Presbyterian Church

1100 Austin Avenue / 1911–12

F. M. Mann (Urbana, Illinois), architect

Scott, Pearson and Dean (Waco), associated architects

This was the third building for the First Presbyterian Church. The congregation included many leading Waco families: the Madison Cooper family, Jesse and Sallie McLendon, Edward and Kate Rotan, and the William Brazelton family. After almost three decades at 812 Austin Avenue (now a parking lot next to a candy store), the congregation purchased a lot at Austin and Eleventh.

In 1911 they hired the architect Frederick M. Mann, a New York native who had studied at the University of Minnesota and the Massachusetts Institute of Technology. After practicing in Philadelphia for a few years, he taught architecture and engineering at Washington University and then at the University of Illinois. When hired to design the Waco church, Mann had recently designed the University Methodist Church in Austin, built from 1907 to 1909. Mann may have visited Waco on stopovers between Austin and Urbana, but he did not supervise construction; that fell to local architects Scott, Pearson and Dean.

The cornerstone was laid on September 27, 1911, after much preparatory work had been done. A highlight of the ceremony was the church choir singing "The Church's One Foundation Is Jesus Christ, Her Lord." The walls of the church had gone up twenty feet by mid-October 1911, and the *Waco Morning News* reported that rapid progress was being made on the building. The contract called for the church to be completed by January 1, and it seemed likely that this deadline would be met.

First Presbyterian was traditional Gothic Revival—or, as church leaders put it, "old English Gothic." They further asserted that "in point of elaborateness it will not be excelled by any ecclesiastical structure in the state" and that it was to be "equipped with every modern convenience." The composition was anchored by a three-story tower at the corner. According to the *Waco Morning News* the brick was "gray." The handsome Gothic Revival front door is a rare example of an original door surviving on a historic Waco church. Above this, two buttresses divided the large Gothic window into three parts; originally, the window was divided even further by the use of more traditional Gothic tracery. At the base of the tower Mann designed a second entrance facing Eleventh Street, with a nicely carved wooden porch. On the side walls buttresses alternated with Gothic windows.

The front door led into a vestibule that stretched across the front of the building. The main auditorium was intended to seat some five hundred of the faithful; the gallery could hold another seventy-five or one hundred. The church was to cost between $50,000 and $60,000, including the pews. The sanctuary itself was a simple rectangle, with a gallery above the vestibule. The pews were solid oak and had elliptical tops, which were also pierced by a pair of trefoils, looking for all the world like tracery from a Gothic window. There were five fine stained-glass windows on each side wall, which rested on a high wainscot. Within each window were two windows that had round, arched tops.

The crowning feature of the interior was the hammer beam ceiling. The hammer beams were the short beams projecting from the tops of the wall, which were supported by curving struts. The hammer beams, in turn, supported the upper part of the roof, including the principal rafters. (The narrower rafters between the principal ones were called common rafters.) Hammer beam roofs had been devised for churches and large halls in England in the Gothic era, the later thirteenth and fourteenth centuries. An earlier use of a hammer beam ceiling in Waco was at St. Paul's Episcopal Church, designed by the Boston architect William Pitt Wentworth.

The church was built by Fell and Ainsworth. W. Frank Fell had been a Waco carpenter and contractor for close to a decade; Homer J. Ainsworth was new to town. This church seems to have been their only joint project. Fell was later the contractor for the William E. Terrell House on Bosque Boulevard (see *Historic Homes*, 94), and Ainsworth built the 1925 two-story addition to Provident Heights Baptist Church—now known as Calvary Baptist Church. The subcontractor for stonework was J. B. Huffman of Fort Worth, who donated the cornerstone of granite from Carthage, Missouri.

In 1928 the church building received an unusual note of appreciation. William J. Battle, a professor of classical languages at the University of Texas and from 1920 to 1948 chairman of the Faculty Building Committee, wrote an essay for the *Southwest Review* titled "Art in Texas: An Outline." His discussion continued into the twentieth century, and his short list of "outstanding examples, some of them worthy to be counted with the best of their class anywhere," included the First Presbyterian Church in Waco. ▪

First Presbyterian Church

4. Deutsche Evangelische Zions-Kirche
(German Evangelical Zion's Church; later New Branch Worship Center)

629 S. Eighth Street / 1914–15

Germans had been immigrating to Texas in large numbers since the 1840s. Many came to Waco, though not in the numbers that settled in Houston, San Antonio, or the Hill Country. Nevertheless, Waco had a large enough German population to justify a German-language newspaper, the *Waco Post*, which was published from 1891 to 1927. The cornerstone of this church was in German, and the congregation continued to pray to their God in German until 1931.

This congregation was part of the German Evangelical church, which was started in the 1530s, the era of the Protestant Reformation. Nowadays this church is associated with the Lutheran church but originally had plainer services than the more liturgically minded Lutherans. In the early twentieth century the minister was the Reverend Joseph Jaworski, whose children included Hannibal Jaworski and Leonidas Jaworski, better known as Leon, who became a prominent attorney and served as the special prosecutor in the Watergate scandal.

The Mailander family, leading members of the congregation, came from Württemberg, which was a center of the Evangelical church in cities such as Stuttgart, Ulm, and Heilbron. Charles Mailander (also known as Christian) came to Waco in the early 1880s, starting as a carpenter and building the Mailander Company, which specialized in manufacturing showcases for bank, drugstore, and general store fixtures. By 1914 Charles was retired and living in his cottage on North Fifth Street (see *Historic Homes*, 29). His son Fred had taken over the business and was living in a house on Austin Avenue.

The Waco congregation erected a frame building in 1881, which was replaced in 1914 by this building. Charles and Fred Mailander took a leading role in the project. Fred was a member of the consistery, the church's board of directors, and Charles was a member of the building committee, along with Martin H. Hille, a draftsman at the Mailander Company. The church was to cost $10,000, and some $7,000 had already been raised before construction started. Charles Mailander agreed to loan the church the remaining $2,750. The building was started in June 1914, and the cornerstone was laid on September 6, which stated the name of the church and the date 1914. It was completed in January 1915 and dedicated on January 31.

Charles Mailander was certainly familiar with the Gothic churches of Baden-Württemberg, which had been built as Catholic churches before the Reformation. These grand Gothic structures served only as distant prototypes for this simple, indeed, humble Texas church. The walls were brick with two porches made of wood. The largest windows have Tudor Gothic arches. A three-story tower anchored the left front corner, and buttresses supported the walls and the tower. The most Evangelical—or, more broadly, Protestant—thing about it was the very compact and centralized floor plan, which brings preacher and congregation together, negating any sense of differentiation between shepherd and flock as might be found in the long, narrow floor plan of a more liturgically based church. ◼

Chapter 1

Deutsche Evangelische Zions-Kirche (German Evangelical Zion's Church; later New Branch Worship Center)

5. First Lutheran Church
(later Grace Church)

1008 Jefferson Avenue / 1916–17
Milton W. Scott, architect
Wiedemann and Salmond, architects for 1956–58 enlargement

This church is usually known as the First Lutheran, but it was designed by Milton W. Scott as the "Scandinavian Lutheran Church" in September 1916. The congregation was founded in 1884 for Norwegian immigrants who had been settling in Bosque County to the northwest of McLennan County, some of whom moved into the big city of Waco.

Scott had been involved in the design of the First Baptist Church while in partnership with Glenn Allen, and the second Temple Rodef Sholom, with some assistance from Roy E. Lane, who probably created the perspective view of that building. Both of these earlier church buildings were in a somewhat freewheeling version of the Neoclassical style, but for the Lutherans Scott turned away from the Neoclassical toward the Gothic Revival.

From the facade one can tell that there are usable rooms on the ground floor, a sanctuary on the main floor, and a gallery above. The emphasis of the design was on the northeast corner, which had the entrance and a steeple above that faced the corner of Tenth Street and Jefferson Avenue. The entrance in the tower was a lovely double door, and each of the two panels had a circular window at the top. Scott marked these as "art glass," though in the actual door the pattern was redesigned as a Gothic quatrefoil.

The trio of stained-glass windows in the center of the facade lit the vestibule on the main floor and the balcony above. The squat tower on the southwest corner seems something of an afterthought, but this was not true on the interior. Families were to enter the church under the steeple, climb half a flight of steps to the vestibule, and then drop off their children in the nursery, which had windows on the front and side, before proceeding into the sanctuary.

The sanctuary consisted of the nave, the chancel, the choir room, and the pastor's study. (Originally, the external stairs on the north side of the building led directly into the study.) The chancel had a semicircular communion rail and was lit by two stained-glass windows on the west wall; in addition, there were stained-glass windows on the back and side walls of the choir room and pastor's study. The choir room had only one door, which opened into the chancel.

After processing into the chancel, the choir was to turn right and proceed into the choir area. The pastor had a door opening into the chancel, closer to the back wall, but also had a door directly into the pulpit, which was attached to the right front corner of the chancel. Many churches of the time had side walls with rows of evenly spaced stained-glass windows, but the Lutheran church had pairs of stained-glass windows framing a trio of windows in the center. Above the vestibule was a gallery, not for the choir but for additional seating. The chancel was expressed on the west end by its lower roof and narrower width.

First Lutheran Church (later Grace Church)

In 1925 a parsonage was built behind the church. This was an American Foursquare, two stories tall. The parsonage was demolished to make way for the enlargement of the church building between 1956 and 1958. The new addition was designed by Wiedemann and Salmond, who also made additions to St. John's Methodist Church in the 1950s and designed the Moody Liberal Arts Building at Paul Quinn College. The changes were carried out by contractor A. C. Reed, who also built the Bishop Abraham Grant dormitory at Paul Quinn College in 1954.

New offices and classrooms were built, and the sanctuary was enlarged. With the massive expansion of educational spaces to the west, the old nursery became the mother's room. A large plate-glass window was installed so that mothers would have a view into the sanctuary, and a small bathroom was created opposite this, with a lavatory and a toilet. (At a later date, this space was abandoned so that an elevator to the gallery could be installed.)

At the other end of the sanctuary, the original chancel, choir room, and pastor's study were dismantled, creating a pair of very shallow transepts. The stained-glass windows from the west walls were saved and placed in the transepts. The original chancel was beyond a Tudor arch; a new, windowless chancel was created beyond a low Gothic arched opening. A new reredos was created, possibly manufactured by L. L. Sams of Waco; a new pulpit was placed at the right edge of the new chancel, echoing the arrangement of the original. In the new configuration, there were pews for the senior choir on the south side and pews for the junior choir on the north side.

The enlargements meant that the exterior articulation of the chancel was swallowed up by the addition; a single roofline runs from the front to the back of the building. While the enlargement was necessary, the 1950s design attempted to obliterate the distinction between the old and the new and thus made it difficult to appreciate the original Milton W. Scott design. ▪

6. St. John's Methodist Church
(later Greater New Light Missionary Baptist Church)

925 N. Eighteenth Street / 1921–22
Cason Brothers, architects

St. John's Methodist Church was founded in 1887 as the Morrow Street Methodist Church. In 1919 the church building burned, and the congregation decided to move farther away from downtown so they would not compete with the Austin Avenue Methodist Church. They acquired a temporary building and began planning a new and more impressive church. Ground was broken in October 1921, and the building was occupied in August 1922.

The architects were the Cason Brothers, Herman and Harry, and the contractor was their father, Joseph F. Cason. To say that the architects and builder were local would be a serious understatement: the late-Victorian house of J. F. Cason was at 1202 N. Eighteenth, one block away from the site of the new church building. (This house remained on its original site into the twenty-first century, but it was bought and moved out of town.) Moreover, the Casons were Methodist and probably expected to worship in the new building.

Joseph F. Cason was a native of South Carolina. He brought his family to Waco in the early 1890s and was soon working as a carpenter and contractor. By 1907 his son Herman was a draftsman for T. Brooks Pearson, and when Pearson joined forces with Milton W. Scott to form Scott and Pearson, Herman worked with them. At this time the firm was designing the Shear-Callan and Smith-Parker-Migel houses (see *Historic Homes*, 33), so Cason learned a great deal about high-end housing. After the demise of that firm Cason joined forces with another draftsman, E. McIver Ross, to form Ross and Cason. In 1915 they designed the Texas Telephone Company Exchange at 119 N. Ninth Street (see 49 in this volume). By 1919 Herman was practicing on his own, though he briefly worked with his younger brother, Harry, who was a veteran of World War I. It was during this interval that he designed St. John's Methodist.

St. John's Methodist Church was a serene example of the Neoclassical style. It was a pure temple form, with a front portico of six columns, which were not carved from blocks of stone but formed by a concrete aggregate. The columns (and the pilasters behind them) were a very scholarly reference to an ancient palace as interpreted by a famous British architect. In the 1760s the architect Robert Adam studied the ruins of ancient Rome and also published a book about the palace of the Roman emperor Diocletian in Split, which is now in Croatia. Adam noticed a pilaster in the palace that blended fluting with some of the acanthus-leaf decoration of a Corinthian column, and 160 years later Herman Cason selected this order for a church in Waco, Texas.

The main facade has two front doors separated by three blind arches (arches without a door or window). The reason for this was that the altar area of the main auditorium was against the front wall, and one entered the space from either side. Inside both front

St. John's Methodist Church (later Greater New Light Missionary Baptist Church)

doors were staircases that led to the ground floor. This lower floor could also be reached by steps on both sides. Apparently this passage was open from side to side, which was another allusion to ancient architecture, known as a crypto-porticus, a passage beneath a more prominent space. The auditorium floor sloped down toward the altar, allowing for better acoustics and sight lines. Simple but lovely stained glass filled each window; between the windows were sober Doric pilasters.

Having the altar area at the front made it easier to expand the church to the rear, and this did in fact happen. In 1938 a two-story frame building with a brick veneer was added to house the Sunday school and other educational activities, and soon a parsonage was built. In 1955–56 the brick addition at the back of the auditorium was constructed, designed by the Waco architect Newell E. Wiedemann. Wiedemann had designed the synagogue of Congregation Agudath Jacob (see 17 in this volume), and with his partner, Don E. Salmond, enlarged the First Lutheran Church (see 5, also in this volume) and designed the Moody Liberal Arts Building at Paul Quinn College. (Like the Casons, Wiedemann lived close to the church: he and his wife, Annah Bell, lived at 1905 Bosque.) Wiedemann designed the expansion of the auditorium to the east, including a shallow gallery. This addition disrupted the purity of the temple form on the exterior, but the oldest part of the building is reasonably intact.

In 1988 St. John's merged with Brookview United Methodist Church. In 1991 they purchased land at Franklin and New Road and built an activities center, but in 1994 they moved to Highway 6 and Bagby Avenue. The old St. John's was purchased by an African American congregation, Greater New Light Missionary Baptist Church, which has cared for the property ever since.

915 N. Sixth Street / 1922–23

Little more than five years after the notorious lynching of a young African American man, Jesse Washington, the oldest African American congregation in Waco rose up and built this church, a fine example of the Neoclassical style and a remarkable example of hope in a time of terror. New Hope was founded in 1866, one year after the Civil War brought an end to slavery in Texas. After worshipping in temporary facilities for nearly two decades, the congregation built a brick Victorian church at 700 N. Sixth in 1884, which served the congregation for nearly forty years.

Ground was broken for this building on January 2, 1922. The program proceedings began at 2:30 with a number of invited speakers, which was followed by the procession to the new site. The *Waco News-Tribune* reported that "an immense throng" attended. In addition to the sanctuary the building was to include rooms for the Sunday school, double parlors (one for men and one for women), a library, gymnasium, natatorium, nursery, dining room, kitchen, offices, and even a rooftop garden. The space not occupied by the church would be used as a playground. When the church was dedicated in May 1923, the newspaper noted that it was "one of the largest churches for coloreds in the south."

The only thing that seems to have been removed from the plan was the natatorium, which was probably desired because African Americans were not allowed in public swimming pools. Another feature mentioned in the newspaper was the presence of drinking fountains, a public utility that blacks dared not use. The church also included a "radio receiving room," an indication that many African Americans were interested in this new medium but not wealthy enough to purchase a receiver for their home.

Although the cornerstone of this church did not mention an architect, one month after the church was completed, the *Texas General Contractors Association Monthly Bulletin* reported that Birch D. Easterwood was making plans for a Sunday school for the "Colored Baptist" church in Waco, which would have been New Hope. A Sunday school, which was expected to cost $30,000, was never built, but the fact that Easterwood was working for an African American congregation suggests that he may have been the architect for their church building as well.

The cornerstone did list the members of the building committee, which included J. Newton Jenkins, the pastor; George S. Conner, a Waco physician who led the choir at New Hope for many years; and John C. Ashford and William S. Willis, Waco contractors who were perhaps the two most responsible for turning the architect's plans into a reality. The first service in the new sanctuary was held May 20, 1923.

The portico showed a sophisticated grasp of the Ionic order as codified by the Italian Renaissance architect Vincenzo Scamozzi, which was used in British colonial architecture of the eighteenth century and in more recent neoclassical buildings. Rather than having Ionic volutes (or scrolls) on opposite sides of each capital, New Hope used angled volutes—that is, the volutes project out at all four corners. The shafts of the columns were unfluted, less fussy than fluted columns, and showed a sober dignity. There were six

New Hope Baptist Church

columns on the portico, with the outer two paired, in the manner of eighteenth-century French classicism. This resulted in three openings onto the porch, which aligned with the three doors into the vestibule sanctuary.

One reason the congregation was able to afford such fine architectural detailing was that the columns, windowsills, and other features were made of a composite stone, possibly Waco Art Stone. These features were made in molds and reinforced with thin steel bars. At this time Baylor University was using Waco Art Stone for the trim of the new Brooks Dormitory. In a few years St. Francis on the Brazos Catholic Church (see 12 in this volume) would use Waco Art Stone to create a facade based on Mission San José in San Antonio.

The medium brown color of the brick contrasted with the light-colored portico and the quoins that visually bound the walls together on all corners. These were "tapestry bricks," which had a rough texture, unlike the pressed bricks that had been popular in the preceding two decades. In the 1920s and beyond tapestry bricks were utilized in most fashionable Waco buildings, so in this regard New Hope was up-to-date. Blocky modillions ran around the entire building, visually supporting the cornice. Less colonial and more modern was the width of the windows, which were analogous to paired windows on Colonial Revival houses of the 1920s.

Just inside the door was the vestibule. This space had doors into the sanctuary, parlors at both corners, and two staircases leading to the gallery and a large meeting room. The sanctuary floor sloped to the front, and a gallery curved around on three sides. Originally, all seating was like that used in theaters of the day, with wooden seats and backs. A large number of these are still in use, both in the gallery and against the side walls of the main floor, though the central part of the main floor now features cushioned pews, which have a streamlined style that was popular in the 1970s.

The pulpit and seats for the choir were on an elevated stage. Above this was a landscape painting of a river (perhaps an imagining of the Jordan River), and painted on the wall in an arc of gold letters on a blue background was the first half of an Old Testament verse from Proverbs: "Where there is no vision, the people perish." Pastor Jenkins and his flock knew full well the second half: "but he that keepeth the law, happy is he."

The interior featured stained glass throughout: on both side walls of the sanctuary, both meeting rooms off the vestibule, the large room above those, and in the back corners the pastor's office and the choir room. The double windows in the two front meeting rooms were the gifts of the Willis family and the intermarried Cobb, Bledsoe, and Smith families; George Conner and his wife, Mattie, paid for a large window on the south side of the sanctuary. The windows were of excellent quality; the congregation was able to afford them because the windows were all in the same abstract pattern. That pattern was economical but also managed to be stylistically progressive: the abstracted floral pattern echoed the works of Frank Lloyd Wright and other Prairie school architects. All of these windows have been carefully preserved to this day.

When A. J. Armstrong, chair of the English Department at Baylor, arranged for the famed contralto Marian Anderson to perform in Waco Hall in 1939, he turned to Pastor Jenkins to find a place for her to stay. Pastor Jenkins turned to George Conner and his second wife, Jeffie Obrea Conner, to host Anderson in their home at 617 S. Twelfth (see *Historic Homes*, 51). The pastor also promised to announce the concert from his pulpit during every service and predicted that a large number of congregants would want to attend. When Anderson performed from the steps of the Lincoln Memorial in Washington a few weeks after her Waco performance, doubtless many members of this congregation crowded into the radio receiving room to hear the national broadcast.

The church went into debt to pay for this grand structure, and it took twenty years to pay off the mortgage. At a special service on December 12, 1943, Jeffie Conner (now a widow and possibly the person who paid off the remaining debt) burned the mortgage papers, and the choir burst out with the hymn, "Victory," which was written in 1897 by Barney Elliott Warren. The refrain included the lines, "Hallelujah I am free, Jesus gives me victory." ■

8. St. James Methodist Episcopal Church

600 S. Second Street / 1924

Adams and Adams (San Antonio), architects

H. W. Hawkins, contractor

The congregation that built this impressive church in 1924 had been founded fifty years earlier by former slaves and their children. Their first home was on the south side of Jackson Street between First Street and the river. It was a simple rectangular frame structure, but it had a seventy-foot spire rising from the ridge of the roof. It faced a cotton seed oil plant and an oil company. In 1885 the block on which the church sat had a few houses and stores; four years later it was crowded with one-story frame houses that the Sanborn Map maker labeled "Negro tenements."

In 1889 the congregation built a new structure on Second Street south of Clay—just a bit south of where the current building stands. Though only a few blocks from the original location, the new neighborhood was less congested. (The old site had been turned into a gravel pit; perhaps the congregation had made enough money on the deal to pay for the new building.) The new building was brick and had two stories, which probably meant the sanctuary was on the upper floor and the Sabbath school and other spaces on the ground floor.

The current building was not only a remarkable testament to the growth of the congregation over fifty years but an impressive civic gesture as well. At a time when many African American churches were designed by a committee rather than by an architect, the members of St. James not only resolved to use a professional architect but also chose to hire one from out of town, Adams and Adams of San Antonio, which had been founded by Carl C. Adams and his nephew Carleton W. Adams. Together they had designed the big house of the King Ranch (1916–17). Carl died in 1918, but Carleton continued the firm and took it to new heights, designing the Kerr County Courthouse in Kerrville, Thomas Jefferson High School in San Antonio, and the Texas State Highway Building in Austin.

All these buildings were in the future when this congregation hired Adams, but they were definitely aware that he had designed St. Paul's Methodist Church in San Antonio for an African American congregation. St. Paul's had been contracted to be built for $80,000 and St. James for $85,000. Both were in the Tudor Gothic style. Moreover, the contractor for the San Antonio church, H. W. Hawkins, agreed to move to Waco to supervise construction of this church. Hawkins, who had been a member of St. Paul's, presumably planned to worship here and even paid for one of the stained-glass windows (in the northwest corner) with his own money.

The Tudor Gothic was most evident in the use of red brick with a decorative pattern of beige-colored bricks and in the pointed arches—flat, not curved—on the upper-level windows of the front and side elevations. The main entry was framed by a pair of octagonal towers. The steps to the entrance and the windows near ground level indicated that there was substantial usable space in the basement. The vestibule was floored with subway tiles,

St. James Methodist Episcopal Church

white with a black border in a Greek fret pattern. Each side had a staircase to the balcony, with an octagonal newel post echoing the towers outside.

There was little of the Tudor Gothic inside, save the pointed tops of the upper windows. The choir was seated in a recess with a segmental arch at the top; the area was bounded with turned balusters in a Colonial Revival style. The sanctuary sloped down from the vestibule to the pulpit and choir, allowing everyone to have a good view. Originally the sanctuary had wooden theater-type seats, but these were replaced in more recent times by long pews. Almost entirely original are the beautiful stained-glass windows, mostly abstract save for a couple depicting Jesus in prayer, as the Good Shepherd, and welcoming the little children. The balcony has retained its original wooden theater seats and stepped wooden flooring. The basement had a large space in the middle, with a floor that sloped in conformity with the sloping ceiling above and with smaller rooms on both sides.

In the early twenty-first century, membership in the church declined, as more African Americans moved away from downtown. In 2016 the building was sold to a Waco couple, Lane and Amy Murphy, who hoped to make it an event center or community center. They successfully applied to have the building entered into the National Register of Historic Places.

To the east of St. James was the Union Baptist Church, built in 1918 for an African American congregation. The simple wooden building has exposed rafter ends, showing the influence of the Arts and Crafts style. ▪

1101 Columbus Avenue / 1924
Milton W. Scott, architect

This church was originally built in a simple Colonial Revival style. The walls were covered with wooden clapboards, above which was a tall hipped roof. An inset porch was under a pediment supported by Ionic piers made of Waco Art Stone or some other concrete replication of stone. It was completed to the designs of Milton W. Scott in April 1924. The board of directors praised the work of Scott in a 1932 endorsement, stating that "this church has been a source of joy to the members, and strangers always express pleasure for its simplicity and beauty."

Sometime before 1950 Walter Cocke Jr. was brought in to remodel the church. The structure was enlarged on the north side, creating a T-shaped footprint. The new part was built of tile, and the entire building was given a new stone veneer. The original nine-over-nine sash windows were replaced with modern one-over-one windows. The pediment on the side facing Eleventh Street was removed. The steeple, clad in copper, was added at this time. Even the front of the pediment was filled with a stone veneer; the additional weight may have caused the fragmentation of the Waco Art Stone entablature beneath it. Sometime after 1950 the building was enlarged again on the west side.

First Church of Christ, Scientist (later Olive Branch Christian Fellowship)

1300 Austin Avenue / 1924–25
R. H. Hunt Co. (Dallas), architect
Walter Cocke Jr. (Waco), architect for 1955–56 reconstruction

Though Waco is often thought of as a predominantly Baptist community, many pioneers were Methodists, including the Fort and Trice families. The original congregation built the Fifth Street Methodist Church, designed by Wesley C. Dodson. The tornado of 1953 blew down its spire, but it did not destroy the church. Not until 1963 did the congregation decamp for the greener pastures of Cobbs and Lake Air. Austin Avenue Methodist was formed in 1900 because Fifth Street Methodist was growing too large.

The original church building was designed by W. A. Cann of St. Louis. Local architect Dodson supervised construction. The cornerstone was laid on December 2, 1901, and the church was finished the next year. By the early 1920s the congregation had outgrown their first structure. Not only was the church too small; the lot went back only to the alley. The new lot went all the way to Franklin, which allowed for critical support spaces.

The church leaders turned to the firm of R. H. Hunt to design their new building. Hunt, a native of Georgia, was a practical builder who evolved into an architect. His firm, based in Chattanooga, Tennessee, specialized in churches, schools, and public buildings throughout the Southern states east of the Mississippi. In 1919 he established a second office in Dallas to handle work west of the Mississippi. Hunt was making plans by June 1924 for a church complex that was to cost some $200,000. The cornerstone stated that it was built in 5925, which counts 4,000 years before the birth of Christ and 1,925 after.

The church was fireproof—built of concrete with a brick and stone veneer. There was also substantial terra cotta ornament, provided by the Atlantic Terra Cotta Company, who also contributed to the stylishness of the Bankers Trust Building (24 in this volume), the Hilton Hotel (60), and Waco Hall (79). The Austin Avenue facade had one large window with a rose window set underneath a low Tudor Gothic arch. The tall steps were necessary because inside the entrance the floor began to slope down, allowing everyone good sight lines. On the side elevations, buttresses alternated with tall windows. The horizontal stone spandrels in the middle of these windows marked where the galleries ran along the side wall. At the back of the sanctuary on the Thirteenth Street side was a prominent bell tower. Designed and built at the same time was the three-story Sunday school building, which had classrooms on the first and second floors and a gymnasium on the third.

The Hunt firm had designed a mighty concrete fortress for the Methodists, and the 1953 tornado did little structural damage. However, a fire on November 13, 1954, inflicted massive damage on the building. The steel and tile roof collapsed onto the burning pews, both side walls collapsed, and the stained glass of the front window melted out of its frame. (The delicate tracery at the top of the bell tower had been removed at an earlier date.) When morning came, only the front wall and the bell tower at the southeast corner of the church

Austin Avenue Methodist Church (later First Methodist Church Downtown)

were still standing. The only examples of original stained glass can be seen in the entrance on the east side, which opens into this tower.

Waco architect Walter Cocke Jr. was retained to design a new interior. The reconstruction of the exterior was so respectful of the original building that it is hard to tell when 1925 bricks leave off and 1955 bricks begin. The sloping floor was retained, and new theater-type seats were installed, traditional but with a streamlined feel. The stained-glass window in front was not replaced; rather, the space was filled with limestone blocks except for the shape of a cross. Handsome stained glass was installed in the new side walls. This new sanctuary was dedicated in 1956. ◾

1100 Washington Avenue / 1924–25
Birch D. Easterwood, architect

Although Birch D. Easterwood is strongly associated with Baptists because of his long association with Baylor University, he also worked with other denominations. He designed St. John's Lutheran Church near Bartlett (south of Temple and northeast of Georgetown) and Central Christian Church in Waco. Easterwood was working on the plans for Central Christian in July 1924, and the contract was awarded to the J. S. Harrison Construction Company in September. The initial plan was for a two-story building that could seat eight hundred. Apparently, the congregation decided to dream bigger, as the contract was for a three-story building with a rooftop garden. Though the architectural style was more or less Gothic, the construction was to be of reinforced concrete throughout, a thoroughly modern material. The initial estimate for the two-story church had been for $150,000, but the contracted figure for the three-story church was just $125,900, perhaps because three other contractors were bidding for the job.

The steps leading up to the front door are a good indication that there is a usable basement here. In addition, there are classrooms and a fellowship hall on the third floor, all lit by large windows with pointed arches. The sanctuary occupies the main floor and has a gallery that curves around on three side. Originally the seats were individual auditorium chairs. Those on the main floor were replaced with pews and more recently with modern auditorium seating, but the seats in the gallery appear to be original, as are the stained-glass windows on both of the side walls. On the rear wall of the sanctuary were three niches framed by Tudor Gothic arches. In the central niche was a built-in baptistery, which was necessary because the Church of Christ required total immersion of the body in baptism. The current baptistery may not be original, but it would be quite normal to have a baptistery in this location. ◾

Waco Central Christian Church (later the Mighty Wind Worship Center)

315 Jefferson / 1928–31
Roy E. Lane, architect

The Mexican Revolution, which started in 1910, and the political and social upheavals that followed led to dramatic Mexican immigration and resulted in large Mexican populations where there had been few before. Waco was one of those destinations, and the refugees tended to settle on the north side of downtown in the area that had, until recently, been the Reservation, Waco's precinct for legal prostitution. Because of the new immigrants from the South, Second Street became known as Calle Dos. In 1924 Franciscan priests arrived to minister to these newest Wacoans in a simple, wood-frame building. Even after the construction of the present building, the congregation consisted of recent immigrants, and all services were in Spanish.

In 1926 Father Pablo Puigserver, a native of Llucmajor, Majorca, an island off the coast of Spain, arrived to serve as pastor of the new parish. Father Puigserver hoped to build a church edifice that would remind all Texans of their Hispanic heritage, and he found a willing partner in architect Roy E. Lane. They decided to create a building closely based on the church of Mission San José y San Miguel de Aguayo in San Antonio. The mission was founded in 1720, but the church being imitated here was built between 1768 and 1777.

The decision to base the Waco church on San José was something close to visionary, as in 1927 the church formerly known as the "Queen of the Missions" was a ruin. The roof of the mission church, along with the dome and much of the north wall, had collapsed in 1868. The complex was in no way usable, but Lane went to San Antonio to study it, bringing back a number of photographs that are now among his papers at the Texas Collection at Baylor University. Indeed, not long after Lane visited, the bell tower behind the main tower also collapsed, though it was quickly rebuilt. Mission San José was not reconstructed until 1933–37, after the Waco church had been planned and built.

Lane was hard at work on his plans in late 1928 and early 1929. An early Lane drawing for "a modernized reproduction of Mission San Jose, to be erected as a memorial in Waco, Texas" showed the church on a flat piece of real estate and had the one tower and sacristy with a very ornate window on the right side, as they were in San Antonio. However, in the actual building Lane flipped the facade of San José so that the tower was at the principal corner and the ornate window, based on the famous sacristy window known as the "Rose Window," would face Jefferson Street rather than the front yard of the rectory. Possibly Lane had hoped that the church would acquire a site on the south side of Jefferson, which was generally flat, but had to settle for the northwest corner of Third and Jefferson, which sharply slopes from north to south.

The most remarkable thing about the facade of St. Francis on the Brazos, however, is the elaborate portal, which is very closely based on the one at San José. At the top is Saint Joseph with the Baby Jesus, and Mary, with the attributes of Our Lady of Guadalupe, is just above the door. As in San Antonio, the statuary also includes Saint Francis, Saint Dominic, and Saints Joachim and Anne, the parents of Mary. The poses were all closely

St. Francis on the Brazos Catholic Church

based on the original sculpture by master mason Antonio Salazar and his talented assistant, Pedro Huizar. The biggest difference was that on the original mission the statues on the left and right side all leaned in toward the center, a sophisticated touch that created a complicated rhythm. Given that the church was featured in advertisements for Waco Art Stone, these are likely to have been of a composite stone rather than cut from solid stone. And leaning bodies may have been too much for Waco Art Stone to replicate. Whatever the case, the replication in Waco was a remarkable appreciation for a heritage that in 1931 seemed on the verge of disappearing.

The contractor was August A. Vuillemin, a native of Indiana who came to Texas in the first decade of the twentieth century. He was in Waco by 1917 and was contractor for many houses; St. Francis seems to have been his biggest project. Much of the ornamental work was made by Waco Art Stone Company, which was founded by J. Fred Simon, a native of St. Louis; most of the ornament on the original Brooks Hall at Baylor was made by his firm. Roy Lane made special note of Frank J. Johnston, a native of Canada who was living in Dallas by 1910. Johnston carved the molds for the art stone on the façade and for interior ornamentation, most likely the side altars and the pilasters, and also carved the front doors and the transom above it. Inside of the communion rail, the choir rail (in the space above the vestibule) and other ornamental turnings were created by Carl A. Trautschold. A native Wacoan of German descent, Trautschold opened his own planing business in 1902. (For his longtime residence, see *More Historic Homes*, 195.)

Construction did not start until March 15, 1931. Apparently Father Puigserver dismissed any admonition to "beware the ides of March" as a heathen superstition. The church was dedicated on November 26 of that year, which was Thanksgiving Day. The frame was steel, provided by the Central Texas Iron Works.

The mural in the curving half dome above the altar is unsigned, but in the Souvenir of the church dedication Roy E. Lane thanked "Mr. Raggi:" Gonippo Raggi, a Roman-born painter who specialized in church decoration, who had settled in New Jersey in 1921. Also original to the church is the painting of Our Lady of Guadalupe above the left side altar. It was donated in 1931 by Archbishop Leopoldo Ruiz y Flores. It was painted in the early twentieth century by Father José Mosqueda, a Mexican priest perhaps best known for a portrait of Father Junípero Serra, the founder of the California missions. His Guadalupe is a detailed copy of the original image of Our Lady that has been venerated in Mexico since 1531. The painting was installed and dedicated in St. Francis in December 1931, the four hundredth anniversary of the appearance of the Blessed Virgin.

Most other paintings in the church were done by Pedro Juan Barceló, of Mallorca, the island off the east coast of Spain. The murals above the dado in the sanctuary depicted the history of the Franciscans in the New World and are signed by Barceló but not dated. The painting to the right of the altar is signed and dated 1942, and the painting to the left of the altar 1943. The six murals on the side walls of the nave are dated 1946 and Mallorca is named as the place they were done. The paintings are murals—that is, applied to an expanse of wall—but they are not frescoes. Rather than being painted on fresh plaster, many strips were painted in a studio and then shipped to Waco. ▪

13. Herring Avenue Methodist Church
(later St. Paul African Methodist Episcopal Church)

1302 Herring Avenue / 1932
Birch D. Easterwood, architect

The original building for the Herring Avenue Methodist Church was said to have been "built in a day"—that day being January 12, 1911. All materials had been assembled, and sixty workmen commenced at 8:00 a.m. and were finished by 5:30 p.m. The wood-frame sanctuary was thirty by sixty feet and cost only $1,500. The location on Herring Avenue was very close to the Methodist Children's Home, and many members of the congregation lived or worked there.

The little frame building sufficed for nearly two decades, but by 1929 the congregation was planning for a larger and much more impressive structure. They hired William C. Meador, a Fort Worth architect, to design a church building. (In 1922 Meador had designed the Glenwood Methodist Episcopal Church in Fort Worth.) His design for Herring Avenue was quite monumental, with a ground floor and an imposing set of steps leading to the main level and the sanctuary. It was similar in scale to the Austin Avenue

Herring Avenue Methodist Church (later St. Paul African Methodist Episcopal Church)

Methodist Church of 1925 (see 10 in this volume). Behind the church was to be a three-story Sunday school building. The whole thing was to cost $75,000. (The Methodist Home was planning to chip in some $10,000.) The site was to be the same as that for the little frame church, which would be pushed to the back of the lot and used as a Sunday school.

Apparently fund-raising stalled, and in December 1931 the congregation hired local architect Birch D. Easterwood to design a building for only $10,000. It was to be much smaller, with the sanctuary on the ground floor. It was also to be built in two phases, the sanctuary first and the educational building later. In January 1932 it was announced that Wacoan N. A. Palmer had won the contract to build it for $8,970, well under the antici-pated cost of $10,000. A Nebraska native, Palmer was in Waco by 1925 and for a decade or more did a brisk business erecting houses and commercial buildings. Both Easterwood and Palmer were Baptists; it is somewhat surprising that the congregation did not hire Herman F. Cason, a Methodist who lived one block to the east.

The building designed by Easterwood was built of red brick (true load-bearing walls, not a brick veneer as had become the norm in many Waco buildings in the 1920s) with a modicum of Gothic trim. Most notable was the large lancet window at the north end of the building. The two lower stained-glass windows on that wall provided light to small rooms to each side of the altar. The cornerstone of Texas red granite reminded all com-ers that Jesus Christ is the chief cornerstone. On the longer, side walls were engaged but-tresses, another typically Gothic feature. Except for the large stained-glass windows, all others had a lower arch, characteristic of the Tudor Gothic, which was amplified by the cast-stone molding above it.

The education building was built much later; it was visible on the Sanborn Map of 1950. It had two and a half stories, a concrete frame, and a concrete floor. It is unclear whether Easterwood designed this later wing, but it is certainly compatible with the church building. The main entry into the sanctuary is through the double doors where the two buildings come together.

Since 2003 the building has been home to St. Paul African Methodist Episcopal Church, which had formerly worshipped in a building at Second Street and Webster Avenue, the design of which has sometimes been attributed to Milton W. Scott. (This was part of the block later occupied by the Hotel Indigo.) ▣

14. St. Mary of the Assumption Catholic Church

Washington Avenue at Fourteenth Street / 1942
Walter Cocke Jr., architect

Roman Catholics have been in Waco since its early days; by 1870 they had grown in number to merit the establishment of their own parish. In that year a small church was built at the northeast corner of Washington Avenue and Sixth Street, on what is now part of the lawn of the present McLennan County Courthouse. In the early 1880s they moved three blocks west to the corner of Washington and Ninth Street and in the early 1940s to the corner of Washington and Fourteenth Street, where the parish remains today.

In 1885 the Sanborn Map showed that the second church building was still not complete, and the Diocese of Galveston sent help in the form of Nicholas Clayton, who was emerging as one of the leading architects in Victorian Texas. A native of Ireland and a devout Catholic, Clayton trained as an architect in Cincinnati and Memphis and was in Galveston by 1872; he became the go-to architect for the Catholic Church in Texas. In addition to St. Patrick's Church and Sacred Heart in Galveston (the latter, alas, destroyed in the great storm of 1900), Clayton also designed Catholic churches in Austin, Dallas, Houston, Palestine, and Waco.

Clayton was working on the drawings for Waco's Assumption Church in March 1883. This was the first of his churches to use Romanesque round arches rather than Gothic pointed arches. He used brick to emphasize the sturdiness of the walls. A seventy-five-foot spire faced the corner of Washington and Ninth Street. Apparently, Clayton had dreamed too big for the parish, because nothing had been done when the Sanborn Map maker started his fire insurance map in April 1885. Clayton was back at the drawing board in September and December 1885. The completed structure was dedicated in 1886.

By 1910 the church was in need of enlargement, and the diocese hired Sanguinet and Staats of Fort Worth to add new transepts and a new altar. At this time the firm was busy designing the Amicable Life Insurance Company Building. The transepts did not conform to Clayton's rounded arches but instead utilized pointed arches. Interior work included the main alar and two side altars dedicated to the Blessed Virgin Mary and Saint Joseph.

Next door was the Academy of the Sacred Heart, a Catholic school not operated by the parish but by Catholic nuns from Belgium. Initially this consisted of two joined two-story brick buildings, but W. W. Larmour was brought in to give the school a third story under a mansard roof. The academy closed in 1946, four years after the parish moved away. By 1950 the school was being used as an office building and an awning factory; the Clayton church had been demolished, and the site had become a used-car lot.

The continued growth of the parish led to the decision to move five blocks west and build anew. Waco architect Walter Cocke Jr. was hired in July 1940 to design a new church costing $100,000. He was still working on the drawings in February 1941, and the budget had grown to $135,000, which included the land on which the building stood and the furnishings inside. The contractor was C. C. Ramsey. The building was dedicated in April 1942.

The new church building had a frame of steel and a concrete floor, but the exterior face was limestone, often known in Texas as Austin Stone. The church was properly oriented, with the entrance at the west end and altar at the east end; the plan was cruciform, a traditional shape that recalled the crucifixion of Christ. Originally the stained-glass windows were traditional art glass. In 1950 architect Cocke designed St. Joseph Catholic Church in Bellmead and in 1968 designed St. Louis Catholic Church in Waco.

In 1967–68 the interior of St. Mary's was dramatically remodeled to accommodate the reforms instituted by the Vatican II Council. Among the changes were a new altar (turned to face the people) and new windows of faceted glass, which had a much more modern appearance.

In 1948 St. Mary's School was built on the eastern part of the block. Unlike the Academy of the Sacred Heart, this school was operated by the parish. Like the new church building, the school had a steel frame and a concrete floor. The outer walls were tile blocks, veneered with Austin Stone. Walter Cocke Jr. was again the architect and C. C. Ramsey the contractor. When the church moved to this location, the congregation was able to acquire the old John T. Davis mansion at 1401 Washington as the rectory. Davis was the owner of the Brazos Valley Cotton Oil Mill, which later became the Magnolia Market at the Silos. However, this burned on February 4, 1971, and was replaced with the present nondescript ranch house. ▪

St. Mary of the Assumption Catholic Church

1300 Columbus Avenue / 1906–07, 1949–51
W. W. Larmour, architect, 1906–07
Walter Cocke Jr., architect, 1949–51
Sunday School Annex, Birch D. Easterwood, architect 1924

This complex is the work of many hands; in the first half of the twentieth century three important Waco architects took turns in shaping the buildings. The original church building was a small frame structure, but it was quickly replaced by a much grander building, one of the last projects of W. W. Larmour, who had been a dominant figure among Waco architects for more than two decades. The original Sunday School Annex was designed by Waco architect Birch D. Easterwood during one of his busiest decades. And the church was dramatically remodeled by Walter Cocke Jr., who gave the building its Colonial Revival character that became the basis for all future parts of the complex.

W. W. Larmour had made his name with Victorian-style buildings, notably the first William Cameron house, the Main Building and Georgia Burleson Hall at Baylor University, and the Victorian First Baptist Church at Fourth and Mary. For the start-up Baptist congregation—then known as Columbus Street—he designed a thoroughly up-to-date structure in the Neoclassical style. Just a few years earlier McLennan County had built a new courthouse in the style, and Baylor built Carroll Science and Carroll Chapel and Library. Columbus Avenue was originally built of buff-colored pressed brick, not unlike that of the new Baylor buildings. The main entrance was under a portico of four Ionic columns, and there were prominent stained-glass windows in the middle of each side elevation. The only hint of Larmour's affinity for the earlier Second Empire style was the mansard roof, but this was deemphasized by the dome above it. The cornerstone was laid on September 17, 1906, and the building was ready for use on June 9, 1907. Contractor James S. Harrison built it for $25,400; Harrison also built the First Baptist Church and the Grand Karem Shrine Building (see 2 and 87 in this volume).

The congregation continued to grow and by 1924 decided to build a Sunday School Annex immediately behind the sanctuary. Lee B. Smyth, a trustee of the church, had recently built a house at 2211 Colcord, designed by Birch D. Easterwood (see *Historic Homes*, 62). Smyth must have been satisfied with the result because Easterwood got the job to design the annex. The architect's deference to the Larmour building is almost touching; the building extended from the sanctuary all the way to the alley and to the sidewalk on Thirteenth Street, but Easterwood recessed the part next to the sanctuary so it would not detract from the corner of the main building. Easterwood had the plans ready by March 5, 1924, and the building committee had hired S. B. Swigert to build it. The annex was ready by September 14.

The complex was dramatically expanded and remodeled between 1949 and 1951 to the plans of Walter Cocke Jr. The church trustees at this time included Harlon M. Fentress, publisher of the local newspapers; Oliver Winchell, president of Central Texas Iron Works; W. A. Lanning, a local banker; and Floyd Casey, after whom the old Baylor football stadium

Columbus Avenue Baptist Church

was later named. The sanctuary was thoroughly remodeled. The footprint was unchanged, as was the pattern of windows, but virtually everything else was changed, giving it a look close to that of the newer Baylor buildings such as Pat Neff Hall. The old buff brick was covered over with red brick; the Ionic portico was replaced with a Corinthian one that projected farther toward the street; a new sixty-foot steeple was erected; a balustrade was added; the dome was removed; and new stained glass was installed. New pews and interior trim also spoke the language of the Colonial Revival. Remarkably, the only thing that remained of the Larmour building was that old-fashioned mansard roof.

Also added at this time were a chapel and a new education building, which doubled the size of the Sunday School Annex. The cornice was removed from Easterwood's building so that the annex would match the new buildings. To the west was the Spencer Memorial Building, the old Victorian Spencer house at 1324 Columbus. Eventually this was demolished to provide more programmatic space.

For the houses of Harlon Fentress, see *More Historic Homes*, 190; for the house of Oliver Winchell, see *Historic Homes*, 115; and for a house built for Wilton Lanning Sr., see 3721 Austin Avenue. ▪

16. St. Alban's Episcopal Church

305 N. Thirtieth Street / 1949–50, 1952–53
Walter J. Cocke Jr., architect

The Episcopal Diocese of Texas started St. Alban's as a mission in January 1945 to serve the rapidly expanding western parts of Waco, including Castle Heights. The first part of the project was a parish house, which had an auditorium; this space was used for services until the church proper was completed. Waco native Walter Cocke Jr. was hired to create a master plan. Cocke was deeply involved in designing and remodeling several church buildings in Waco. He designed St. Mary of the Assumption Catholic Church for Waco's Catholics and the educational building and chapel at the First Baptist Church and oversaw the rather emphatic remodeling of Columbus Avenue Baptist Church.

Phase 1 of St. Alban's was built in 1949 and dedicated in January 1950. The structure was reinforced concrete and tile, with a veneer of limestone. The *Waco News-Tribune* reported that "the exterior follows the simple lines of an English country church and the interior is in keeping with advanced design for modern liturgical church buildings." The building could seat 175 people comfortably. The dedication incorporated both the architect and the builder, William W. Smith, a native of England and long-time Waco contractor. Cocke presented the plans for the church to Bishop Quin, and Smith presented the key to the main entrance.

Phase 2 was undertaken just two years later, after a building fund campaign raised $60,000. The building was extended sixty-five feet toward Thirtieth Street, which increased the number of pews to forty-six. Fund-raising was completed by February 1952; the Reverend Charles Higgins preached from a text in which King David declared, "The house which is to be builded for the Lord must be exceedingly magnifical." The enlarged St. Alban's was ready for use at Christmas in 1952, though some work remained to be done on the exterior. To modern eyes the building may not be "magnifical," but it is simple and dignified and serves as an anchor for its neighborhood. ▪

St. Alban's Episcopal Church

17. Congregation Agudath Jacob
(later Sul Ross Senior Center)

1414 Jefferson Avenue (originally 405 N. Fifteenth Street) / 1950
N. E. Wiedemann, architect

Congregation Agudath Jacob, the Orthodox congregation in Waco, was formed in 1888. (The other and earlier synagogue, Temple Rodef Sholom, was a Reform congregation.) In 1894 Agudath Jacob built a frame synagogue at 620 Columbus, which is now a vacant lot at the corner of North Seventh Street. The frame synagogue was destroyed by a tornado in 1913, and a brick synagogue was built in 1914. In the 1920s the congregation built the Hebrew Institute next door at 618–620 Columbus to the designs of Milton W. Scott. (This brick-veneered building is extant, but its facade has been remodeled.)

Congregation Agudath Jacob (later Sul Ross Senior Center)

By 1950 the congregation was looking to move to more modern quarters. It acquired a lot at Jefferson Avenue and North Fifteenth Street and hired local architect Newell E. Wiedemann, who arrived in Waco after World War II, to design its new home. The plans were complete by mid-April. The synagogue proper would seat five hundred in opera-style seats—that is, individual seats rather than pews.

The exterior was austere yet churchly: the synagogue was under one roof, with corbels outlining the juncture of wall and roof on the Fifteenth Street facade. The main entrance was set within a semicircular arch. To the east was the Memorial Building, which included a gymnasium, six classrooms, and an auditorium that would seat a thousand. The floors were concrete, and the frame was steel; the outer walls were cinder blocks faced with a light tan brick; interior walls were simply cinder blocks.

In the late 1960s the congregation decided to build a new home at 4925 Hillcrest Drive, which was dedicated April 1972. The congregation sold its old building to the Waco Lions Club, who in turn sold it to the City of Waco. It became the Sul Ross Recreation Center (now Senior Center), operated by the Waco Parks and Recreation Department. Lawrence Sullivan "Sul" Ross, son of one of the founding families of Waco, served as a general in the Confederate States Army, governor of Texas, and president of Texas A&M University. ▪

1717 N. New Road / 1961
MacKie and Kamrath (Houston) with Bush and Witt, architects

Congregation Temple Rodef Sholom was founded in Waco in 1879. The first two buildings were in the same location: 918 Washington Avenue, which in 1881 was on the edge of downtown. For the design of its first house of worship the congregation turned to W. W. Larmour, a recent arrival in town who had already designed the home of William Cameron on Austin Avenue and the First Baptist Church at Fourth Street and Mary.

The Larmour building was brick and very similar to Christian churches of the time, with Gothic arches for doors and windows, a rose window above the central door and smaller ones above the side windows, and buttresses between the windows on the side walls. The only variant from a typical Gothic Revival religious building was that on the twin spires: the left one was topped with an elongated onion dome, while the right one had a roof with eight sides. Two additional onion domes framed the first bay on each side.

Onion domes might be found in Russia, and some of the earliest families of the congregation had emigrated from Russia in search of religious freedom. Isaac Goldstein, a prominent member of the congregation, recalled that the synagogue "was considered a model of architecture in its day" but that finally "the congregation decided to build a new and modern temple suited to changed conditions and needs of the present."

In 1909 the congregation hired Milton W. Scott to design a new temple that blended the Neoclassical and Italian Renaissance styles. The building committee included Isaac Goldstein, Louis Migel, Sam Freund, and Jacob Levinski. The building was of buff pressed brick (as was Columbus Avenue Baptist Church and the newest buildings at Baylor) with white stone columns and trim, copper cornices, and a red tile roof. The auditorium was octagonal with an octagonal dome crowned with an art-glass skylight six feet in diameter.

The *Jewish Herald* of Houston reported that the new temple was "constructed in the semi-classic style." The dome of tile was very much in the style of the Italian Renaissance, while the portico of Doric columns—two freestanding and two half columns engaged to the side wall—were in the Neoclassical style. There was not a single onion dome to be found, but set within the pediment was a six-pointed star. Such stars had long been a motif in the arts but increasingly became known as the Star of David, especially after it was embraced by the First Zionist Congress in 1897. It became the central symbol of the new nation of Israel in 1948, long after the Waco temple was dedicated on September 23, 1910.

As the first temple had been doomed by "changed conditions and needs of the present," so, too, was the second temple. The growth of the congregation and its Sabbath and Sunday school led to the decision to build a new temple on Forty-First Street, now known as New Road. The decision to move was made in January 1955, but work did not start in earnest until 1958. The congregation hired the firm of MacKie and Kamrath of Houston, who in 1949 designed Temple Emanu El near the campus of Rice University in Houston in a style inspired by the American master Frank Lloyd Wright. Bush and Witt of Waco were the local associates on the New Road temple. It was dedicated October 20, 1961.

The exterior was dominated by a tall, steep roof, which was inspired by the "Tent of Meeting in the Wilderness" that the Israelites had used in their years of exile. The congregation was also aware that the vast shingled roof recalled the great shingled synagogues of Eastern Europe, many of which had been destroyed in the Holocaust. The south end projected forward in three increasingly narrow planes; in the central wall bricks projected out of the wall in the shape of a menorah. The space between the three planes was filled with vertical strips of stained glass. The menorah was a candlestick with seven branches, one for each day of the week, with the tallest representing the Sabbath. Unlike the Star of David, there was clear evidence for such a candlestick in the Torah, the first five books of what Christians call the Old Testament. There was no applied ornament on the exterior—the menorah was part of the wall, and the only color came from the fascia boards (the edge of the roof), which were triangles and diamonds stained red and green. The only interruption of the main roof was on the west side, which had a horizontal band of stained glass covered by a shed roof.

Under the great roof were the sanctuary and the social hall, which on special occasions could be opened into one large space. The entrance was just to the east of this as was a lower wing. On entering the building, the business office and the rabbi's study were to the left and a built-in bench was to the right. Straight ahead was a six-sided space, enclosed with glass but open to the sky, with a fountain in the shape of the Star of David. Later a skylight was installed, the glass windows were removed, and an inlaid floor with a Star of David replaced the fountain. The one-story wing had a floor plan in the shape of a Star of David with ten triangular rooms, many of which could be opened to create larger spaces. These were mainly classrooms but also included a library and a board room.

The great space containing the sanctuary and social hall was created by seven pairs of ceiling beams painted Cherokee red. The pews were upholstered in turquoise, and the carpet was bright red. (All of these were colors of which Frank Lloyd Wright would approve.) The bimah, a raised platform for reading scripture, was at the center of the south end, near the ark, where the Torah scrolls are kept. (In earlier times the bimah would have been placed in the middle of the synagogue, as at the Touro Synagogue in Newport, Rhode Island.) To the left of the ark was the pulpit, a sophisticated use of Wrightian geometries. On the brick wall to the right of the ark was a menorah with the tallest candle not in the center but on the left. Behind and to the left of the pulpit was a wooden screen, behind which was the organ and a door to the rabbi's study. Most lighting was artificial, except for the vertical stained glass that accented the lighting of the bimah and the horizontal band of stained glass that faced west. ■

Temple Rodef Sholom

4901 Cobbs / 1962–63, 1967, 1975–76, and after
Steinbomer and Duffin (San Antonio) architects,
then Bush and Dudley (1975–76)

Methodists were among the earliest settlers of Waco. For many years they worshipped in a Gothic Revival building on Fifth Street, one of the earliest Waco designs of Wesley C. Dodson, who designed the McLennan County Courthouse at about the same time. Among the prominent members of the congregation were the family of William and Dionitia Fort, who lived just a few blocks away, and William Berry Trice, who chaired the Building Committee. Contrary to popular legend, the tornado of May 11, 1953, did not destroy the building. The steeple was blown down, but the congregation hired Birch D. Easterwood to design a new steeple and continued to worship there for nearly another decade.

The decision to move to the corner of Lake Air and Cobbs came at exactly the time when the Lake Air subdivision was being developed. Dezzie and Ella Janes donated the six-acre tract; they lived nearby at 2000 Lake Air. In 1962 the congregation hired a notable San Antonio architect, Henry J. Steinbomer, to design the new building. Steinbomer began his career in the 1920s and at first embraced the traditional Beaux-Arts Neoclassical style and the period revivals of Bertram Grosvenor Goodhue, but after World War II he began to design in a more modern style. He specialized in the design of churches. By the late 1950s he had become associated with Jack L. Duffin. This was one of Steinbomer's last buildings, as he died in 1964.

Ground was broken on the new building in April 1962. While it was under construction, services continued to be held at the downtown church, but there was also an 8:30 service at the "town hall" of the new Lake Air Center on Bosque Boulevard. (The ideology of 1960s suburbanism held that new communities would completely replace the old: one could live, shop, and even worship in suburbia and need never go downtown.) The last service in the old church was March 24, 1963, and the first service in the new church was March 31, which was Easter Sunday. The design was clean, with little applied ornament. Steinbomer was an enthusiast for modern stained glass, and First Methodist was no exception.

Over the years the congregation and its campus have grown so much that it is hard to recognize the original building. Steinbomer designed a long, rectangular building; the only elements that projected forward from this rectangular block were the entrance facing Cobbs Drive and the steeple just to the right of the door. Double doors with a large stained-glass window above led into a broad hallway; the sanctuary was on the left, and a wing with offices, meeting rooms, and restrooms was to the right. Immediately inside the front door was a small chapel, now known as the prayer room, lit by a stained-glass window on the east wall; this was set into the base of the tower. The sanctuary was oriented toward the west wall, which had another stained-glass window as a focal point. Most of the fittings were modern in style, but one item brought from the old church on

First Methodist Church

Fifth Street was the organ, which had originally been used in the Hippodrome Theater but was no longer needed after the advent of movies with sound. It was acquired by the congregation in 1928, when the Hippodrome was rebuilt.

The focal point of the exterior was the modern steeple; however, the congregation delayed its construction until 1975, preferring to enlarge program space first. In 1967, as ground was broken for the first of several additions, the *Waco Tribune-Herald* reported that the steeple would cost $52,000 and that "members hope to add the steeple later because they believe and have been told that it adds to the pictorial beauty of the building." The original design was Steinbomer's, but Bush and Dudley created new working drawings. As completed in 1976, the steeple did not rise from the roof but was engaged with the front wall of the building and contained a great deal of functional space. On the first floor was a small chapel; on the second floor, a Sunday school room; and above this, storage space. The belfry contained three bells, each hanging from a pair of crossed steel I beams. The steeple proper was built of ultramodern stainless steel with a satin finish. At the peak was a twelve-foot-high cross.

One of the earliest additions to the church campus was a large chapel built between the sanctuary and Cobbs. A new door was created in the wall opposite the door to the old chapel, opening into a hallway against the south wall of the sanctuary, with the new and much larger chapel to the left. In 1984 a large new worship center was built to the north of the original sanctuary, which created a new main axis from the parking lot on the western side of the property. The new worship center allowed the original sanctuary to be adapted for use by the children of the congregation. (The chancel fittings, including the historic organ, were sold or given away; the remodeling made it difficult to see the stained glass on the west wall.) The building has been expanded to the east several times and now extends to Lake Air. First Methodist is a prominent landmark of the Lake Air neighborhood. ▪

Commercial Buildings

20. Cornish Building
(later Kestner's Dry Goods Store)

445 Elm Avenue / 1897, remodeled 1914

Though it has fallen on hard times, this building is an important remnant of Waco's commercial architecture from around 1900. The Cornish family came to Waco just after the Civil War. Both John Lucas Cornish and Eliza Bonner Lucas were natives of Alabama. They had two sons, John Bonner and Victor Hugo Cornish. In his shop on Elm Street John L. Cornish sold both prescription drugs and groceries. After the senior Cornish died in 1884, John B. Cornish carried on the business and continued to live with his mother and brother, Victor. At various times he sold paints, oils, and stationery, but always drugs. Victor tried a variety of jobs, including dealing in coal, and briefly worked with his brother as Cornish Brothers. However, in the mid-1890s John turned his focus to real estate.

Before this building was erected, a simple one-story frame house occupied the site. The present two-story building of industrially made pressed brick went up in 1897 and originally was divided into two stores, 501 and 503. The original arrangement of the first floor facing Elm Street has been lost, but the upper floor, with nine round-arched windows, and the brickwork on the cornice above, all date to 1897. There was a partition wall between the two stores, and a narrow stair to the upper floor ran against this wall. (It had its own door on Elm Street.) This partition wall did not extend to the upper story, allowing for one larger open space. On the east side the upper floor had round-arched windows grouped in trios, fifteen windows in all; on the west side were another thirteen windows with segmental arched tops. Initially John B. Cornish's real estate office was in the building, but it is unclear how the rest of the space was used.

John B. Cornish died in 1910. His widow, Laura, indicated that she planned to continue the real estate business but had no use for the Cornish Building. It was rented to the Clifton-Coffield Manufacturing Company, which made awnings, tarpaulins, and wagon covers, for a couple of years. Apparently the building was caught up in probate, and the trustee for the Cornish estate, Peyton Randle, decided to auction the building from the steps of the courthouse in November 1913. His ad in the *Waco Morning News* cited Waco contractors J. T. Cason and Jimmie Harrison as saying that it would cost at least $13,000 to build in 1913.

On November 4 the building was purchased at auction for $10,000 by Samuel Kestner, who sold dry goods on the south side of the Square on the other side of the Brazos. The purchase allowed Sam to set up his oldest son, Isaac "Ike" Kestner, in business in East Waco. The Kestners had the two stores united into one with a single, centrally located front door. This allowed for a large window display of his goods. A canopy also seems to have been added at that time. The partition wall was replaced by wooden posts, and the staircase was moved to the back wall. The store was successful enough that Ike and his wife, Kate, could eventually afford a nice house in Castle Heights at 3724 Chateau (see *Historic Homes*, 110). Kestner's remained in business until 2003. ▪

Cornish Building (later Kestner's Dry Goods Store)

600 Elm Avenue / 1901–2

Although this building has been dated to the late 1800s, it was actually built at the beginning of the twentieth century. Samuel H. Clinton had been selling groceries and feed in East Waco for years—first in a building on Elm Avenue west of Archer, then at the northeast corner of Elm and Dallas, facing the Cornish Building. In 1899 this lot, at the northeast corner of Elm and Sherman, was occupied by a frame store and frame warehouse. By 1902 Clinton was in this building, selling groceries, cotton, and farm implements.

The new brick building held two stores, at 600 and 602. The storefront clearly had two entrances, although it was used from the beginning just for Clinton's store. (He may have been thinking about resale value.) Above were mezzanine windows and on the second floor six windows that were segmentally arched. There were six more windows on the Sherman Street side, but none on the east side, which was expected to be a shared wall with another building. Clinton never lived above this store; he lived at 116 Dallas, then moved across the Brazos to a house on Columbus Avenue. One of Clinton's clerks was Duard Pippin, who lived with his brother John at 502 Dallas (see *More Historic Homes*, 131). In fact, the store was briefly called Clinton & Pippin before reverting to S. H. Clinton.

Clinton spent a decade at this location before moving his shop to 506–508 Taylor, which backed up to the Cornish Building (Kestner's). His Elm Avenue building was taken over by the Andrew G. Smith Furniture Store. Smith was there from 1913 to around 1920, when the Elmer Barrett Furniture Company took its place. ◼

S. H. Clinton Grocery and Feed Store

618 Austin Avenue / 1911–12

A native of Scotland, William Cameron immigrated to the United States in 1852, fought for the Union in the Civil War, and came to Texas in the 1870s. He created a lumber company that grew to be one of the largest in the Southwest. The company sold lumber, lath, and shingles as well as premade window sashes, doors, and blinds. After Cameron died in 1899, his son, William W. Cameron, and son-in-law, Edward R. Bolton, became president and vice president.

In July 1911 Wm. Cameron & Co. requested a permit to build a three-story brick building at Seventh and Austin, to cost $45,000. Previously, the site had been occupied by two brick stores, which had sufficient space on the upper levels for Hill's Business College and the lodge hall of the Knights of Pythias. The Cameron Building had two stores on the first floor and offices above. Originally there were three doors, one to each store and a third in the middle that led to an elevator. The walls were demure beige brick, but the outer bays were ornamented with green- and ivory-colored glazed terra-cotta. Cartouches with a "C" for Cameron flanked the outer windows on the third floor. The terra-cotta continued onto the first bay of the side elevation facing Seventh Street.

The store closer to the side street was the Cameron Company retail store, selling paints, oil, varnish, window glass, and wallpaper. The second floor had a dozen or so offices, which could be rented singly or in groupings. The company advertised the availability of "several new and thoroughly modern offices on the second floor [of] our Austin Street building. All southern exposures, accessible both by stair and electric elevator, and affording all usual conveniences." Their ad opined that it would be appropriate for doctors, dentists, brokers, or commission men.

In the first several years, the occupants included an insurance company, a photographic studio, a dressmaker, and an architect, George C. Burnett. Burnett may have designed the building in return for office space; he stayed there for a couple of years before moving his practice to El Paso. Later, other Waco architects officed there: Harry L. Spicer in 1921 and Herman F. Cason in 1923. The third floor had the offices of Wm. Cameron & Co., of which William W. Cameron was president, and Bolton Farms, Inc., the real estate company of which Edward R. Bolton was president. The number of renters declined throughout the 1920s, and by 1930 Herman F. Cason was there by himself. After that, the second floor was vacant.

Around 1950 the building was remodeled for McCrory Stores, a department store. A single central entrance was created on Austin Avenue, along with display windows. The partition walls were removed, and both elevators were removed, replaced with a staircase and a Peelle freight elevator (from Long Island, New York) on the southwest corner. A new concrete floor was poured on the first floor, and iron posts were installed; the wooden floors remain on the second floor, as does the pressed metal ceiling. The painted McCrory's name is still visible on the east side of the building. ■

The Cameron Building

23. Commercial Building

This two-story brick building, which replaced an old one-story frame house, was essentially two stores in one building. The current entrance was originally for 208, and access to 210 was from the door on the right side. The entire facade was divided in half; there were three brick pilasters, one at each end and one in the center. Each unit had three front windows, and the dichotomy was repeated in the cornice as well. The pilasters, which were entirely of brick, were subdivided into squarish blocks, a treatment often found in French classical architecture. The canopy supported by seven struts was very characteristic of commercial buildings of the 1910s.

The left half, originally 208, was the shop of Lawrence S. Henry, a printer. This was a logical location for Henry because the *Waco Times-Herald* had its shop at 426 Franklin—the empty lot to the left of this building. The paper had its own presses at 420 Franklin, the spot now occupied by a public house—but Henry may have hoped to get smaller job for advertisements and the like. Henry used the left half of the building and also the entire back of the building, which had a loading dock on the south and a connection to the *Times-Herald* printing press on the north. The right side was briefly the shop of a chemist, Robert B. Tenney. This was also a logical address, given that Waco Drug Company was across Fifth Street to the southwest, and Behrens Drug was just to the southeast, facing Fourth Street. At some point the brick walls were painted a muddy red, but in 2018 the walls were brightened with a light gray color. ◼

Commercial Building

526–528 Austin Avenue / 1915–16
Sanguinet and Staats (Fort Worth), architects

Historically, banking houses in Waco had been in the Victorian style, but this ornate building set a new tone. Technically, a trust company offered more services than a bank, as it could act as an agent in managing real estate, placing investments, or collecting income; it could also execute wills or serve as the custodian of a trust for minors. Edward Rotan was president and E. W. Marshall was vice president of Bankers Trust. (Rotan had built the grand Victorian house at 1503 Columbus; in the 1920s Marshall would buy the Lazenby house at 1525 Morrow; see *Historic Homes*, 12 and 32.) Previously Bankers Trust had been on the third floor of the ALICO Building.

The building was designed by Sanguinet and Staats of Fort Worth, who had recently designed the ALICO Building with Roy E. Lane associated. For Bankers Trust the associated architects were Ross and Cason, formerly draftsmen for T. Brooks Pearson and Pearson and Scott. Ross and Cason were paid for their work with rent-free offices in the new building. The contractor, A. Alford, agreed to build it for $40,000; he began work in June 1915 and was finished by January 1916. Like the ALICO, Bankers Trust had extensive neoclassical ornament fashioned from terra cotta—provided by the Atlantic Terra Cotta Company of New York City, who later provided terra cotta ornament for the Hilton Hotel (60 in this volume), the Austin Avenue Methodist Church (10), and Waco Hall (79). The building was said to be strong enough to have three floors added at a later date.

The first floor had four retail spaces as well as space for a barber's shop. One early occupant was the Mohan Floral Company. On the second floor was Bankers Trust; Rotan's realty company; Marshall's insurance agency; the office of Charles Hamilton, who lived at 1521 Austin; and two architectural offices: Ross and Cason and T. B. Pearson. Also officed there was the Exporters and Traders Compress and Warehouse Company; the secretary of this company, Andrew J. Dossett, had recently purchased the home of Edward Rotan.

By 1919 Bankers Trust had apparently gone out of business, but most of the other occupants remained. In the early 1920s the occupants included the American Red Cross and the realtor Charles A. Weathered, who purchased a bungalow at 1821 Morrow designed by Milton W. Scott (see *Historic Homes*, 47). By 1926 the banking space was occupied by National City Bank.

The integrity of the building was seriously damaged in two separate campaigns. Originally the Austin Avenue facade was divided into three equal parts by pilasters in the Composite order (blending Ionic and Corinthian). The entrance was in the eastern (left) bay; the central and western bays had windows, above which were mezzanine windows. (Amazingly, the original three-part windows are still present in the upper floor.) Above this was a meander (sometimes called a Greek fret) with an eagle centered above each grouping of windows. On the first floor were commercial spaces, and above were offices. Originally the only entrance was on the left, opening into a hall with subway tiles. Just inside the door to the left was a small office, behind which was the main staircase. Both

Bankers Trust Building

the staircase and the neoclassical pressed-metal ceiling above it are amazingly intact. Upstairs the larger rooms on the west side benefit from large windows but were later updated and lost much of their historic character. The second-story windows facing Austin Avenue have survived into the twenty-first century. A passage ran from the upper landing of the staircase to the rear of the building; the smaller offices to the left had less light, as their windows faced the side wall of the building just a few feet to the east.

Around 1930 the first floor was "renovated" for the first time. A new entrance was created leading into the large commercial space; this door required destroying the bottom half of a pilaster and removing the mezzanine windows, creating windows to each side of the new door that were narrower and taller. The upper part of the pilaster was now supported by the void, which any classicist would see as utterly illogical. At this time a large neon sign was attached at the corner of Austin and Sixth. A second renovation around 1970 completely covered the 1930s ground floor with large blocks of red granite.

Between this building and the alley was the Colgin Building, designed by Roy E. Lane and built around 1912. Lane claimed that it was built strongly enough to be the base of a tall office building. Directly across Austin Avenue was the Goldstein-Migel Department Store, which was destroyed by the tornado of 1953. ■

25. Commercial Building

625 Franklin / 1923
Birch D. Easterwood, architect

Early in 1923 local businessman Lee B. Smyth hired Birch D. Easterwood to design a two-story commercial building at the corner of Franklin Avenue and Seventh. This site had formerly housed the C. M. Trautschold planing mill. By May, the Waco contractor James S. Harrison had signed a contract to build the structure for $50,000. Originally, there were three shops in front—619, 621, and 623—but by 1950 first-floor partitions had been removed so that the first floor of the building was open on Franklin and on the Seventh Street side halfway to the alley. This converted the three stores into a fully covered filling station, plus a shop to sell and service automobile tires.

From the beginning the back part of the ground floor and the entire second floor were referred to as auto storage—essentially covered parking. This is a reminder that in 1920s Waco parking lots were just coming into existence, and some Wacoans were willing to pay a premium to protect their new autos. Apparently, Smyth was pleased with Easterwood's design because in the fall he hired the architect to design an elegant house at 2211 Colcord Avenue (see *Historic Homes*, 62).

Commercial Building

922 Austin Avenue / 1923

Down the block from Central Motor Company (see the next entry) was the Cruger Company, where Harry T. Cruger sold Wacoans Ford and Lincoln automobiles and Fordson tractors. Cruger had been a dealer of Ford autos and accessories since 1907, with locations on Austin Avenue, Franklin Avenue, and South Sixth and Seventh. The *Waco News-Tribune* announced in January 1923 that a new building at Austin Avenue near Tenth Street was being built by Waco mayor Ben C. Richards, to be occupied by the Cruger Company, authorized Ford dealers. By April, bricklayers were making good progress on the walls of the building. The Cruger Company moved in mid-June, and the Wilson Brothers Motor Company moved into the former Cruger Company space.

Whereas Central Motor opted for the progressive Prairie style, the Cruger Company opted for a more traditional Tudor style. The Sanborn Map noted that the roof was full of wire-glass skylights, and ten were still on the roof in 2017. The architect of the Cruger Company Building is unknown; the cornice of the building echoes that of the Hebrew Institute by Milton W. Scott, but James P. Baugh designed a house for Harry T. Cruger at virtually the same time (see *More Historic Homes*, 176) and may well have designed his business site as well.

Between Central and Cruger were another auto repair shop at 920 and a store (now a vacant lot). Across the street at 913 was the two-story brick Victorian house of Lula Clark, who offered furnished rooms for rent, surrounded on all sides by shops relating to the automobile industry. By 1950 the house had been demolished and replaced with a bowling alley. ◼

The Cruger Company Building

904, 906, and 908 Austin Avenue / 1924–25
Milton W. Scott, architect

By 1925 virtually this entire block was set aside for the sale, storage, or repair of automobiles. Joseph M. Nash and W. Pitt Barnes founded Central Motor Company in the 1910s. They were distributors of Dodge Brothers Motor Cars and sold accessories and repaired autos. In the mid-1920s they built a new building on the former site of Nash's father Elihu's business, the Nash, Robinson and Company Lumber Yard, which had moved to 1600 Franklin.

On the principal facade white glazed terra-cotta enlivened dark brown brick. The terra-cotta on the top of that facade, which marked the three entrances, echoed the Prairie style that had become popular for commercial buildings in Chicago and its hinterlands. The building stretched from Austin Avenue to Franklin; it could hold seventy-five cars. The building had no posts supporting the roof; rather, the roof was framed with steel trusses. A satisfied J. N. Mitchell wrote a letter of recommendation for Scott in 1932, noting that Scott "drew plans and supervised the construction of my business house, embracing some 50,000 square feet." ▪

Central Motor Company

28. Texas Fireproof Storage Company
(later Balcones Distillery)

225 S. Eleventh Street / 1923

In 1923 the Texas Fireproof Storage Company was a start-up that offered "moving, packing, storage, distribution, and long distance hauling." The moving and hauling were facilitated by the railroad tracks on the south side of the building. The *Texas General Contractors Association Monthly Bulletin* reported in October 1922 that the company was working on plans for a four-story building that was expected to cost $100,000. No architect was mentioned. The contract went to J. E. Johnson and Company of Waco; this firm was simultaneously rebuilding the Carroll Library on the Baylor campus, which had been gutted by fire. Between October and November, the cost of the building decreased from $100,000 to $56,400.

The building erected the next year was thoroughly modern and adapted for business. It had a reinforced concrete frame, floors, and roof and brick curtain walls. And as if that were not fireproof enough, there was an iron water tower on the roof. There was a covered loading dock on the south side, facing the railroad tracks, which was long enough to load or unload five cars. The only hint of ornament was the marble door surround at the Eleventh Street entrance, which hinted, just barely, at the Neoclassical style. One floor of the building was devoted entirely to the storage of furniture. There was a vast open space that was dust-proof and also "many separate rooms for extra careful storage of pianos, rugs, Victrolas, and similar articles."

One feature of the original building indicated that an expansion was anticipated from the very start. On the north side of the building, the pattern of concrete floors and piers was left clearly visible, and the capitals on the piers projected beyond the plane of the wall.

The president of the company, Roy B. Albaugh, was a native of Greencastle, Indiana, who served in World War I and moved to Waco with his new wife, Omah. Soon after this building was completed, Roy and Omah hired Waco architect Milton W. Scott to design a house for them at 2201 Colcord (see *Historic Homes*, 75).

The company was sufficiently successful that the plant was expanded sometime before 1950. The addition was not to the north, however, but to the west. It was only one story and extended to Twelfth Street. The materials and method of construction were quite different from those of the original building. The floors were concrete, like the original floors, but iron posts supported steel trusses, and the walls were made of tile, not unlike those of the nearby Brazos Valley Cotton Oil Mill (see 46 in this volume), now known as the Magnolia Market at the Silos. ◼

Texas Fireproof Storage Company (later Balcones Distillery)

514 Austin Avenue / 1926–27
Harry L. Spicer, architect

Harry L. Spicer needed Citizens National Bank a lot more than Citizens National Bank needed Harry L. Spicer. A native of Norwalk, Connecticut, Spicer found himself in Waco in 1913, working for Roy E. Lane just a year or so after the completion of the Amicable Building. Spicer may well have assisted on the design of the new house of Alfred and Sadie Abeel on Austin Avenue—known as "the Castle." Although he had his own practice as an architect and structural engineer by 1916, over the next decade the only major project that Spicer was able to snag was the Stratton Building at Austin Avenue and Eighth Street (see 59 in this volume).

The bank commission proved critical. This was a bank that had been in business in Waco since 1884, and its directors included Walter G. Lacy, Madison A. Cooper Sr., Albert T. Clifton, E. W. Marshall, Abram C. Patton, and George K. McLendon. Even before selecting an architect, bank president Lacy stated their desire that the building would be in the Doric order and that it "would include large columns, which will give it a massive setting. There will be a restroom for ladies, and only one floor will be used by the bank for the transaction of its business." This was not a building committee to be trifled with.

Citizens National Bank expected the building to cost at least $75,000, but Spicer delivered what they wanted for only $65,000. Austere piers frame full-height fluted Ionic columns. (The Ionic columns were apparently a Spicer upgrade from the desired Doric order.) Between the tall columns were windows that provided light to the banking hall inside. Above the central window was an ornamental eagle with spread wings; above the left and right windows were neoclassical festoons (also known as swags). The lion's share of the material came either from Wm. Cameron & Co. or from W. F. and J. F. Barnes Lumber Company.

This commission was the turning point in Spicer's career. Within a few years he was designing the new Waco City Hall; he was associated with Lang and Witchell of Dallas as structural engineer for Waco Hall, and with Birch D. Easterwood in a similar role for Women's Memorial Dormitory. His firm became the go-to architects for buildings that might not be exciting but arrived on time and within budget.

Citizens National Bank

30. Commercial Building (later Simply Irresistible)

1018 Austin Avenue / 1927–28

Harry L. Spicer, architect

N. A. Palmer, contractor

This set of stores (now made into one) was built for A. C. Patton on the site of the old C. H. Higginson house. Patton had hired Birch D. Easterwood to design his house at 2402 Colcord, but for the one-story commercial block he turned to Harry L. Spicer, who had earlier designed the Stratton Building at 800 Austin, the Clemens Building at 701 Austin, and Citizens National Bank at 514 Austin. Spicer also designed Waco's City Hall and would be a consultant on the design of Waco Hall on the Baylor campus.

In September 1927 it was announced that N. A. Palmer had won the contract. Palmer had been in Waco for only a few years but had became a well-known Waco builder; among the houses he had built was the home of A. C. Patton. On October 23 the *News-Tribune* reported that the "four handsome brick store buildings" would cost $19,000. "The framework of these stores is showing up now in good form, with construction being rapidly pushed." The main facade was largely windows; above this was a modern row of buff brick with a bit of terra-cotta ornament. There were no windows on either side, but clerestory windows on the back wall provided abundant light, especially in the morning.

In the 1920s one-story commercial structures such as this—and those across Austin Avenue—picked up the nickname "taxpayers." They were definitely not an ambitious project like a skyscraper or even a commercial building with several floors of offices above, but they were better than an empty lot. That is, unlike an empty lot such a building could pay for the property taxes, even if it was not seen as a major development or even as very permanent. However, this building and its neighbors have shown their utility, and their structural soundness continued into the twenty-first century.

Commercial Building (later Simply Irresistible)

1023, 1025, and 1027 Austin Avenue
(originally 1017, 1019, and 1021 Austin Avenue) / 1927
Herman F. Cason, architect
N. A. Palmer, contractor

In the late nineteenth and early twentieth centuries this block consisted largely of Victorian houses, some one story and others two stories, but downtown was growing to the west. By 1926 the middle of this block had a filling station with a sixty-five-car parking garage, which later evolved into a building for car sales and service. (This was the western part of the present parking lot.) At the end of the block was the two-story frame Tom McMullen house. This was not originally a corner lot, because Eleventh Street coming from the south stopped at Austin Avenue. Opposite this was the two-story brick Victorian house of Jesse and Sallie McLendon, designed by W. W. Larmour by 1889. Sometime before 1926 this house was demolished to make way for North Eleventh. The McMullen house was demolished in late 1926 or early 1927 for the present building.

David George, an emigrant from Persia, purchased the land and built a trio of stores. The architect was Herman F. Cason, a former draftsman for Milton W. Scott who was later in partnership with E. McIver Ross before setting out on his own. The design was complete by May 1927, when the contract was awarded to N. A. Palmer, who also built the set of stores across the street soon thereafter.

All three stores had large glass windows for displaying the wares inside and a clerestory window above the awnings—now covered by signage, as is often the case. Unifying the three stores was a red brick upper wall with a cast-stone molding at the top, which gave the building just a hint of the Tudor Revival style.

The corner lot remained empty until after World War II, but before 1950 it was occupied by Reed's Flower Shop. The enterprise was founded by an emigrant from England, Albert Harry Reed, and after Albert's death was run by his son, Harry. Like the stores to the east, the building is glass below and red brick above; however, the entrance was at the corner. The highlight of the building, however, was the neon signage. Having survived the make-do years of the Great Depression and World War II, America was ready for an era of exuberance and high energy. ◼

Commercial Building

32. McDermott Motor Company

1125 Washington Avenue / 1928–29
Milton W. Scott, architect

The earliest Dodge and Ford/Lincoln dealerships were in the 900 block of Austin Avenue; this building housed the earliest Buick dealership. The client was Wilford Dees McDermott, who lived on Colcord Avenue in a house designed by Birch D. Easterwood (see *Historic Homes*, 98). The twenty-eight-year-old Arkansas native was looking to make his mark in the Waco business community and turned to the old lion of Waco architects, Milton W. Scott, who had been in practice for more than two decades and had designed the Dodge dealership, Central Motor Company, on Austin (see 27 in this volume). A more personal connection was that Scott had designed the house of Mrs. Mary McDermott's sister, Omah Albaugh, which sat across Colcord from the McDermott house.

Scott was working on the plans in the summer of 1928 and had finished them by September. The garage was to be two stories, 72 feet by 160 feet. The construction was fireproof, with concrete frame, floors, and roof. This heavy construction allowed for exterior walls of brick and plenty of glass—a sure sign of modernity in 1928. A set of four brick-faced piers divided the facade into three parts, with three windows in each part of the second floor. A somewhat anemic row of red tiles attempted to top off the building. More successful was the copper awning above the main entrance, which complemented the curving tile steps that led to the front door.

Immediately inside the door was a most impressive space: tall-ceilinged and light-filled, thanks to the row of plate-glass windows flanking the door and the mezzanine windows just above. The concrete floor in this space was covered with earth-toned tiles, and on the back wall were two floors of arcades, with wrought-iron balconies on the upper level. And on the right (east) side wall was a large fireplace, framed with even more earth-toned tiles. The exterior had been somewhat light on the architectural symbolism, but this principal showroom more than made up for it. Toward the rear, a concrete ramp on the right side wall allowed for easy delivery of heavy objects to and from the second floor; in 1950 the upper floor was occupied by a printing company.

Earlier this site was associated with the homes of Isaac Goldstein and Louie Migel, who were partners in one of Waco's most prominent stores. The site where this building now stands was the location of the one-story frame home of Isaac and Janie Goldstein before they built their grand late Victorian at 1229 Washington; and the parking lot for 1125 was the site of the one-story frame Victorian home of Louie and Rebecca Migel, who in the 1920s moved to the Smith-Parker house at 1425 Columbus. (For both of these later houses, see *Historic Homes*, 21 and 33.) ■

McDermott Motor Company

33. Gulf Filling Station

1425 Washington Avenue / 1929

By 1928 there were already five Gulf Refining Company service stations in Waco, and in 1930 that number rose to nine. This station was the most recent addition, and now it is the only survivor. It was very typical for stations to be built on street corners and to have the canopy built at an angle so that cars could pull in from either the main street or the side street. Gulf stations were built with porcelain-enamel paneled siding, which was one of the key features of an art deco gas station. For all its modern look, the building was built of good old brick, and the canopy had a wooden frame. The station has been enlarged: the three bays in the rear were added sometime after 1950. The transition from brick to cinder block is evident on the east side of the building. The building was restored in 2014 by owners Gary and Randy Balusek. ◼

Gulf Filling Station

525 S. Eighth Street / 1928

Before there were Magnolia Homes or Magnolia Market, there was the Magnolia Petroleum Company of Dallas. It is perhaps most famous for its trademark flying horse, Pegasus, but Magnolia eventually became Mobil and, after a season of corporate mergers, Exxon-Mobil. This little filling station was its fourth Waco location.

Filling stations were often oriented toward the corner rather than directly to the street; this made it easier for autos to pull in from either side. The bay for filling the cars has now been enclosed, but the brick corner piers are still visible. The office had brick-veneered walls, and the hipped roof covers both the office and the service bay, with exposed rafter ends typical of a bungalow.

Two more filling stations were created just a block north. Across Webster from the Merrick Medicine Company (what is now the Findery) was a Gulf "refilling" station, which still exists, and across Eighth Street from the Gulf station was a Humble station, demolished long ago.

Early filling stations were especially vulnerable to technological updates. For many years the Magnolia Filling Station has housed Mama and Papa B's Bar-B-Que. The slogan, which reveals the depth of the company's support for the sporting teams of Baylor University, is painted across the building: "If the Bears Kill It, We'll Cook It!" ■

Magnolia Filling Station (later Mama and Papa B's Bar-B-Que)

826–828 Austin Avenue / 1928
Harry L. Spicer, architect

This simple commercial building of two stories was built for John Sleeper, whose name remains on the building. Sleeper's family had moved to Waco in 1868, when John was a teenager. A longtime Waco businessman, Sleeper was also involved in the development of the Medical Arts Building, across Ninth Street from this one (see 61 in this volume). His half brother, William Markham Sleeper, became a prominent Waco attorney and long-time chair of the Water Commission who oversaw the construction of the Waco Water Pumping Station in East Waco (see 66). The architect for the Sleeper Building was Harry L. Spicer, who six years earlier had designed the Stratton Building at the other end of the block (see 59), and who in 1927 had designed the commercial building at 1018 Austin (see 30). The contractor was G. J. "Gus" Olson, who was much better known for building Waco homes. The original tenant was a Montgomery Ward store; the mail-order giant was opening thirty-five stores in Texas to give it a local presence. Construction began in May, and the building was finished by the end of September.

The walls were built of demure beige brick—"pearl gray" was the preferred name—enlivened by four terra-cotta panels at the upper level. The main floor was lit by large plate-glass windows across the entire front and another forty-foot "show window" on the Ninth Street side, with additional mezzanine windows above the awning. In addition to the main entrance into the first-floor commercial space, a second door to the left led to the space above. Montgomery Ward intended to use the upper floor for large items such as furniture; the separate door from the street indicated that it could also be used for office space. The large picture windows were a huge asset for retail stores; however, their historic function is obscured by the current smoked-glass windows. ■

Sleeper Building

36. Clemens Building

701 Austin Avenue / 1929
Harry L. Spicer, architect

In 1928 the heirs of William and Kathinka Clemens of New Braunfels decided to invest the residue of their estate in a new commercial building at Austin Avenue and Seventh Street in Waco. They hired Waco architect Harry L. Spicer to design a two-story building with a basement. The building was to have a narrow front—only 25 feet—but a depth of 165 feet. When the bids were opened, however, the cost exceeded what the heirs were able to pay, and all bids were rejected. In February 1929 William W. Smith agreed to build the store for only $40,000. Smith, a native of England, emigrated to the United States in 1907 and was in Waco by 1911. He was a Waco contractor for four decades and was responsible for building phase one of St. Alban's Episcopal Church in 1949–50 (see 16 in this volume).

The building was constructed with concrete blocks covered with a veneer of light brown bricks and with spare use of ornament. The Waco Art Stone Company produced whatever ornament the building had. At the top of the side elevations are winged orbs, a bit of Egyptian detail rarely seen in Waco or, for that matter, in Texas. Though the Clemens name was prominently placed atop the facade, the first occupant was Snaman and Co., which sold ladies' furnishings, millinery, and shoes. It had previously been located a few doors up the street at 725 Austin. The owner of the shop, Joseph Snaman, lived with his wife, Rose, at 905 N. Eighteenth Street (see *More Historic Homes*, 155). ◼

Clemens Building

724 Austin Avenue / 1913, rebuilt 1929
Lang and Witchell, architects, with Roy E. Lane associated, 1913–14
Unknown architects, 1929
Rehabilitation by Bell, Klein and Hoffman (Austin), 1986

The original Hippodrome was designed by the Dallas firm of Lang and Witchell in association with Waco architect Roy E. Lane. The chief draftsman for Lang and Witchell, Charles Erwin Barglebaugh, had studied for a year with Frank Lloyd Wright in Chicago and obviously shared Wright's admiration for the commercial work of Louis Henri Sullivan. A sketch of the Hippodrome Theatre was signed by H. McKay, who was Hunter McKay Jr., one of three Lang and Witchell draftsmen who were supervised by Barglebaugh. This commission was considered important by the principals of the firm: Otto Lang was on the original board of directors for the Waco theater.

In 1912 the firm had designed a Hippodrome Theatre in Dallas at 1209 Elm Street. The front of the Dallas Hippodrome was divided into three equally sized spaces, a central entrance flanked on each side by a store. At each corner was a tower, which sloped inward above the first floor (giving it a somewhat Egyptian feel) and topped with diminutive domes that sported flagpoles in the middle. At the base of each tower was the entrance to a store, and to the side was a large show window. Two brick piers had Egyptian capitals, which framed the entrance into the theater. These piers also supported a curving canopy, which lent an art deco aspect to the front. The building had a steel frame protected by concrete, reinforced-concrete roof and floors, and brick walls. The building was planned both for live vaudeville performances and "moving pictures."

The Waco Hippodrome was organized in a similar way, with stores to each side of the entrance. Like the Dallas Hippodrome it had towers at each corner, both containing the entrance to a store, but the sides did not lean inward, and there were no pilasters with Egyptian ornament. Rather, Barglebaugh used a frame of Prairie style ornamentation in the upper half of each tower, in the frames of the windows, and at the top of the curving cornice, which echoed the curve of the awning over the entrance to the theater. Working with Barglebaugh and supervising the construction of the Waco theater seems to have increased Lane's appreciation for the Prairie style, as within a few years he designed the Richey house on Colonial Avenue, one of the few early Waco houses in that style (see *More Historic Homes*, 150), and the National Bank of West in northern McLennan County, one of the finest Sullivanesque banking houses built in Texas (demolished).

The Waco Hippodrome was designed to show moving pictures, but its backstage area, thirty feet deep, was only two feet less than the Dallas Hippodrome, and thus it is not surprising that the Waco theater also hosted vaudeville acts in its early days. In 1926 the Sanborn Fire Insurance Map noted that the building had fireproof construction—except for its wooden roof. This proved prophetic, because around 1928 the building burned, and it did not reopen until it had been entirely rebuilt.

The Waco Hippodrome

On February 7, 1929, Dent Theatres, Inc. announced that a new theater would be built on the site of the Hippodrome; it would be renamed the Waco and would cost approximately $150,000. The building had an entirely new front, and the floor of the main auditorium was ripped out and the plane of the seating was lowered to allow for better sight lines. Projection equipment was updated to allow talkies—in fact, the projection booth was sound-proofed for the first time. The new seating on the main floor had 1,000 seats, and another 650 were placed in the new balcony. And perhaps most attractively for Wacoans, the theater would have "an air purifying cooling and ventilating system" for the comfort of moviegoers.

After nearly two decades the Prairie style was no longer stylish and gave way to the currently trendy Spanish Colonial Revival. On the upper level of the facade two round-arched windows framed by Composite columns provided ample light for the upper lobby. Two scalloped vents and a few rows of red brick at the roofline gave the building a bit of Spanish flavor. More visible at street level was the awning, which arched upward in the middle and was faced with a row of *torcheres*.

In both versions of the theater small stores took up a third of the front, resulting in a small and narrow lobby. In 2012 Shane and Cody Turner purchased the structure, restoring it and reconfiguring the seating to allow eating and drinking during shows. As part of the business plan a restaurant was added on the Eighth Street side, which was enlarged in 2017–18. ▪

Chapter 2

38. Losavio Grocery Store

1528 Austin / 1938–39
J. Scribner Dunne, architect

This ultramodern grocery store featured goods from the Old World. Mariano (or Mario)
Losavio was a native of Palermo. He married Marie Celestine Di Gioia shortly before they
immigrated to America (and Waco) in 1906. At first, he tried his hand as a shoemaker, but
by 1910 he was selling groceries, fruits, and tobacco at 119 S. Third Street. This address was

Losavio Grocery Store

closer to Franklin, so the store did not face City Hall but the side of the stores on the south side of the Square. His store differed from most in Waco in that he offered a variety of foods from foreign countries. As Waco grew and more Wacoans purchased automobiles, parking became a serious concern as the Square became more and more congested. In August 1938 Losavio announced that he was relocating the store to Austin and Sixteenth.

The architect was J. Scribner Dunne, who signed the perspective view of the new store that was published in the *Waco Tribune-Herald*. Dunne was a self-trained designer; he had a day job as a draftsman at the Mailander Company, which manufactured showcases and other fixtures for banks, drugstores, and other types of stores. Thus, Dunne was in his element designing stores. In the 1950s Dunn provided designs for Paul Quinn College in East Waco, including Abraham Grant Hall and possibly the Bishop Joseph Gomez Administration Building.

The facade was largely white, with black tiles underneath the large plate-glass windows on front, wrapping around the angle where the corner would be and ending under the only large plate-glass window on the side. The angle at the corner of Austin and Sixteenth was the most outstanding feature of the design: segments of the wall projected forward and to the side, highlighted with vertical rows of black tiles. Three rows of black tiles rose to the top of the wall, where they intersected with horizontal rows of tiles that defined the top of each wall. At this corner a slim tower rose, topped with an abstract cupola. The windows on the Sixteenth Street facade allowed afternoon light to filter into the space. Inside were white porcelain cases for vegetables and dairy. At the back was a large storage room, with a mezzanine above, allowing for offices and a lounge for employees that provided a view of the entire store.

The whole thing was very modern, not in the sense of modern materials, structure, or spaces, as one expects in the Bauhaus or International style, but in the sense of facades with a crisp, abstract decorative pattern, which is characteristic of the Art Deco style. Losavio reveled in its modernity, telling the *News-Tribune* that "we had experts design the store and experts to construct it, thus assuring a scientific arrangement as well as modernistic appearance." ▪

39. Elite Café
(later Magnolia Table)

2132 S. Valley Mills Drive / 1941, 2018
Herman F. Cason, architect

The Elite Café at 608 Austin Avenue had been an institution in downtown Waco since 1919; this was a storefront coffee shop that served breakfast and home-style meals. The owners were brothers George and Michael Colias, emigrants from Greece. In spite of the Great Depression business was good, and they decided to add a second location on the Circle south of town. They hired architect Herman F. Cason to design the new building. Cason had been a Waco architect since the 1910s; he designed St. John's Methodist Church, the Fentress house on Austin Avenue, and houses in the Karem Addition and Castle Heights. More recently he had worked with Franklin D. Roosevelt's Civilian Conservation Corps on Mother Neff State Park near Moody, designing two of the park's most iconic structures, the Concession Building/Clubhouse and the Lookout Tower/Water Tank.

The Colias brothers asked Cason to design a building in the Spanish Colonial style that was oriented toward a traffic circle with roads angling off in all directions; a simple box

Elite Café (later Magnolia Table)

would not do. Cason created a two-story octagonal entrance tower, from which one-story wings projected at right angles. The wing on the left aligned with what is now South Valley Mills Drive, while the wing on the right lined up with what is now Circle Road. Both terminated with square pavilions with pyramidal roofs; Cason rotated these so that one corner of each pavilion touched the outer corner of the adjoining wing. Spanish Colonial came from the white plastered walls, the red tiles of the roof, and the shallow iron balconies on the upper level of the tower. On top of each wing, just above the couple of rows of tiles, "ELITE CAFE" was spelled out in neon. For a roadside diner, it was pretty sophisticated.

Parking was plenteous, and though the interior was pretty standard American Diner, it was air-conditioned, which was a huge advantage for a restaurant in 1941. Soon business was hopping, and within a year the Colias brothers had enlarged the building. Sadly, Herman F. Cason was not involved with the addition, as he had died of a heart attack in November 1941 at age fifty-one. In 1952 the brothers added a banquet room and renovated the interior, though the only change to the exterior was the addition of a small protrusion atop the main tower, which seemed to be a cross between a lighthouse and a Sputnik space capsule. (This feature was later removed.)

The Elite Café was sold in 1986 and remodeled by new owners and remodeled again in 2003. The restaurant had its ups and downs, as Interstate 35 allowed cars to whiz by without even hitting the brakes. By the time the building was purchased by Chip and Joanna Gaines, there was little of any age inside the building. Their renovation made one drastic change: new rows of clerestory windows atop the roof of the wings, which allowed light to trickle into the interior. The change was clearly marked by the use of metal roofs, and the new walls rose to roughly the height of the old neon signs, which were removed as part of the rebranding to Magnolia Table.

40. Sachs Austin Avenue
(later Sironia)

1509 Austin Avenue / 1953–54
Harris H. Roberts and Associates, architects

This midcentury modern building was a direct result of the 1953 Waco tornado. It was built by brothers Aubrey and Jacques (or Jack) Sachs, sons of retail dry goods merchant Harry Sachs. Their original store was near the town square at 509 Austin. Devoted especially to women's clothing, it was named with a knowing nod to a somewhat more famous establishment on Fifth Avenue in New York. The store on the Square was destroyed in 1953.

Aubrey and Jack resolved to build anew, but farther up Austin Avenue. Their new shop replaced a Victorian house with a wraparound porch. Designs for the new complex were drawn up by Waco architect Harris H. Roberts, who is perhaps best known as the local

Sachs Austin Avenue (later Sironia)

architect overseeing the designs of Houston architects Farnsworth and Chambers for the Heart O' Texas Coliseum, also built in 1953. Roberts arrived in Waco just after the war and practiced until his death in 1958 at age sixty-eight.

In 1953 this new development was considered "uptown." The shopping center was to cost $500,000; Jones and Williams were the contractors. Both "architecture and landscaping" were to be "of California Style." Roberts characterized the design as "a contemporary interpretation of practical, modern architecture." The design was strongly horizontal and featured large plate-glass windows and three freestanding display cases, each of which could contain a life-sized mannequin, thus showing off the latest fashions in a striking manner. The landscaping features consisted of a pair of palm trees on the sidewalk and another pair in the parking lot. A canopy that engaged with the building projected to the east side, framing the entrance to and exit from the parking lot. The complex extended to the east with a two-story building on the downtown side; this unit was also attached to the canopy. Between the two units was a driveway that led to a parking lot that could hold sixty cars.

In the early 1980s new owner Diane Henderson created her own shop, naming it Sironia. This was a nod to the lengthy two-volume novel written by Madison Cooper Jr., which was published in 1952. The novel was written just a few blocks away in the Cooper house at 1801 Austin Avenue (see *Historic Homes*, 30). ▪

41. Pioneer Savings Association

823 Washington Avenue / 1955
E. H. Hezner (Chicago), architect

T. B. Taylor founded Pioneer Savings Association in 1922. The original office was a single room on the fifth floor of the Provident Building at Franklin Avenue and Fourth Street. In 1938 the institution built an art deco building at 706 Austin, designed by T. Brooks Pearson and J. Scribner Dunne, which survives in a mutilated state. Less than twenty years later, however, they were ready for an even more modern building at the corner of Washington and Ninth, which was emerging as Waco's financial row.

Pioneer retained E. H. Hezner of Chicago as its architect. Hezner was an in-house designer with the Chicago Bank Equipment Company and had extensive experience designing banks and savings and loan associations. The idea was to have a building compatible with that of the First National Bank (which was to be built at the opposite end of

Pioneer Savings Association

the block) but still have "its own distinct character and identity." The bank building was to cost $1 million; the savings association, half a million. McClellan Construction Company was the contractor for Pioneer, and soon close to one hundred men were laboring at the site.

That identity was distinctly midcentury modern, though its design was nothing that would win accolades from the high priests of the International style. The most notable feature was the veneer of black and white marble, with expanses of black marble framing a central feature of white marble on the upper level. The *Waco News-Tribune* noted that the "wide expanses of glass in vast windows, contrasting color schemes, a two-story-high corner entrance way, floodlights and unique-for-Waco design throughout are among the features of the new savings center." President Taylor claimed that "the building and furnishings were designed primarily to appeal to the women who stand behind 98 percent of our savings accounts and mortgages." The building also had over five thousand feet of space for rent, which was air-conditioned, had a private entrance, could be partitioned, and was in a convenient location. ▪

42. First Federal Savings and Loan
(later Guaranty Bank)

1226 Austin Avenue / 1958–60
A. C. Lenander (Columbus, Ohio), architect
Spicer, Bush and Witt, associated architects

Some financial institutions, such as Pioneer Savings Association and First National Bank, built modern banking houses in the 1950s (see 41 and 62 in this volume). First Federal Savings and Loan went in the opposite direction, making it one of the last full-blown examples of the Colonial Revival before Baylor University revived the style once again in recent years. The architect was A. C. Lenander of Columbus, Ohio, who made a specialty of designing for financial institutions. Lenander associated with Spicer, Bush and Witt to execute his plans.

The traditional look came from the red bricks, made by the Texas Brick Company in Brownwood, Texas (some 120 miles west of Waco), and especially by the ten fluted Doric columns that spanned the facade. These were made from Indiana limestone quarried and

First Federal Savings and Loan (later Guaranty Bank)

carved by the Indiana Limestone Company. The roof was built of Vermont slate, which was "durable enough to last for several lifetimes." Even the drive-in window was clothed in colonial garb. Tradition stopped with the expansive windows, which were insulated glass framed in aluminum.

The floor of the bank lobby was covered in Roman travertine, and all the woodwork was walnut, "hand-rubbed to a stain finish," provided by H. J. Upperman and Sons of Amlin, Ohio, who specialized in fixtures for banking houses. The domed ceiling featured ornamental plaster moldings and three colonial chandeliers, each with twenty-eight lamps.

Though it is not apparent at first, the building contained two upper floors of rentable office space. These were accessed by a separate door at the east end of the building, which led directly to stairs. The freestanding sign to the left of this door was designed to contain a directory of tenants.

As did most Colonial Revival buildings of the twentieth century, the style drew both from truly colonial buildings—built before the American Revolution—and from the neo-classicism that was embraced in the years after the war. Indeed, the *Waco Tribune-Herald* felt compelled to explain that "the Colonial building is not the informal colonial of residential character nor the provincial Williamsburg style. It is the heavier classical colonial associated with many top financial institutions."

Lenander also designed a branch at Highway 6 (now Valley Mills Drive) and Lake Air, which opened in January 1958. The location of the branch bank acknowledged that Waco was growing toward the west. Later both the downtown and suburban buildings were bought by Guaranty Bank. About 2013 Bank of America demolished the branch to erect a nondescript modern building. In 2017–19 local developers Shane and Cody Turner purchased the downtown building and renovated it into office space.

The president of First Federal Savings was Harry Jeanes, a major supporter of Baylor University, especially the Strecker (now Mayborn) Museum. The 2004 Mayborn building, with its redbrick, classical columns and Monticello-inspired dome was precisely to his taste. ◼

CHAPTER THREE

Wholesale and Manufacturing

43. Artesian Manufacturing and Bottling Co. (Dr Pepper Museum)

300 S. Fifth Street / 1906
Glenn Allen and Milton W. Scott, architects

The location of this building at Fifth Street and Mary was critical, and the reason can be seen on Mary Street—the remnants of railroad tracks that shipped Dr Pepper and other soft drinks far and wide. To the south was a wholesale grocery company, first known as the Rotan Grocery Company, named for President Ed Rotan, then as the Shear Grocery Company, named for President Herbert H. Shear. At the opposite end of the block, facing Fourth Street, was the Cooper Grocery Company, a wholesale grocery firm that supplied mom-and-pop grocery stores all over Central Texas. By 1953 the Cooper Grocery had expanded to include the old Rotan-Shear building, but the company was soon on a downward trend thanks to the rise of supermarkets. The Artesian Manufacturing and Bottling Co. had a loading deck—what they called a "wharf"—facing the Mary Street tracks and that continued east along Mary, connecting with the Cooper loading dock. Another wharf was on the south to facilitate trucks picking up finished soft drinks to deliver locally.

Glen Allen and Milton W. Scott were designing this building the same year that they were designing the First Baptist Church just a few blocks away (see 2 in this volume), and they were just as freewheeling in their design ethos here. (Scott seems to have been the lead designer here, and Allen at First Baptist.) The building was described at the time as Romanesque, but like Dr Pepper itself it was actually a blend of flavors—or styles. All arches were heavily rusticated—which gave it a medieval feeling—but the arches on the ground floor all landed on sober neoclassical piers. Yet the entrance on the Mary Street side was completely encompassed within a rusticated arch, which might be seen as Richardsonian. Scott would soon design a similar rusticated arch for the Mary Street side of the McLendon Hardware building two blocks down the tracks (see the next entry). Moreover, the arcade on the upper floor leaned out above the main wall, giving it a medieval character. Complicating things even further were the hipped roof tower and the cupola on the Mary Street facade, which had something of a neoclassical character.

The walls were built of Elgin brick, from Elgin, Texas, with stone trimming. Had this building been erected just a few years earlier, it would have looked quite different. The Elgin Press Brick Company had been founded in 1891, northeast of Austin, but in 1904 was reorganized under M. T. Smith. Originally its pressed bricks were a deep red color, but in 1897 shale clays were discovered near McDade, six miles from Elgin, and this allowed the company to expand its product line to include a yellowish "buff-pressed brick." Very similar brick was used on the First Baptist Church, a few blocks south on Fifth Street.

The company hoped for a "model bottling establishment" that would also "be in keeping with the vim, vigor and vitality of Dr. Pepper and the snap and sparkle of Zu Zu Ginger Ale." The building was divided into two distinct parts, with offices at the Fifth Street end of the building and the bottling area behind. The Fifth Street door led into a lobby with a staircase; to the right was a corner office for the president and the general office, while to the left was the advertising room. The president's room had generous windows on the south and west, with a fireplace at the southwest corner. The general office included a bay widow on the south side, assuring plenty of sunlight in that space. An elevator connected the bottling area on the first floor with the distilling plant and sugar storage on the third floor. In between on the second floor were laboratories for product development.

The structure was seriously damaged in the tornado of 1953. The roof on the front part of the building and the upper wall on the Mary Street side were ripped away. Ultimately, the end of the building as a soft-drink producer came not from the move of corporate headquarters to Dallas but the transition from soft drinks sold in glass bottles to soft drinks sold in aluminum cans. This facility could fill the former but not the latter. The building was restored in 1989–90 as the Dr Pepper Museum and Free Enterprise Institute and has remained a popular local museum. The Mary Street scar from the 1953 tornado was preserved as a memento of a most trying time for the building—and for Waco. The Rotan-Shear building has now been adapted as part of the Dr Pepper Museum, providing the museum with much more space for exhibits, work space, and even a soft-drink counter. ▪

Artesian Manufacturing and Bottling Co. (Dr Pepper Museum and Free Enterprise Institute)

44. McLendon Hardware Company
(later River Square Center)

213 Mary Avenue / Circa 1908,
severely damaged 1953, renovated 1995–97
Milton W. Scott, architect

This large brick block for a wholesale hardware company went up several years before the neighboring Hanna-James-Taylor Building, but both were located here for the same reason: the railroad tracks on Mary Street. The McLendon Hardware Company proudly advertised that the building had "300 feet of trackage on Mary Street," which allowed it to promptly ship all mail orders. Waco's Union Depot was one block to the west, at the corner of Mary and Fourth. Mary Street was thus an important artery for both people and products coming into and going out of Waco. The architect of the building was Milton W. Scott, who had recently made a splash in conjunction with his partner, Glen Allen, on the First Baptist Church and the Artesian Manufacturing and Bottling Company, the home of Dr Pepper.

Adapted in the 1990s to house shops and restaurants, the building is now experienced in a completely different way than when it first opened. The current parking lot was a fully developed city block, with the New Exchange Hotel at the west end and other businesses filling out the rest of the block. The north wall of the McLendon Hardware building, which presently has the main entrances to stores and eateries, originally faced an alley. The south wall was devoted to moving things on and off railroad boxcars; the main entrance was actually on Third Street, where three round-arched doors are now windows, lighting the main dining room of a Mexican restaurant.

At 350 feet the McLendon Hardware building was longer than a football field, and Scott chose to create two sections. To the east, in the workaday storage areas, the walls were pilastered with wide banks of windows in between, anticipating Hanna-James-Taylor next door. The focal point of the building was at the west end, where the three central bays and corner bays projected forward and were marked by round-arched windows, classical pilasters, and an ornate cornice. On the Mary Street side Scott created a freight entrance set within a massive round arch with voussoirs of light-colored stone. (This echoed the arched opening that Scott and Glenn Allen had designed for the Artesian Bottling Company two blocks to the west.) The building was featured on more than one postcard, one of which declared that it was "one of the most ornate commercial buildings in the South."

However, pride goeth before a tornado, and in 1953 the building was badly damaged. The destruction was concentrated on the west end, and as a result the third floor and the cornice above were removed. A neighboring block of buildings has become the parking lot, and the former entrance is now a side wall. The great arched entrance from the railroad has been bricked up, the voussoirs covered with drab red paint, and a new brick wall erected in front of it to hide the garbage cans. Though the tornado and its aftermath obscured much of its historic character, the old building has been successfully adapted and given a new life. ■

McLendon Hardware Company (later River Square Center)

501 S. Eighth Street / 1908

Dr Pepper was not the only popular product produced in Waco. The Merrick Medicine Company manufactured Baby Percy Medicine in this building for more than a hundred years. Albert W. Percy was a traveling salesman who came across a prescription that helped settle the stomach of one of his young sons. After moving to Waco, he requested that pharmacist William S. Merrick re-create the solution, which was to relieve "intestinal and stomach upsets"—in particular, diarrhea.

The fledgling company rented a couple of locations until this building was completed sometime between 1907 and 1910. The building replaced a one-story frame Victorian house; the neighborhood had been working class but was on the edge of Waco's home for the construction industry. Just across Eighth Street was the W. F. and J. F. Barnes Lumber Company.

This is—and always was—a no-nonsense, let's-roll-up-our-sleeves-and-get-to-work sort of building. It was two stories with a raised basement—note the basement windows on the Clay Street side. The walls were of red brick, with a very limited amount of ornament at the top of the front. In the center of that facade six steps were recessed behind the front wall. To each side were paired windows; three more pairs were on the second floor. Immediately above the first-floor openings was a flat canopy, above which were three mezzanine windows. Such windows were designed to provide additional light when first-floor windows were shaded.

The company believed in using its building to market its product, so at the top of the Clay Street elevation and the rear elevation is painted these words: "Percy Medicine— for Intestinal and Stomach Upsets." This would have been painted on sometime after 1938, when "Baby" was dropped from Baby Percy Medicine.

The company moved to a more modern facility in 2010. Just a few years later the location became prime for retail with the opening of the Magnolia Market one block to the east, and this building was reopened as The Findery in 2015. The adaptation from manufacturing to retail was done with great respect for the original fabric. The biggest change was a small addition for an elevator, and this was clearly marked as new by the use of concrete blocks painted white, which contrast with the neighboring red brick without competing with it.

The new occupant also continued the tradition of painted advertisement, with the store name painted on the right corner and a motto and a hashtag printed on the side of the stair addition. The only departure from the original design is that the awning, also emblazoned with the business name, obscures the mezzanine windows, which, fortunately, were retained. ▪

Merrick Medicine Company (later the Findery)

601 Webster Avenue / 1910 main building
seed tanks (silos) between 1943 and 1950,
complex remodeled 2014–15

Before Chip and Joanna Gaines spent $1.4 million to create the Magnolia Market, this was the site of a large lumber company and then of a cotton oil mill. In early Waco, this block was known as Farm Lot No. 13 because it was so far out of town. However, when railroad tracks were laid down Jackson Avenue, this neighborhood became a prime location for early Waco industry. Beginning the late 1880s this block and the land across Webster were the home of the Waco Lumber Company.

Essentially this was the turn-of-the-century equivalent of a big-box home-improvement store. The buildings were all one story and wood-framed. The office was at the corner of Webster and Sixth Street—anticipating the office of the cotton oil mill—and behind this was the supply of architectural moldings, flooring, nails, and shingles. To the west of this was a large lumber shed and beyond this a warehouse for doors, window sashes, and blinds. (Later this became a furniture warehouse and then a shingle warehouse.) Across Webster were the planing mill, which was run by a 50-horsepower engine, and a carpenter's shop. A railroad switch came off the Jackson Avenue rails, which also served a beer refrigerator storing cold beverages made in St. Louis.

In 1910 the site became the home of the Brazos Valley Cotton Oil Mill, which was founded by J. T. Davis. His office was at the corner of Webster and Sixth Street in a twelve by fourteen brick block, which originally had a frame porch running across the front. This is now occupied by the Silos Baking Company. Over time there were single-room additions made to the office. The most recent came sometime after 1950; this had a curved wall with glass blocks for a window and is visible when walking on Sixth Street. What are now known as the Silos proper were actually referred to as seed tanks. They were made of iron and rose sixty feet to the eaves and ninety feet to the apex. Each tank could hold up to four thousand tons of seed.

Between the silos and the railroad tracks on Jackson was another seed house, this one with a wooden frame. A railroad switch allowed seed to be dropped off here, and the process of cleaning the seed began. In a second brick complex just west of the frame seed house was the room for hulling the seeds, removing the lint, and pressing the oil. A metal conveyor belt shipped the product into the seed house, now known as the Magnolia Market. It had a steel frame resting on exterior tiles and, inside, on concrete pillars on concrete floors. An exterior platform ran across the north wall. A second railroad switch came up to the northeast corner of the building so that the finished product could be shipped out. The oil could be used in cooking or in industry.

The Gaineses saw the potential of the rusty old structures, and the taxpayers of Waco and McLennan County provided incentives, specifically $208,376 in tax increment funding (TIF), which is reserved for downtown improvements. Working with the Texas Historical

Brazos Valley Cotton Oil Mill (later Magnolia Market at the Silos)

Commission, Chip and Joanna Gaines were able to successfully adapt this old structure to retail purposes while retaining the historic character of the office, the silos, and the seed house. The biggest change from the original character was painting the tile blocks of the seed house white, but the original color was a workaday beige color that added little to the appearance of the building. Pearson Construction, the general contractor for the project, won an award for outstanding construction in a historic renovation. ▪

220 S. Second Street / 1913

The Hanna-James-Taylor Company was in the wholesale grocery business, which was a tough business to be in when the Cooper Grocery Company dominated the market in Waco and McLennan County. Sam Hanna Jr., Frank K. James, and Peter G. Taylor were the officers of the firm; Taylor stayed the longest in Waco, probably because he and his wife, Eva, purchased and remodeled the old house at 1705 N. Fifth Street and lived there for many years (see *More Historic Homes*, 170).

The headquarters was a three-story red brick building with a slightly raised basement visible on the Second Street elevation. The Sanborn Fire Insurance Map noted that it had "pilastered walls," which projected forward and created a steady rhythm on three of the four facades. At the top of each pilaster was a round concrete ornament with the initials of the firm, "HTJ Company," in each roundel. Presumably these pilasters enclosed steel beams; between them were wide banks of windows. The location was probably seen as a critical advantage; the building was connected to the outside world by the railroad switch on the Mary Street Side.

This was a no-nonsense building with just the right amount of ornamentation. In the years around the construction of this building there was a fourth officer who did not live in Waco: M. B. Orde of Chicago. In the decades surrounding 1900 Chicago had emerged as a leader in the design of tall buildings and commercial blocks that were functional yet also had a formal dignity. Although the architect for this building is unknown, he seems to have drawn inspiration from the Windy City.

The Hanna-James-Taylor Company did not last a decade. By 1919 the building was the home of the Meadows Grocery Company, but apparently this did no better against the Cooper juggernaut. By 1926 it was the home of the Herrick Hardware Company wholesale facility; this was no retail hardware store but a facility for selling automobile accessories and tires wholesale. It was also briefly the office of the Castle Heights Company, selling lots in what they called "Waco's Ideal Exclusive Homesite." William T. Herrick was an officer of both companies.

In the second half of the 1930s the building was the home of Central Freight Lines and other businesses of W. "Woody" Callan. After World War II, the building became the home of Hammond Laundry Cleaning Machinery Co., which manufactured laundry and dry-cleaning machinery. In the late 1990s the building was converted to Holiday Hammond Lofts. ◼

Hanna-James-Taylor Building (later Holiday Hammond Lofts)

401 S. Third Street / Circa 1914–15

Built in two phases, this utilitarian building housed two start-up companies that were chasing the dominant company in their business. As late as 1913 the site was occupied by two frame houses, but by 1916 the front part of the current building had been erected. Initially there were two occupants: Hamilton-Turner Grocery Company and the Cash Mercantile Company. Hamilton-Turner, which occupied the part of the building closest to the tracks, was a wholesale grocery business—that is, its business was to supply retail stores with the groceries they would sell.

In so doing, Hamilton-Turner was competing with the Cooper Grocery Company, whose building was nearby. Given that Cooper Grocery dominated the market, the start-up faced a difficult task. The other part of the building was occupied by the Cash Mercantile Company, which was trying to create a chain of corner grocery stores (in 1916 it had twenty-one branch stores in Waco), which the company itself supplied. By 1921 both companies had moved on.

In the early 1920s the building was often vacant, though in late 1922 and early 1923 it was rented by the Mason Transfer and Storage Company, which occupied another building at 217–219 Jackson, catty-corner from this building. Its business was moving, storing, packing, and shipping. The company name was painted on the north wall of the building and is still visible. (For a similar business, see 28 in this volume, the Texas Fireproof Storage Company building at 225 S. Eleventh Street.)

By 1926 the entire building was occupied by the Crawford-Austin Manufacturing Company, which was chartered in 1924. The company made tents, awnings, camp furniture, wagon covers, tarpaulins, and cotton-picker sacks. (The latter were especially useful in an area in which cotton was an important crop.) The product line was listed in paint on the north side of the building, just below the cornice.

As Hamilton-Turner had challenged Cooper Grocery, so Crawford-Austin challenged the Clifton Company, which made canvas products at its plant in East Waco. Crawford-Austin tried innovative techniques to market its products, such as advertising its "Teepee Tents for Boy Scouts" in 1928 in *Boys' Life*, the magazine for scouts. At the beginning of World War II it won two federal government contracts to make army tents, folding canvas cots, and other products. Production pressures were such that Crawford-Austin rented the Hanna-James-Taylor Building at 220 S. Second Street.

As it was for many commercial buildings in Waco, proximity to railroad tracks was seen as a key advantage. A frame platform ran along the north side of the building, facing the tracks, which after 1950 was replaced with a concrete platform. The building had brick load-bearing walls, with four rows of stretcher bricks (laid with the long side visible) to one row of header bricks (laid with the short side visible). The front of the building had seven bays, separated by pilasters with large glass windows between them; the corner bays were marked by a higher cornice. Originally there were awnings shading the first-floor windows. Inside, the upper floor was supported by wooden posts.

Commercial Building

Perhaps during World War II, but definitely before 1950, Crawford-Austin expanded the building to the alley. The new part of the building had concrete rather than wooden posts, and the concrete frame was clearly expressed on the exterior. The tent factory was on the second floor, while the first floor had offices at the front and the shipping department at the back. ◼

119 N. Ninth Street / 1915–16
Ross and Cason, architects

The proliferating number of telephones in Waco necessitated the construction of this building. The architects were E. McIver Ross and Herman F. Cason, who until recently had worked for Milton W. Scott. J. S. Harrison and Son were the contractors. Sam Herbert issued the building permit in October 1915 for a $60,000 building.

The Neoclassical style and brick facades conceal reinforced-concrete floors and roof, making the building fireproof. The bricks on the front were in a variety of colors laid in what was known as a "tapestry" pattern, making for a lively appearance. They were even used for the shafts of two-story columns, with contrasting stone for their simple bases and Doric capitals. The ornate door was also of stone.

Cheaper, orange-tinted brick was used on the south side, which faced the alley. Ross and Cason may have expected that any new building across the alley would hide this economy measure, but as of 1950 there was an auto sales lot on the corner and a group of one- and two-story stores between that and the Hotel Raleigh.

The recessed entrance was on the left. Inside was a narrow stair lobby, which opened into a public lobby, with general offices and six private offices beyond. There were also two cashier's cages and three public telephone booths, which in 1916 was a novel public amenity but has now been made obsolete by cell phones.

The upper two floors were divided by gender. On the second floor were the terminal room and other mechanical functions, which were the domain of male workers. At the rear was a locker room. On the third floor was the operating room, which was the domain of young women who operated the switchboard. This was a large room with three windows on the front and nine windows on the side. All of these windows were oriented to catch the Gulf breeze. At the rear was a "rest room" for the workers and a small café. Part of the roof was floored over, creating a rooftop garden that could hold more than one hundred people. ■

Texas Telephone Company Exchange

50. Williams Dry Goods Company
(later Waco Dry Goods, later Altura Luxury Lofts)

216 S. Sixth Street / 1917

Like the Waco Drug Company building to which it backs up, this is how Waco built when it meant business. Built for a wholesale dry goods company, the floor, roof, and frame were all made of reinforced concrete. This is visible on the east side of the building, where the horizontal and vertical lines of concrete were left exposed. The remaining space was filled with windows and a brick curtain wall, which was not load bearing. The south and west facades were organized by brick pilasters (which, as on other Waco buildings of this vintage, were not actually structural) capped with abstract cartouches where one might expect to find a capital on a neoclassical pilaster. The concrete construction was frankly expressed inside by concrete columns approximately every fifteen feet.

The Williams Drug Company was founded by Hugh L. Williams, who was new to Waco but had secured financing with the Mercantile Trust Company of St. Louis. He was president from 1917 until the early 1920s, when the other officers bought him out and changed the named to Waco Dry Goods Company. (For the rented home of Williams, see *More Historic Homes*, 128.) In the 1940s the building housed the J. M. Wood Manufacturing Company; and in the 1990s, the Gradel Printing Company.

In 2015 the building was converted to luxury loft condominiums. By and large the adaptation was respectful to the original fabric, with the glaring exception of the original windows being removed and replaced with modern ones; in addition, the window openings on the Sixth Street elevation—which were only half the size of the ones on the south front—were dramatically enlarged. The retention of original windows on the adjacent Waco Drug Company Building should have been a helpful example but was not.

One original opening was retained on the alley side: a metal door that is hung from a rod at the top and slides to open. This is often associated with barn doors, but in the early twentieth century it was also used in industrial contexts and would be known as a fire door. This door came from Chicago and was made by the Allith Manufacturing Company. ◼

Williams Dry Goods Company (later Waco Dry Goods, later Altura Luxury Lofts)

<h2 style="text-align:center">51. Miller Cotton Mill
(later L. L. Sams and Sons Manufacturing Company,
now L. L. Sams Historic Lofts)</h2>

2000 S. First Street / 1919–20, 1946
Wyatt C. Hedrick, architect

This complex was created for the processing of McLennan County's principal crop, cotton, into blue denim for overalls and into twine. It was noted at the time that Texas grew huge amounts of cotton but manufactured very little. The more prominent, three-story building had five thousand spindles and a large number of looms to spin and weave the denim; the two-story building behind it could process two thousand pounds of cotton twine per day. By 1929 the complex sat on thirty acres. These two main buildings were made of reinforced concrete, brick, and ribbed glass. The concrete columns are visible on the south wall of the three-story building: the capitals flare out from the wall, anticipating an addition to the south that was never built. Nevertheless, the words "Miller Cotton Mill" can still be seen at the very top of the tower.

The complex was begun in 1919 and completed in August 1920. The builder (and presumably designer) was Wyatt C. Hedrick, a thirty-two-year-old Virginian with a degree in engineering from Washington and Lee University. He moved to Texas in 1913 and started the W. C. Hedrick Construction Company the next year. In October and November 1919 he was advertising in the Waco paper, first for carpenters who could construct concrete forms and then for laborers. He promised to pay the latter forty cents an hour and to pay eleven hours a day for ten hours of work. Hedrick, who went on to design many buildings in Fort Worth and much of the early campus of Texas Tech University in Lubbock, probably had no idea that some thirty years later he would return to Waco as the lead architect of the Armstrong Browning Library (see 83 in this volume) and the earliest part of the First National Bank complex on Washington Avenue (see 62a).

The cotton mill was founded by Byron Miller, who started his business in Fort Worth and expanded into Dallas and Waco. Local investors included Waco businessmen E. W. Marshall, Harold Shear, and George McLendon, as well as Rufus Higginbotham of Dallas. The complex included not only the mill buildings but also some twenty one- and two-story houses for mill workers. In 1919 this complex was just beyond the city limits of Waco at what is now Daughtrey Avenue. Initially business was good, but a variety of factors led to the company going into receivership in February 1929.

The complex sat empty for nearly two decades, but after World War II the buildings were acquired by L. L. Sams and Sons. This was a furniture-making company, founded in Waco in the 1920s, which specialized in making pulpits and pews for churches. The sons of L. L. Sams, Ross and Rowe, bought the company from their father in 1927, and under their leadership the business grew dramatically. In 1997 the company moved to Cameron, Texas. Both the city and Baylor University continued to grow toward the complex, and the buildings were converted into loft apartments, principally for Baylor students. ■

Miller Cotton Mill (later L. L. Sams and Sons Manufacturing Company, now L. L. Sams Historic Lofts)

52. Waco Drug Company
(later Insurors of Texas Building)

225 S. Fifth Street / 1910–11, enlarged 1922–23

Pearson and Scott, architects, 1910–11

E. McIver Ross, architect, 1922–23

This building has been a bit of mystery to Waco historians because a 1911 drawing of it in a local newspaper does not match the present building. The confusion is due to a dramatic enlargement of the structure during the Roaring Twenties.

The Waco Drug Company was a start-up in 1911. Robert L. Cartwright, the founder, was new to town but was a grandson of Matthew and Amanda Cartwright of San Augustine, Texas, who were among the wealthiest Texans after the Civil War. Robert attended Vanderbilt University, then formed a real estate and livestock company in the Hill County with his father and brother. While living in Waco in 1903 and 1904, he was president of another family company that drilled for oil near Beaumont in the aftermath of Spindletop, but their company was liquidated in 1905. For the Waco Drug Company he had financing from the Mercantile Trust Company of St. Louis, which also provided funding for the Goldstein-Migel Building, the R. T. Dennis Building, and the neighboring Williams Dry Goods Company Building.

The original building was the left five bays of the current building. The architects were Milton W. Scott and T. Brooks Pearson, and the contractor was J. E. Johnson. The building was well under way by May 1911, and completion was expected by August 1. The pattern of horizontal and vertical reinforced concrete is today exactly as it was in the drawing by Scott and Pearson in 1911, down to the door for the loading dock on the Mary Street side. The front of the original building had brick pilasters framing the outer bays, but there was a much more elaborate classical cornice. Instead of the present single-wide windows in the outer bays, there were two narrower ones. A canopy over the front door was suspended by wires. Scott and Pearson were quite busy in 1910–11; they oversaw construction of the Waco High School (see 75 in this volume) and the Smith-Migel and Shear-Callan houses on Columbus Avenue (see *Historic Homes*, 33), but the partners decided to go their separate ways.

Robert L. Cartwright led the firm only briefly; by 1913 he was in real estate and at other times claimed to be a farmer or a rancher. James M. Penland, who had been vice president in 1911, was president in 1913 and remained in that position for more than a decade. In the early 1920s business was so good that Waco Drug decided to more than double the size of its building. Plans for the addition, which was anticipated to cost some $50,000, were drawn not by Milton W. Scott but E. McIver Ross, who often worked as a draftsman for Scott. Scott was the architect of the new Penland house on Park Place near Cameron Park, but Ross was the draftsman who signed the drawings (see *Historic Homes*, 60). In February 1923 Ross provided a perspective view of the enlarged building, which was published in the *Waco New-Tribune*, but ground had not yet been broken. In 1926 Ross designed the house of C. Samuel Appel, who was second vice president of Waco Drug (see *More Historic Homes*, 179).

Waco Drug Company (later Insurors of Texas Building)

In the new building another five bays like those in the early building were placed at the other end of the block, separated by three bays in the middle. The new middle section had a sloping parapet that looked somewhat like a pediment, and in the central bay below was an actual neoclassical frame for the steps up to the front door. The heavier classical cornice of 1911 was removed, and the Fifth Street facade was veneered in red brick. Like the original building, the enlarged structure was built with reinforced concrete—floors, frame, and roof—with a brick curtain wall. The difference between the two phases of construction are best seen on the west (parking lot) side, where both the concrete and brick are of a slightly different shade, and on the concrete platform where the old left off and the new began.

Insurors of Texas bought the building in 2006, when it had been vacant for some seventeen years. The company restored the building and adapted it for use at its corporate headquarters, winning several preservation awards in the process. ■

1201 Austin Avenue / 1938
Robert V. Derrah (Los Angeles), architect,
with T. Brooks Pearson, associate

While Waco prides itself as the birthplace of Dr Pepper, Coca-Cola also had a considerable presence in town, especially after the construction of this streamlined art deco bottling plant. The architect was Robert V. Derrah of Beverly Hills, California, who was also designing a Coca-Cola plant in South Central LA at the same time. Derrah, a native of Salt Lake City, attended MIT and Harvard and moved to Southern California in 1924. Among his best-known designs were the Brown Derby Restaurant on Wilshire Boulevard and the Walt Disney Studios on Hyperion Drive. Derrah may not have visited Waco; local architect T. Brooks Pearson oversaw the project. Pearson was well positioned to provide this service, as his office in 1939 was a few feet away at 115 N. Twelfth Street.

The Waco Coca-Cola plant was in a severely simplified classical yet modern style that might be called "Greco-Deco." The "Greco" part is most evident around the entrance: the vertical grooves resembling the fluting on a classical column, the elongated urns above this, and the piers framing the opening, each of which has half of an Ionic capital. The "Deco" part is seen in the metal-frame windows—a wide window to the right of the entrance, the second-story window that wraps around the corner—and the porthole windows, one in the door and two in the wall above. The original building was only half of the present structure, which was dramatically enlarged after 1950.

A report in the *Waco Tribune-Herald* noted that the building would be "pure white, and built of solid concrete, reinforced with steel." Large plate-glass windows on Austin and Twelfth would allow pedestrians to view the bottling works in action. The use of tile, stainless metal, and glass would "insure absolute sanitation." The building would also include an internal street for delivery trucks. The trucks would enter at the northeast corner on Twelfth, unload empty bottles that would travel by conveyor belt to the bottle washer, then continue on to another conveyor belt bringing newly filled bottles. There would also be an automotive maintenance shop on the west side and nighttime parking on the second story. The exit would be onto Austin Avenue west of the main entrance.

The Coca-Cola Bottling Company building must have presented an extraordinary contrast to the house that occupied the western two-thirds of the block, the William Cameron house by W. W. Larmour. This High Victorian mansion was built in 1878–79; it burned in 1966 and was demolished shortly thereafter. The bland and boxy addition on the west side of the Coca-Cola building stands where the Cameron family had their garden and, at the very back of the lot, where the Cameron carriage house stood.

Across Twelfth Street at 1125 Austin is an original Texaco gas station. The strong horizontal lines are a characteristic feature of the streamlined design prototype by Walter Dorwin Teague. And across Austin from the gas station is the former location of the 1904 Waco Public Library, which was a fairly typical example of the Beaux-Arts classicism utilized for many Carnegie libraries. ◾

Coca-Cola Bottling Company

54. Southwestern Bell Telephone Company
(later McLennan County Archives)

824 Washington Avenue / 1947–48

The earliest telephone systems required conversing with an operator to make a call, but by the early 1940s new phone systems allowed each customer to dial the numbers for their calls. In 1947 it was announced that Waco would get a $1.7 million dial telephone system in a new building, which would cost around $300,000. It would be attached to the old Texas Telephone Company Exchange, which was around the corner at 119 N. Ninth but would also include business offices that were until then at 819 Austin Avenue. Building permits were issued in August 1947, but the building was not completed until 1948, and it took until 1949 to install the new dial telephone system.

The new building was two stories with a basement. The frame of the building was reinforced concrete, making it thoroughly fireproof, with a beige brick veneer and stone and aluminum trim. The building was wide and had a nearly flat roof; to counter this, first- and second-floor windows were arranged with aluminum spandrels between them. Just above each second-story window was a stone panel in the shape of a bell, the logo of Southwestern Bell. The off-center stone entrance had just enough classic detail to echo the classicized art deco of the 1930s, sometimes called "Greco-Deco." Though striving for modernity, the building did not originally have air-conditioning, which had become very popular in Texas. This was installed in 1954, providing cooling for both the old and new buildings. ■

Southwestern Bell Telephone Company (later McLennan County Archives)

CHAPTER FOUR

Skyscrapers

55. Amicable Life Insurance Company Building (ALICO)

425 Austin Avenue / 1910–11, remodeled 1964–66
Sanguinet and Staats (Fort Worth), architects, with Roy E. Lane, associate
Jay Frank Powell (Midland), architect for remodeling of 1964–66

A Waco icon, the Amicable Life Insurance Company Building was one of the tallest in Texas for almost two decades. In addition to serving as the home office of the insurance company, it was a prestige address for doctors, lawyers, and other professionals. For a while it was the home of Waco's first radio station, WACO. Constructed with a steel frame and reinforced concrete, the lower two floors were terra-cotta with two-story granite columns of the Doric order. Terra-cotta was also used on the top three floors. Between the terra-cotta sections, the building was clad with brick, referred to as "light cream" in color. The letters "ALICO" were spelled out in the terra-cotta, though these letters are now dwarfed by the gigantic neon letters above. Inside, the lobby was finished with imported marble.

The architects were Sanguinet and Staats of Fort Worth, in association with Roy E. Lane of Waco. This Fort Worth firm was responsible for a great many of the tall office buildings in Texas before 1920. In their home town they designed the Flatiron Building, the Hotel Texas, and the Burk Burnett Building; in Houston, the Carter Building; in Austin, the Scarborough Building; and in San Antonio, the Rand Building. Lane is not known to have designed any other skyscrapers, and his role seems to have been the local architect riding herd on the contractors. Most of the drawings for the project are dated June 23, 1910. Excavation of the site was under way by August, and the steel frame was coming out of the ground by December.

Eleven of the first twenty-two drawings for the ALICO Building were done by Herman Paul Koeppe. A native of Leipzig, Koeppe immigrated with his family to Galveston around 1880. After apprenticing in Galveston, he moved to Fort Worth in 1904 to work as a draftsman for Sanguinet and Staats. He remained with the firm after it was purchased by Wyatt C. Hedrick and designed many of Fort Worth's art deco buildings, including City Hall and the Will Rogers Memorial Auditorium, Coliseum, and Tower. Two other drawings were by Alfred C. Finn, who worked for Sanguinet and Staats from 1904 to 1912. He then moved

Amicable Life Insurance Company Building (ALICO)

to Houston, where he became the local architect for Mauran, Russell and Crowell of St. Louis for the Rice Hotel—the same type of position Roy Lane had performed on the ALICO project. Among Finn's later buildings were the Gulf Building in Houston (1922–29) and the San Jacinto Monument (1935–36).

When the ALICO was finished, only the Carter Building in Houston was taller—by one story. In 1921 a Dallas skyscraper tied the ALICO in height—the Magnolia Petroleum Company Building, whose neon Pegasus was as emblematic of Dallas as the neon letters "ALICO" later became for Waco. It was not until the late 1920s that the ALICO was surpassed by three skyscrapers that were thirty stories or more: the Niels-Esperson Building and the Gulf Building in Houston (both by Alfred C. Finn) and the Smith-Young Tower in San Antonio (by Ayres and Ayres).

The sturdy steel frame withstood the force of the tornado of 1953, as did the veneer of terra-cotta and brick, but flight to the suburbs in the aftermath of the tornado made the building something of a cream-colored elephant. An attempt was made to revive its fortunes by creating a motor hotel, the ALICO Center Inn (now a parking lot facing the Roosevelt Building), and by adding a multistory parking garage (1964–66). Jay Frank Powell, a young Midland-based architect, designed and developed the project; Waco Construction Company built it.

Although the idea was well-intentioned, the original facade of the three lowest floors were remodeled to match the modish design of the inn and the garage. Initially the plan was to sheathe the lower floors in aluminum, but ultimately it was covered in pebbledash, a plaster or cement surface mixed with sand, gravel, and pebbles. In either case it was a sorry substitute for the original granite columns and terra-cotta.

Still visible at the east end of the Austin Avenue elevation there are a few feet that were originally part of the ALICO Center Inn; when the inn was demolished, this part had to be retained because it housed a skywalk connecting both the old and new buildings to the parking lot. In spite of such indignities, the building still towers over the Central Texas landscape. ▪

56. Riggins Hotel
(later the Raleigh Hotel, now an office building)

801–807 Austin Avenue / 1912–14, 1925, 1929
Lang and Witchell (Dallas) architects, with Roy E. Lane, 1912
Henry T. Phelps (San Antonio), architect, 1929

This grand old building has survived several changes of ownership and a very unsympathetic restoration. The original owner/developer was J. W. Riggins, who had served three one-year terms as mayor of Waco in 1900, 1901, and 1902 and who would serve again in 1914 and 1915. He hired the prominent Dallas architects Lang and Witchell, with local architect Roy E. Lane to be the man on the scene. (Lang and Witchell were responsible for three other important Waco buildings: the first version of the Hippodrome and, more than a decade later, the Hilton Hotel and Waco Hall on the Baylor campus.) Riggins chose as his contractor the Westlake Construction Company of St. Louis. This was no random decision: Westlake had recently built the Gunter Hotel in San Antonio, designed by the St. Louis firm Mauran, Russell and Gardner.

Otto Lang was a German immigrant who specialized in engineering; Frank O. Witchell had been a draftsman for J. Riely Gordon and for Sanguinet and Staats (before they designed the ALICO Building). The firm was created in 1905, but in 1907 it made a crucial hire: Charles Erwin Barglebaugh. A native of Arkansas, Barglebaugh worked with Frank Lloyd Wright for one year around 1900 or 1901. By 1902 he was in Dallas, working as a draftsman for J. E. Flanders, including the years in which Flanders designed the first Grand Masonic Lodge in Waco, at Franklin and Sixth. After four years with Flanders, Barglebaugh went out on his own, but within a year he had joined Lang and Witchell. He started as a draftsman but by 1911 was named chief draftsman. At this time the firm had begun to incorporate the progressive tendencies of the Chicago school in commercial buildings and the related Prairie school in residences. In Dallas notable examples were the Sanger Brothers Department Store (1910) and the Southwestern Life Insurance Building (1911–12).

The oldest image of the Riggins Hotel, from the time of construction, was signed "Orlopp," which would be either Donald, Harry, or Stanley Orlopp, all young architects in Dallas specializing in drawing. (They were nephews of Maximilian A. Orlopp Jr., architect of the 1890–92 Dallas County Courthouse.) At least one other Lang and Witchell drawing, for the Boren and Stewart Building in Dallas (1913), is also signed "Orlopp."

Especially noteworthy on the Waco hotel were the foliate panels on the mezzanine level, which echoed the organic ornament of the Chicago master Louis Sullivan. The design emphasized the building as a series of stacked floors by running light-colored bands of stone across the facade just under the windowsills. At each corner of the Austin and Eighth Street facades the last bay projected forward and the course of stone stopped, resulting in an emphasis on the verticality of the building. At the ninth floor of these outer bays were stone balconies supported by brackets (these balconies were later removed). As on the nearby Praetorian—and on many skyscrapers by Sullivan himself—

Riggins Hotel (later the Raleigh Hotel, now an office building)

the back facades were extremely plain, presumably because it was expected that nearby skyscrapers would soon be blocking views not on the street sides.

The Chicago influence continued inside: the entire hotel was furnished by Albert Pick and Company. This Chicago firm specialized in furnishing restaurants, cafeterias, and lunchrooms but expanded to supply everything a hotel could need, from ashtrays to armoires. The hotel also had a complete telephone system, made by the Stromberg-Carlson Telephone Manufacturing Company of Rochester, New York.

An early advertisement for the hotel announced that it was "absolutely fireproof" and that it had "over 200 rooms of comfort and good cheer." The hotel had a "beautifully decorated dining room" and rooms for social events: the ad stated that it was "the center of all Waco activities." It was also an excellent resting spot for traveling salesmen, as it had a large and light-filled room where they could display their samples. Basic rooms were $1.00 a night; a room with a private bath cost $1.50.

Although the Riggins attracted some major meetings, such as the Texas Bankers Association in May 1915, the hotel went into receivership late in that year. It emerged from bankruptcy with a new owner, the Central Texas Hotel Company; Robert E. Pellow moved from Chicago to Waco so he could take over as president. Pellow renamed it the Hotel Raleigh.

By the end of the 1920s, however, the hotel again changed hands, now owned by Albert Pick Hotels. (Having been in the business of furnishing hotels, the company decided to start buying them.) The hotels tended to be in midsize cities in the Midwest, mainly Ohio. Pick hired the San Antonio architect Henry T. Phelps to remodel the building with a budget of $150,000. This included modernizing the guest rooms and introducing air-conditioning to the lobby, the dining room, and the Purple Cow Coffee Shop. As newer hotels were built, the hotel shut down and the Raleigh was later repurposed as an office building. All windows were replaced with single panes of glass, which seriously damaged its historical integrity. ■

601 Franklin Avenue / 1913–15
C. W. Bulger and Son (Dallas), architects

The Praetorian Order was a recently founded fraternal insurance company headquartered in Dallas. It hired Charles W. Bulger to design a fifteen-story skyscraper at 1607 Main Street in Dallas, which was built between 1905 and 1909. Just a few years later the company decided to erect a second building and chose Waco as the location. Bulger was again the architect.

The Praetorian Building

The Praetorian Building in Waco was half the size of its Dallas predecessor. It was seven stories tall and had two elevators in the lobby. The building was fireproof, with a reinforced concrete frame, floor, and roof. On the two principal facades, the walls were covered with a base of gray granite and above this with glazed terra-cotta, mainly white but with colorful details. The other two facades were covered with economical brick. There was a curving canopy above the Franklin Street entrance and an awning along the Sixth Street elevation.

The building was slow to be fully occupied. The large first floor contained the American Express Company and the ticket office for the Missouri, Kansas and Texas Railway; the passenger depot was two blocks away at 811 Jackson. The Waco City Directory for 1916 showed that the tenants included a large number of doctors, as well as cotton brokers and insurance agents. The doctors included Kenneth H. Aynesworth, Charles E. Collins, and H. R. Dudgeon, who practiced together, and Merchant and Irwin Colgin. Most offices needed more than one room. For example, the Colgins, who practiced with H. M. Lanham, shared four rooms, plus a fifth for their newfangled X-ray equipment. A year later only nine rooms were occupied. Among the new renters was the architect Birch D. Easterwood, who had rooms 507 and 508.

Around 1921 the ground floor was occupied by the First State Bank & Trust Company, which had previously been situated across Sixth Street. At that time the building became the First State Bank Building. The president of the First State Bank up to 1921 was James H. Lockwood, who retired and built a fancy retirement house on Austin Avenue called "Casa Grande" (see *Historic Homes*, 73). His son, Lee Lockwood, was a teller at the bank before moving on to other business opportunities. He and his wife built a house in the Karem Addition close by his parents. ■

58. Liberty National Bank Building
(later One Liberty Place)

100 N. Sixth Street / 1922–23
Birch D. Easterwood, architect

Liberty National Bank was founded in 1917 and by 1922 had grown sufficiently to plan a nine-story skyscraper with a banking house on the ground floor, which would cost around $300,000. Birch D. Easterwood, who was emerging as an important Waco architect, followed the classic scheme for an early twentieth-century skyscraper: stone for the base (in this case, artificial stone), brick for the office floors, and a heavy cornice (this one made of metal) at the top. Originally there was a large arched opening on Austin Avenue similar to the one that still exists on N. Sixth. The entrance to Liberty National Bank was at 601–603 Austin Avenue, but the entrance to the elevator lobby, Liberty Pharmacy, and Stringfellow Barber Shop was on North Sixth. The office and display rooms of C. H. Ruebeck, which sold bricks, tiles, and other building materials, were in a two-story annex at 112 N. Sixth Street. Ruebeck provided Acme Brick for the exterior and Waco common bricks for internal uses.

Easterwood concentrated much attention on the interiors of the bank. Unlike the ALICO Building, where the Austin Avenue facade included entrances into both the banking spaces and the lobby, at Liberty the bank took the entire space. The ceiling was twenty-four feet high, and much walnut, bronze, and Italian marble was used. A circular marble stairway led to the mezzanine level, which had the director's room (what we would call the board room), various offices, and a ladies' restroom. The vaults were in the basement, which was also completely occupied by the bank.

The building was complete by April 1923, when Easterwood and Earl M. King, who was briefly his partner, announced that their offices were on the sixth floor, perhaps in partial payment for the design. On the fourth floor was J. S. Harrison and Son, Construction Company, which had been the general contractor; also on that floor was the insurance company of Walter V. Fort Jr., a grandson of William and Dionitia Fort, in whose house he was born (see *Historic Homes*, 4). On the eighth floor were offices for the president and vice president of the bank, J. B. Earle and J. M. Nash. Baylis Earle was a grandson of Waco pioneers Baylis Wood Earle and Eliza (Harrison) Earle and lived in a sturdy Foursquare on Morrow Avenue (see *Historic Homes*, 3 and 44). Joseph Mitchell Nash was involved in a number of family businesses; he had grown up in his family's two-story Victorian house and would soon hire Birch Easterwood to design a Tudor Revival house in Castle Heights (see *Historic Homes*, 15 and 90). On the third floor were the offices of the Ku Klux Klan, who had recently formed a chapter in Waco.

The windows on floors 2–9 were tripartite, all three windows having one sash above another, and with the middle one wider. This was a tip of the hat to "Chicago" windows, except on true Chicago windows the center window was a single, wide pane and did not open. The same brown Acme brick was used on all four sides, giving the building a unity not found on other skyscrapers such as the Raleigh Hotel or the Praetorian Building.

However, the cornice at the top was present only on the Austin Avenue and Sixth Street elevations. (This economy measure could be seen on many early American skyscrapers.) Easterwood was so proud of his design that when he placed an ad in the *Waco News-Tribune* celebrating eight years as a Waco architect, he placed the Liberty Building at the top of his list of "Easterwood Landmarks."

A massive explosion on October 4, 1936, seriously damaged the building, essentially blowing out all partitions on the first four floors. There was one fatality—the janitor—but the losses would have been much higher had the blast not occurred on a Sunday morning. However, there was also serious damage to the adjoining Woolworth Store on Austin Avenue and to the Goldstein-Migel Department Store across Sixth Street.

Time and later owners have not been kind to the structure. All windows, including the tripartite windows on floors 2–9, were later replaced with single sheets of reflective glass, and the "ornamental art stone" has been covered with a thick coat of paint. The annex was either partially or completely rebuilt to house a restaurant. For a long while it has been occupied by Café Cappuccino, which also uses the Liberty Pharmacy space. All of these changes damaged the historic integrity of the building. ■

Liberty National Bank Building (later One Liberty Place)

59. Stratton Building

800 Austin Avenue / 1922–23
Harry L. Spicer, architect

Architect Harry Spicer is better known for his design of Waco City Hall, but he also designed a number of commercial buildings, including this one. He got his start as a draftsman for Roy E. Lane before going out on his own. The Stratton-Stricker Furniture Company was founded only in 1918, but the company experienced explosive growth, prompting it to build its own facility. In the fall of 1922 the company was simultaneously negotiating with Anheuser-Busch to purchase the land and working with Spicer on the design of the building. Initially the plan was for a four-story building but grew to five stories plus a mezzanine and a basement.

The Stratton Building was clad in red brick, but the firm placed more emphasis on the ground floor, which had large plate-glass windows—50 feet on Austin Avenue and 165 feet on Eighth Street. This, they claimed, made it "one of the finest show spaces in this city or section." The furniture company's showroom occupied the ground floor. Above the plate-glass windows was a band of mezzanine windows; inside on the mezzanine was a new department of upholstery, for which the company hired W. A. Crouch away from Goldstein-Migel.

Spencer B. Swigert was the contractor. Excavation of the basement was under way by December 1922, and the grand opening was held June 30, 1923. While not as flashy as the Raleigh Hotel directly across Austin Avenue, the Stratton had a simple dignity. The owners claimed that it would be "modern in every respect" and "a credit to Waco." The facing of white tiles that were later added to the ground floor lent little distinction to the building. Amazingly, the original metal-framed windows of 1923 have survived to the present. ▪

Stratton Building

400 Austin Avenue / 1927–28, enlarged 1929
Lang and Witchell (Dallas), architects, with Milton W. Scott

In 1919 World War I veteran Conrad Hilton bought his first hotel, the Mobley Hotel in Cisco, Texas, and between 1925 and 1930 he opened a new hotel in Texas every year. This was one of them. The architects were Lang and Witchell of Dallas, who had earlier designed the Riggins/Raleigh Hotel and the original Hippodrome Theatre and who would soon design Waco Hall on the Baylor campus. They also designed the Hilton Hotel in Dallas. The first three stories were the base, with brick-faced pilasters with Composite capitals on the second and third floors, followed by eight stories, and capped with a final story with brackets below and arches above each window. The space to each side of the windows was a continuous vertical so that the soaring nature of the building was emphasized. The terra cotta ornament came from the Atlantic Terra Cotta Company of New York, which was also the decoration on Lang and Witchell's Waco Hall. As originally designed by Lang and Witchell, the building was much wider facing Austin Avenue—nine bays wide and only four bays deep. They were designing the building in the summer of 1927; in August of that year contractor J. E. Johnson of Waco agreed to build the structure for $291,000.

The hotel was such a success that Hilton nearly doubled its size in 1929. This time local architect Milton W. Scott provided the plans for another one hundred rooms. This was a wing running along the Fourth Street side, which extended the total length of the structure eight bays deep and running all the way to the alley. The base was virtually identical to that of the original; above this Scott chose a slightly lighter color for the brick. Again J. E. Johnson took the contract, this time for only $68,927. Johnson was also the contractor for Waco Hall at the same time. The addition included a large ground-story dining room, above which was the second-story ballroom, which had larger windows on the east and south sides. This room was the scene of many Waco social events for decades to come.

Hilton was forced to sell the hotel in 1934 as the Great Depression left him near bankruptcy and forced a downsizing of his chain. The new owners renamed it the Roosevelt Hotel in honor of President Franklin D. Roosevelt. The hotel finally closed in 1961, another victim of suburbanization in Waco. In 1963 the building was converted into the Regis Retirement Home, a Catholic facility, and served this function until 2003. The next year Waco builder Mike Clark renovated the building for offices. ◼

Hilton Hotel / Roosevelt Hotel / Roosevelt Tower

61. Medical Arts Building
(later National Lloyd's Building)

900 Austin Avenue / 1927–29
J. N. MacCammon (Dallas), architect

This skyscraper is, unfortunately, a shadow of its original self. It was designed by the Dallas architect J. N. MacCammon between September 1927 and January 1928. (MacCammon is perhaps best known for the Meadows Building in Dallas, erected in 1955.) The Austin Avenue site was owned by John Sleeper, who owned the building across Ninth Street and became one of the developers of this building. As its original name suggested, the plan was to rent to Waco's growing community of physicians, surgeons, and related specialists. The general contractors were Churchill-Humphreys Contracting Company of Dallas, but there were some Waco subcontractors: J. E. Johnson for excavating the foundation and E. Nelson Manufacturing Company for millwork.

The foundations were completed by May 1928, and it was expected that the building would be completed by December 1. However, in September 1928 the newly formed Waco Business and Professionals Club announced it was going to make the eleventh floor its clubhouse and that a twelfth floor would be added as well. This, it was thought, would cause only "a slight delay." William C. Abeel, son of Alfred and Sadie, builders of the Castle farther up Austin Avenue, was in charge of adapting the space for club purposes. Though the *Waco News-Tribune* carried a prediction that the building would be ready by January 1, the building actually opened in April 1929 and the club in June 1929. What was initially planned to cost some $400,000 was reduced to $375,000 on the building permit application. It was finished for $450,000.

The focal point of the ground floor was the lobby entrance, with a grand central arch. Originally there were much larger openings to each side; these were later plastered over, reflecting the diminished standing of the occupants. Above this every original window was later ripped out and replaced by reflective glass. Only at the top can one get a sense of architect MacCammon's design. A double-height round-arched window echoed the Austin Avenue entrance below, and the top floors were partially stepped back, creating balconies at three of the four corners. The clear precedent for this arrangement was the set-back skyscrapers then fashionable in New York and other metropolitan areas. ■

Medical Arts Building (later National Lloyd's Building)

62a. First National Bank Building

811 Washington Avenue / 1954–55
Wyatt C. Hedrick (Fort Worth), architect, and Spicer, Bush and Witt, associated

First National Bank Building

62b. First National Bank Office Building

801 Washington Avenue / 1963–64
Walter Cocke Jr. and Robert S. Bennett, architects

For many decades, the north side of the 800 block of Washington had been the site of St. Mary's Catholic Church and the Academy of the Sacred Heart. The church, built in the mid-1880s, was designed by the Galveston architect Nicolas J. Clayton; in 1910 Sanguinet and Staats of Fort Worth designed an extension at the north end. (The Fort Worth firm was designing the ALICO building at the same time.) The academy was designed by W. W. Larmour, the designer of the earliest buildings of Baylor University in Waco. The church moved to Washington Avenue and Fourteenth in 1942, and the academy closed in 1946. The church was demolished by 1950, when the site was a used-car lot. The First National Bank acquired the entire block in 1953. The company planned to build its own structure but sold the western corner lot to the Pioneer Savings Association so that the block could become Waco's new "financial district."

First National Bank traced its roots back to 1874, when it was the Waco National Bank. For many years, its banking house was at Fifth and Austin, which was vacated to provide a site for the ALICO Building. The company engaged Wyatt C. Hedrick of Fort Worth, who had recently been the lead designer for the Armstrong Browning Library on the Baylor campus, and Waco architects Spicer, Bush and Witt. Thirteen contractors bid on the project, which was awarded to McClellan Construction of Waco.

The present building at 811 Washington, occupying only the middle of the block, was intended to be phase 1. It was three stories, would have side walls of traditional brick, but a more modern front of aluminum and plate glass framed by cast stone. The first floor was slightly recessed so that the front wall was supported by six granite columns or, as modernists sometimes called them, pilotis. In the interior a pair of escalators provided access to and from the main bank lobby on the second floor. This principal business space was decorated with an abstract mural by Stanley Fogel, which stretched across the west, north, and east walls. By the 1950s Americans had become so enamored of their automobiles that there were drive-in restaurants, drive-in movie theaters, and drive-in bank tellers. On the alley side of this building the first floor was recessed by ten feet so that autos were sheltered by the second and third floors above. This was one of the earliest drive-in teller arrangements in Waco.

The plan was to replicate the three-story design all the way to the corner of Eighth, and a fifteen-story tower would rise just to the right of the phase 1 block. The narrow ends of the tower, on the south and north, would have a stone veneer, while the east and west sides would have a curtain wall of glass. The design echoed the United Nations Secretariat Building of 1948–52, designed by the Brazilian architect Oscar Niemeyer and the Swiss-French architect Le Corbusier. Bank president Howard Hambleton hoped that this would be achieved by 1960.

However, the project was not completed until 1964, and the decision was made to place the tower at the corner of Eighth rather than in the middle of the complex. New plans were drawn by Walter Cocke Jr. and Robert Bennett. Both were well-known in the Waco design community, though neither specialized in office buildings. Cocke was best known for his work on churches, notably the St. Mary of the Assumption Catholic Church, St. Alban's Episcopal Church, and the extreme makeover of Columbus Avenue Baptist Church (see 14, 15 and 16 in this volume), while Bennett was known as the designer and builder of houses in Castle Heights and elsewhere in Waco.

The emphasis of the Cocke-Bennett design was decisively vertical. The one feature carried over from the bank building was a walkway around the building created by recessed walls, which exposed the concrete piers supporting the structure. These piers, open at the first floor, were visible as they rose through all ten floors of the building. Flanking these piers on each floor were tall single panes of glass; here, too, verticality was stressed as the black spandrels where the floor met the facade seemed to blend with the windows. Finally, between each grouping of windows was a vertical veneer of white marble. This arrangement was used on the west, south, and east elevations; on the north side was a windowless brick box, containing elevators, restrooms, and utilities.

Since 2010 these buildings have been the home of Baylor University's Diana R. Garland School of Social Work. This was an early and important gesture showing the university's commitment to the revitalization of downtown Waco. ▪

First National Bank Office Building

Public Buildings

63. Waco Suspension Bridge

University Parks Drive between Franklin Avenue and Washington Avenue / 1870, 1914
Thomas M. Griffith (New York), civil engineer, 1870
Missouri Valley Bridge and Iron Co. (Leavenworth, Kansas), 1914

Although this is not as much a historic building as a historic structure, the Waco Suspension Bridge is a Waco icon on a par with the ALICO Building and even the Magnolia Market at the Silos. In the nineteenth and early twentieth centuries this bridge gave travelers an excellent reason to head to Waco. Prior to 1870 humans had to take a ferry across, and cattle simply waded from one side to the other. Originally it was a private venture and a toll bridge, but the tolls were so unpopular that the bridge was sold to the City of Waco in 1889. The bridge also had local ramifications, encouraging both residential and industrial development on the east side of the river.

The bridge was designed by Thomas M. Griffith, a civil engineer and associate of John M. Roebling, the builder of the Brooklyn Bridge and many other American bridges. On each side of the river were two piers, connected above by a single arch. The bridge was supported by cables strung 475 feet from pier to pier; these cables then ran down to two small buildings, which contained a toll house and a house for the toll taker. The cables passed through these buildings and were buried deep underground. The original bridge was medieval in style, with battlements, niches, and other features. The Roebling firm supplied the cables for the Waco bridge; local brickyard owners John Wesley Mann, William Berry Trice, and Sion B. Trice provided the sandy pink Brazos River bricks for the towers. (These are still visible underneath the bridge at the river level.)

Although the approach to the bridge is today set in a park, in the early years the treatment was not so reverential. In 1885 a soda-water manufactory was less than 60 feet south of the bridge, and less than 130 feet to the southwest of the toll taker's house was the livery of W. R. Kellum and Son. It was also 120 feet to Bridge Street, which led to the town square. The part of Bridge Street nearer to the Square had three saloons, a variety theater, and a pit for cock fights. By 1889 there was a long string of small rooms stretching south from Bridge Street to the alley, which were for "female boarding," a euphemism for prostitution. Within a few years these would be gone, as all prostitutes were moved to the Waco Reservation, a zone of legal prostitution that started one block to the north, beyond Washington Avenue. The bridge itself was treated with something less than the dignity it deserved, as the brick piers became billboards advertising Bull Durham tobacco, among other things.

In 1914 the bridge was essentially rebuilt. This was made possible by the completion of the Washington Avenue Bridge in 1902. The city hired the Missouri Valley Bridge and Iron Co. of Leavenworth, Kansas, to reinforce the structure and give it a new look. The arches of the towers were lowered, and another arch was built above it; they were also stuccoed, eliminating the medieval features and the texture of the unstuccoed brick. (Only the toll houses that anchor the cables retain their original battlements.) The new trusses were ordered from Inland Steel, allowing for the addition of pedestrian walkways on each side of the main road. For more than 150 years the Suspension Bridge has been a Waco icon.

Waco Suspension Bridge

115 N. Twelfth Street / 1889–90, remodeled 1933

Though dramatically altered in the 1930s to serve other functions, this was once a Waco firehouse. The original Central Fire Station was on Franklin Avenue, but a new one was built in 1892 on Washington Avenue just north of the town square (the current site of Baylor's Piper Center for Family Studies and Child Development), and there were stations in East Waco, near the new campus of Baylor University, and in the rapidly developing north and west ends of town.

The West End Engine Company was organized in September 1889 with seventeen volunteer members. Their station was built soon thereafter. It was a simple rectangular two-story building made of soft local brick, which is still visible at the northeast corner of the building. On the ground floor were wide double doors to allow the entrance and exit of the horse-drawn fire equipment. Upstairs was a large room for company meetings, which had numerous windows on the two long sides and the front side. The pressed-tin ceiling that is still in place in the upper room is probably original to the fire station.

With the completion of the nearby Central Fire Station in 1931, the old West End was adapted for other purposes, including a commercial space and an architect's office on the first floor and a dance studio on the second. Presumably these changes were designed by T. Brooks Pearson, who created an office for himself at the rear of the ground floor; the double doors were replaced with a shopfront, creating a commercial space within.

At this time the ornate steps and loggia, with red tile roof and cast-iron balustrades, was created on the alley side. Within the round arch was the entrance to Pearson's office. To the left were the steps up to the dance studio, which required a new door into the main space. The steps and supporting wall were made entirely from concrete. The cast-iron balustrades were made by the J. E. Bolles Company of Detroit, Michigan. The brick walls were initially painted but not plastered; the current crude plaster treatment dates to after World War II.

The firehouse meeting room upstairs became home to a series of dance studios: Olivette Pinto (who danced in a number of Cotton Palace pageants), then Catherine Horne and Elmer Wheatly. Pearson kept his architectural office downstairs from 1933 to around 1943; in 1945 he had moved his office to his home at 1824 Mitchell. After Pearson passed away, his son, Brooks W. Pearson, moved the office back to 115 in 1946, where he joined forces with James P. Baugh, a Waco architect of the 1920s who had spent intervening years working in other Texas cities. ▪

West End Fire Station

501 Washington Avenue / 1900–1902
J. Riely Gordon (San Antonio), architect
Wesley C. Dodson (Waco), supervising architect, Tom Lovell (Denton), contractor

The McLennan County Courthouse was one of the most forward-looking buildings erected in Waco's first hundred years. Because the Waco City Hall had been placed in the center of the town square, where county courthouses usually sit, the earlier courthouse was shunted off to the northeast corner of Second Street and Franklin, now the parking lot for the Hilton Waco. That courthouse, in a Victorian style, was an early design of Wesley C. Dodson, a Confederate veteran who moved to Waco in the mid-1870s.

By 1900 that courthouse had been outgrown, and the county planned a new and grander structure on Washington Avenue between Fifth and Sixth. The county hired W. C. Dodson to help evaluate the ten submitted proposals and to oversee the work. Dodson selected entry number 9, which, it was revealed, was by J. Riely Gordon. A native of Virginia, Gordon had come to San Antonio with his family in 1874 and later emerged as the leading courthouse designer in Texas. Dodson praised its "easy and dignified" character and predicted that with a few changes it would give the county "a public building with convenience, elegance, and repose."

Gordon's previous courthouses included those in La Grange, San Antonio, New Braunfels, and Waxahachie, which is now generally considered to be his masterpiece. All of these were in some sort of Victorian style, but around 1900 Gordon adopted the Beaux-Arts Neoclassical style, which had become very popular nationally after the World's Columbian Exposition of 1893. Gordon's first essay in the style was the Harrison County Courthouse in Marshall (now a museum), and the courthouse for McLennan County followed soon thereafter. The contractor, Tom Lowell, had worked previously on buildings by both Gordon and Dodson.

The site for the courthouse sloped sharply down toward Washington Avenue. This factor, combined with the need for a full basement, necessitated high sets of steps on the Washington Avenue and Fifth Street entrances. The steel frame was covered with limestone, except for the lowest course on the ground floor, for which Texas red granite was used. This was from the Granite Mountain quarry just west of Marble Falls; in the 1880s this quarry had supplied the stone for the Texas State Capitol. Domes like the one on this building were not found in the architecture of ancient Greece or Rome but rather during the Renaissance and Baroque eras; Beaux-Arts classicism was open to the selection of features from many different classical eras, not solely from antiquity.

The tall front steps led to a Corinthian portico that was enclosed on both sides. Minor porticoes to both sides of the main entrance were not accessible from the street but were intended as amenities for those whose offices were just inside and to aid in ventilation in a time before air-conditioning. Inside, a short hallway led to an impressive rotunda, which was actually not round but octagonal. Courtrooms occupied the west, north, and east sides, and county offices filled up the rest.

McLennan County Courthouse

A remarkable photo at the Texas Collection at Baylor shows the construction crew posed in front of the nearly completed ground floor. There are two groups of men: these in the foreground overwhelmingly white, those in the background overwhelmingly black. Presumably this segregation extended beyond the photo op to include every workday. The men in the foreground shaped the rough stone into its final form, and the men in the background carefully set these stones in their place. This building is thus an artifact of strict segregation but also a testament to the contribution of African American hands to the building of Waco.

The cornerstone, made of Texas red granite, boldly proclaimed that the courthouse was "Erected by the Tax Payers of McLennan County." ◼

66. Waco Water Pumping Station

101 Mill Street / 1904

In the nineteenth century, providing water to homes and businesses was a private business rather than a public utility. This building was constructed at the tail end of the private and the beginning of the public. The private Waco Water Works Company had a pumping station at South Tenth and Jackson by 1889; ten years later this company had given way to the Bell Water Company, organized by Captain J. D. Bell, which had a pump house at South First and Webster. In 1900 J. W. Mann, the owner of East Terrace, briefly served as a vice president, and Mann may have been the one who suggested supplying water to East Waco. This second pump house was completed by 1902. However, the company went out of business, and the City of Waco purchased the remaining facilities for $405,000 in 1904 and established a city Water Commission.

Mayor Allan Sanford appointed a prominent Waco attorney, William Markham Sleeper, as the first chairman of the Water Commission, and Sleeper served for two decades. In 1916 Sleeper recalled that both pump houses had been built cheaply and that they "were really nothing more than shacks." In 1904 the City of Waco rebuilt both of the pumping stations at a cost of $20,000. Sleeper referred to them as "substantial and commodious structures of brick." The brick walls supported an iron roof and sported a fair amount of ornament for an industrial building. This included rusticated window headers, a bull's-eye window, and urns at each corner. In the north part of the building was a brick tank that was thirty feet deep and nearly thirty feet in diameter, with a Worthington pump at the bottom. The pumping station in East Waco continued in operation until 1917. A new pumping station on the west side of the river, at South Third Street and Vermont (now Colcord), was built around 1923.

By 1926 the building was in use as a storage house for road-building machinery owned by the State of Texas. However, no major changes had been made in case it needed to revert to its original function. This section was used as the warehouse in 1950, while the larger southern section was used as the machine shop. To the southeast was a frame building for spray painting signs and markers. (This building was removed to make way for Waco Drive.)

After the warehouse moved, the building was adapted once again, serving sometimes as a restaurant and other times as a bar. The caboose emerging from the north wall dates to this era. The fence around East Terrace also dates from this era, as sometimes inebriated bar patrons would take their fights across Mill Street to the grounds of the historic house. ■

Waco Water Pumping Station

300 Austin Avenue / 1929–30
Harry L. Spicer, architect

One peculiarity about the layout of Waco is that the center of the town square was occupied by City Hall rather than the county courthouse. A simple brick cube, built 1856–57, served as the first permanent City Hall, but this was replaced in 1888–89 by a grander Victorian structure designed by W. W. Larmour. Waco voters approved the construction of a new City Hall and a new fire station in July 1928. (For the new fire station, designed by T. Brooks Pearson, see 68 in this volume.)

By February 1929 local architect Harry L. Spicer was at work designing a three-story City Hall with a basement, which was expected to cost $225,000. The design process dragged on into the summer, and Spicer may well have had to do some "value engineering" (i.e., cuts) to his plans. When the contract was awarded to the Christy-Dolph Construction Company of Dallas, the cost of the building had been reduced to $187,900. Christy-Dolph had recently built the Eastland County Courthouse to the designs of Lang and Witchell of Dallas.

The businesses of the Square encircled the building on all sides. The main entrance faced Austin Avenue and downtown; there were side entrances on the north and south, but not facing Bridge Street, which was the side of the Square where African American businesses were located. (The east side was also the location of the notorious Jesse Washington lynching, which occurred on May 15, 1916, and became known as the "Waco Horror.") That side of the town square was the side most dramatically changed by the construction of the Waco Convention Center, built in 1972 and enlarged in the late 1980s, which approached the northeast corner of City Hall.

The building had a concrete frame, floors, and roof; the exterior had an appropriately sober veneer of stone; and the interior curtain walls were made of brick or tile blocks. There were four stories, a basement, and a penthouse. The city jail occupied the fourth floor and the severe-looking cube above. In overall form the building was one large block with canted corners. Windows were arranged in vertical strips, in a manner typical of art deco. In between were flat representations of pilasters. At the top were round ornaments, using alternating buffalos and Indian heads, much like an old nickel. These diminutive decorations seem out of scale, but above the main door an eagle carved in high relief spread its wings with authority. ■

Waco City Hall

1010 and 1016 Columbus Avenue / 1931–32
T. Brooks Pearson, architect

The Waco Fire Department was organized in 1873. By the turn of the century there was a Central Fire Station downtown, one in east Waco, one near the Baylor campus, one in the west end (which then was on Twelfth Street between Austin and Washington), and one in the north end at North Ninth Street and Colcord. The previous Central Fire Station was at 313 Washington, just east of where Baylor's Piper Center now stands. Built in 1892, it was a two-story brick building with a sixty-foot cupola, which must have served as an observation post for smoke.

By 1930 this building's Victorian style seemed very out of date, much as the Victorian City Hall was seen as past its shelf life. Moreover, the fire station's location downtown was congested and increasingly valuable. The City of Waco decided to move the station to the 1000 block of Columbus Avenue. The lot was sufficiently spacious to allow for the construction of a drill tower next door. City engineer J. H. Strange retained T. Brooks Pearson, who had been practicing in Waco for more than two decades, to provide the designs, which were to cost $70,000. By October 1931 Pearson had plans out for bids. In November 1931 C. C. Ramsey, a local contractor, agreed to build the station for $34,590, though the next March that figure was increased to $40,000, perhaps to include the drill tower. The contract gave Ramsey 120 working days (six months) to complete the project.

The station was two stories and built of tile blocks stuccoed over to give it a Spanish Colonial style. The roof was to be made of a steel truss, and the floors of concrete. The east part of the building was for fire department administration, and the west for the actual fire station. Both parts had red tile roofs characteristic of the Spanish Colonial style. The roof on the west part was somewhat higher (thirty-four feet rather than thirty feet), and the central section extended beyond the front wall to provide some shelter for the cast-iron balconies on the second floor. A third cast-iron balcony, with its own tile roof, was attached to the west side wall. By and large the exterior is in a good state of preservation, except for the loss of a pair of huge paneled doors, with windows in the middle, roughly where the plain windows are now, originally decorated with two balusters in front of each pane of glass.

The principal ornament on the administrative wing was two columns of the Composite order (combining Ionic and Corinthian ornament). Because of the incised carving that seems to spiral upward, it would also be known as a Solomonic column, because such columns were thought to have been used in the Temple of Solomon in Jerusalem. Mounted to the left of the door was a lamp with golden glass, which was seen as appropriate for Spanish Colonial buildings. Unfortunately, the original door and windows were replaced long ago.

The drill tower was forty-two feet high and four stories, with stuccoed walls and a red tile roof that matched the roof of the main building, though on the tower the roof was hipped. In the early days each member of the fire department was put through a prac-

     Chapter 5

Central Fire Station and Drill Tower

tice here at least twice a year. The structure was quite plain, except for the round-arched entrance and a fourth-floor loggia in which two more Composite columns supported an arcade. Amazingly, the original round-arched door is still in place, although both of its decorative strap hinges have been pried off.

With the completion of the new station the old West End Station at 115 N. Twelfth Street was adapted for other purposes, including Elmer Wheatly's Dance Studio and the offices of T. Brooks Pearson (see 64 in this volume) ■

69. Waco Veterans Administration Hospital
(Doris Miller Department of Veterans Affairs Medical Center)

4800 Memorial Drive / 1931–32, 1937–39, 1945 and after

President Herbert Hoover signed an Executive Order creating the Veterans Administration in July 1930. President Hoover had been concerned by the number of veterans of World War I who were plagued by "shell shock," the period term for what we now call posttraumatic stress disorder. Under his administration twenty-five new veterans hospitals were built across the country, including this one. The VA Hospital Complex is one of the hidden historic gems of Waco.

The government acquired 508 acres at the end of Dutton Avenue, which was then considered to be three miles from the city. (At this time New Road did not exist.) This type of site was preferred to a more urban one; the hope was that a more peaceful country atmosphere would soothe the nerves of soldiers trying to overcome the traumatic injuries of war, both physical and mental. The anticipated cost was $1.2 million. Bids were opened in February 1931; the low bid, $740,000, was submitted by James I. Barnes of Springfield, Ohio. The work progressed quickly, and the facility was opened on May 8, 1932. The actual cost of phase 1 was $1,145,578.

With such a large number of projects under way at once, it is not surprising that a set of standardized architectural plans was developed in Washington. The architects most likely thought that they were designing the complex in the Italian Renaissance style, but we would now call it the Mediterranean Revival style to acknowledge that these forms were used beyond Italy and to acknowledge that it was not a continuation of the Renaissance but a revival. All buildings were modern in construction but clothed with redbrick walls, decorative brickwork and terra-cotta, and a red tile roof.

The main building was four stories above a high basement; a tower rose in the middle, and wings projected forward on both sides. Its importance was emphasized by the boulevard that led from the main entrance. Originally there was only a single flagpole; the present arrangement of two rows of flags is a more recent innovation. The only interior space that received any ornament was the lobby, which had engaged pilasters and a terrazzo floor. A three-story administration building was just to the right of the main building. North of this, near the intersection of present-day New Road and Beverly Drive, were four buildings used as quarters for hospital staff. (These are discussed in *More Historic Homes*, 192.)

The other key area was behind the main building. An oval drive encircled eight more buildings, which faced both the drive and an open green space or mall. Originally this space was treeless and echoed the parade ground of many military installations; over time trees have been planted in a random manner. In 1932 the only completed buildings on the mall were Buildings 4, 5, and 6. Nearest to the main building was Building 4, originally the dining hall; Building 5 was for patient care, and Building 6 was a recreation building. After a pause in construction, four more patient-care buildings (8, 9, 10, and 11) were completed in 1937, and Building 7 was finished in 1939. Like Building 5, these were all roughly

 Waco Veterans Administration Hospital (Doris Miller Department of Veterans Affairs Medical Center)

H-shaped with the main entrance in a central pavilion. This completed the original plan, and the facility could house 1,151 patients.

In 1945, as World War II was drawing to a close, the federal government anticipated a new generation of wounded soldiers needing care. Five more buildings (90–94) were placed on the outer side of the oval drive, continuing the general form and the Mediterranean Revival style of the rest of the complex. With their completion the facility could serve 2,040 soldiers.

Fortunately, most later buildings were placed on the periphery of the complex. The one unfortunate exception is the chapel, a not-terribly-compatible structure near the south end of the mall, built in 1963. The only major change to the historic buildings was the enclosure of large porches, when air-conditioning was introduced. The facility also included a farm, an attempt at occupational therapy that might also make the hospital more self-sufficient. The land was eventually sold or donated to create the City of Waco's Cottonwood Creek Golf Course and, later, the Waco Independent School District football stadium, reducing the hospital's footprint from 508 to 125 acres.

In 1989 President George H. W. Bush upgraded the Veterans Administration to the cabinet-level Department of Veterans Affairs. One of the earliest initiatives of the department was to identify historically significant VA hospitals and nominate them for the National Register of Historic Places. The Waco Veterans Administration Hospital was entered as a historic district in the National Register in 1994, making it the first historic district in Waco. In 2015 the facility was renamed in honor of Doris Miller, the native son of Waco who served with distinction during the Japanese attack on Pearl Harbor and who later lost his life serving in the Pacific.

All the original buildings were dressed in the same uniform and arranged in a careful plan. They all were good buildings individually, but as one walks through the complex, the units visually interact with each other in a way that makes the whole greater than the parts. ■

800 Franklin Avenue / 1935–37
Louis A. Simon, supervising architect of the US Treasury
Neal A. Melick, supervising engineer
W. H. Schimmelpfennig, architect (Washington, DC)

By the early 1930s Wacoans were eager for a new US Courthouse and Post Office. The one at Fourth and Franklin had been built in 1888, designed in Washington and supervised on-site by W. W. Larmour. In January 1932 Waco's old lion Milton W. Scott had written to the assistant secretary of the Treasury hoping to be appointed architect for the building, but he did not get the job and, in declining health, died in June 1933. A younger local architect, Harry L. Spicer, also hoped to win the commission. By February 1933 he was making plans for a $500,000 building and was even aware that the corner of Franklin and Eighth was a likely location. Apparently he was doing this on his own, without having the job in hand. However, most federal buildings were designed in Washington in the offices of the supervising architect of the Treasury, and this building was no exception.

By early 1935 the federal government was ready to move forward on a new building, but Waco's city administrators were dismayed to learn that plans called for a two-story building. A group went to Washington and conferred with Congressman O. H. Cross; soon thereafter it was announced that plans would be revised to allow for a third story. The federal architects went back to the drawing boards, and a new design was approved by the end of June.

As the Roosevelt administration was trying to work the United States out of the Great Depression by rebuilding infrastructure, there were several hundred projects being designed in Washington in 1935. Whether coincidentally or intentionally, the architect assigned to the Waco building was a native Texan, William H. Schimmelpfennig, who was born in McKinney in 1895. When the final plans were released, the *Waco Tribune-Herald* interviewed the architect, who explained that the design was "Spanish renaissance, with strong Mexican feeling." Schimmelpfennig had served as architect for government buildings in Puerto Rico and also offered to show photographs of buildings in Mexico City that had a similar design.

This building is durable and presentable but not a particularly compelling example of the Spanish Colonial style. The only real Spanish Colonial features were the Renaissance classicism of the entrances and the red tile roof. The entrances were clothed with Renaissance classical details, which might pass for Spanish but could be used in neoclassical buildings as well. The red tile roof was partially obscured by the series of low segmental arches placed at the corners. The structure was concrete but covered with buff-colored brick with creamy limestone trim.

Bids were taken in October 1935. Bidders included James I. Barnes of Springfield, Ohio, the contractor for the Waco Veterans Administration Hospital; and A. J. Rife of Dallas, who after World War II would serve as the contractor for the Masonic Grand Lodge on Columbus Avenue, but the contract for the courthouse was won by E. L. Martin of Dallas.

The intention was to have the building finished by Christmas of 1936; this proved overly optimistic, but the building was dedicated in March 1937 with Postmaster General James A. Farley in attendance.

Originally the first two floors, containing the post office on the first floor and offices on the second, had a rectangular footprint, while the third floor, containing the courtroom and associated spaces, was U-shaped, allowing better ventilation for the courtroom. The reason for what seems now to be an out-of-the-way location (compared to that of City Hall or the county courthouse) is that railroad tracks ran down Mary Street, an invaluable asset for the US Postal Service.

In 1939 two sculptural panels were installed in the upper reaches of the lobby: *Cattle* and *Indians*, both in low relief. Made of Texas gumwood, they were carved by Eugenie Shonnard, a native of Yonkers, New York, who had studied in Paris with Auguste Rodin and Antoine Bourdelle before settling in New Mexico. The panels were paid for by President Franklin Roosevelt's New Deal—specifically, the Section of Fine Arts, which succeeded the Public Work of Arts Project. It was more typical for the New Deal to fund painted murals in the lobbies of post offices and other public buildings and for the artist to be male. ■

United States Courthouse

1717 Austin Avenue / 1961
J. W. Bush and James D. Witt, architects

Waco was the recipient of the largesse of self-made millionaire Andrew Carnegie, who promoted public libraries around the United States both as a way of giving back for his success and as a way of enabling a new generation of young people to improve themselves. Carnegie donated $30,000 for a library building, with the stipulation that the City of Waco would pledge to spend at least $3,000 a year on upkeep. The result was a Beaux-Arts Classical structure built in 1904 at the southeast corner of Austin Avenue and Twelfth Street, sharing the block with the First Presbyterian Church. The site is now occupied by an utterly nondescript office building.

The current building is located on the site of the mansion of William W. Cameron Jr., who had succeeded his father as president of Cameron Lumber. His house was built in 1910–11 to the designs of Roy E. Lane. Cameron died in 1939, and in 1941 the house was donated to the Waco Library Association to serve as the new home of the Waco Public Library, on the condition that it was to be used as a library for at least twenty years.

Unfortunately, adaptations such as removing walls between rooms and installing heavy bookcases undermined the structural integrity of the house. By the late 1950s there was considerable sentiment to demolish the mansion and build anew. In spite of intense opposition from Waco preservationists, including Lavonia Jenkins Barnes and Eb Morrow, the decision was made to demolish the mansion and replace it with this midcentury modern building.

The new building was designed by the architectural firm of Bush and Witt. John William "Bill" Bush graduated from Rice University in 1939 and joined the office of Harry L. Spicer in Waco in 1945. James D. Witt joined the Spicer firm in 1950, and after Spicer's retirement in 1953, the firm became Bush and Witt. The contractor was Waco Construction Company, owned by Joe Brownfield, who also built many of the buildings at Baylor University in the latter part of the twentieth century.

The modernity of the structure came from the alternating planes of Alabama marble and plate glass and from the abstract columns at the corner of Austin and Eighteenth, which served as a brise-soleil, shading the plate glass behind it from too much direct sunlight. Above and beneath each marble panel were square windows; the upper ones lit the main floor, and the lower ones, the ground floor, which was essentially a raised basement. Much of the furniture inside was designed by Charles and Ray Eames for Herman Miller Furniture Company. This couple had a national (or even international) reputation as pioneers in modern furniture and industrial design.

By the early twenty-first century, what was once hailed as the height of modernity was seen as drab and uninspiring. Between 2011 and 2013 the building was given a $5.8 million renovation. The interior was remodeled to make it more colorful, accessible, and computerized. The principal entrance was moved from the center of the building to the east end, making it closer to the parking lot and wheelchair accessible. ■

Waco-McLennan County Library

72. Bledsoe-Miller Recreation Community Center

300 N. Martin Luther King Jr. Boulevard / 1971–72
Bush and Dudley, architects

This recreation center on the banks of the Brazos was built in what was originally a park solely for African Americans in a segregated Waco. What was originally Mackey Park was renamed after World War II to honor two native sons of Waco: Doris Miller and Jules Bledsoe. Doris Miller grew up in the country near Waco; he joined the US Navy and distinguished himself at Pearl Harbor on December 7, 1941. Jules Bledsoe grew up in the African American community of North Waco and sang in the choir at New Hope Baptist Church; he distinguished himself on Broadway, singing "Ol' Man River" in the musical *Show Boat*. Bledsoe died in Hollywood in July 14, 1943; Miller, after serving in a war bond campaign, returned to active duty in the Pacific Theater and died in action in November 1943. These two Waco natives found different routes to fame but were remembered in their hometown when the war was over.

In the early 1970s Waco was participating in the Model City Program, which was created in 1966 as part of President Lyndon B. Johnson's Great Society. The city initiated plans for a community center, which would feature a space for athletics (primarily basketball) but also spaces for social, cultural, and educational activities. The budget was set at $400,000, which consisted of $266,755 from the Neighborhood Facilities Program of the Department of Housing and Urban Development and $133,000 in Model City Funds.

For the design of the building the city turned to John Dudley of the Waco architectural firm of Bush and Dudley. The firm was founded by Harry L. Spicer; he was joined by J. W. Bush in 1945, and after Spicer retired in 1953, the firm became known as Bush and Witt. This iteration of the firm designed the Waco Public Library, Westview Village Shopping Center, and Richfield High School, which formed the core of what later became Waco High School. John Dudley, who studied architecture at Texas A&M, joined the firm in 1960 and was made a partner in 1965. With the death of James D. Witt, the firm became Bush and Dudley. This new firm designed the police and courts building at North Fourth Street and Waco Drive (an Urban Renewal project) and also the fire drill tower between Webster and Clay near the banks of the Brazos River (demolished).

Bush and Dudley strove to make the building as modern as possible. While it was in essence a masonry building, several of the exterior walls were concrete (an allusion to the modern style known as brutalism; in French, *béton brut*), and there were several large windows of plate glass. Walls of glazed and brightly colored red bricks were also prominently featured. Bush and Dudley were at work on the plans in late 1970 and early 1971. R. L. Smith Construction Company began work on the project in the fall of 1971, and the building was finished by the end of 1972. ■

Bledsoe-Miller Recreation Community Center

Education

73a. Old Main
1886–87

73b. Georgia Burleson Hall

Baylor University / 1887–88
Larmour and Herbert, architects

These two buildings were in the very first photo in architect W. W. Larmour's *Architectural Waco*. Clearly, he wanted to emphasize the large and impressive buildings for the new campus of the Baptist university. His older brother, Jacob Larmour, had been the architect for the main building at the Texas Agricultural and Mechanical College (now Texas A&M University), built 1873–75. W. W. Larmour had recently been named supervisor of construction for the new Federal Building at Franklin and Fourth (demolished) and formed a partnership with a younger man, Samuel P. Herbert. Larmour was not yet in Waco when the A&M building was designed and built; perhaps he assisted his brother on that project. Herbert definitely knew the building in College Station well, as he was one of the earliest graduates of Texas A&M.

Baylor moved from Independence, Texas, into the buildings of Waco University, with which it had merged. This campus was on Fifth Street between Webster and Clay—the block now occupied by the First Baptist Church. By 1889 both of the brick buildings had badly cracked walls, and the plan was to abandon the buildings when the new Baylor campus was completed. President Rufus C. Burleson probably met Larmour when he was designing the First Baptist Church at Fourth and Mary in 1877, as President Burleson was an elder of the church.

The cornerstone for the Main Building was laid on June 18, 1886. Carved on the outside of a piece of red granite was the phrase "Pro Ecclesia, Pro Texana" (For the Church, for Texas), which President Burleson had devised for Baylor at Independence in 1851. Inside the stone were copies of all the local newspapers, some Confederate money, and documents relating to the founding of Baylor and Waco Universities and their consolidation. Newspapers reported that Larmour and Herbert had completed the plans and specifications and that contracts had already been let for the brickwork and some of the

Old Main

woodwork. The plan was to build it in phases so that part of the building could be occupied by September. The cornerstone for the women's dormitory was in white marble and declared: "ERECTED IN 1887 AND DEDICATED TO FEMALE EDUCATION AND PIETY."

The plan agreed on by the university and Larmour was for an academic building to be flanked by two dormitories. The Main Building was to hold recitation and study rooms and an assembly hall on the third floor. To the south was Georgia Burleson Hall, the women's dorm. An identical dormitory for men was supposed to be built on the north side of the main building. Though Baylor officials told the Sanborn Map Company in 1899 that it would be built, it was never constructed. By 1893 Georgia Burleson had a dining hall on the first floor.

Both buildings were three stories, with four-story towers at each corner and a taller tower in the center of the east facade. The brick walls were load bearing—that is, they not only screen out wind and rain but also hold up the roof. Later Baylor buildings have frames of concrete or steel, and the exterior walls are simply a curtain. On the two earliest buildings all exterior walls have seven rows of bricks laid lengthwise, known as stretchers, then one row of bricks with the narrow end facing out, known as headers. The headers allow the outer layer of bricks to bond with inner layers. The central tower of the Main Building was 110 feet high; the tower in Georgia Burleson was 100 feet. In both buildings, the entrance was in the central tower. The walls were red brick with windowsills and lintels of stone. The roof was slate in multiple colors.

Some of the key features reflected the French Second Empire style, such as the tower pavilions at each corner, the steep mansard roofs above, and the segmentally arched windows throughout. Most of these features had been used on the original building of the Agricultural and Mechanical College, except that the earlier building had twin towers framing the entrance and no towers at the corners. The Baylor buildings were originally lit by gas; in 1889 the heat was provided by a stove in each room, though the installation of a steam heating system was anticipated.

Samuel Gideon, a professor of architecture at the University of Texas and author of much of *The WPA Guide to Texas*, was largely unimpressed with the design of Old Main and Georgia Burleson Hall. He noted that they were in the Victorian Gothic style, for which he had little admiration, but he did concede that "their otherwise unimposing appearance" was "relieved by the tall, ivied 'Baylor Towers.'" Unfortunately, those towers were removed two months after the tornado of 1953, out of fear that a future tornado would knock them over (It was also anticipated that both buildings would be replaced in the near future anyway.) They were re-created in 1978 with modern materials that give them a somewhat surreal appearance. At the same time all original windows were removed and replaced with modern smoked glass. Nevertheless, the two buildings remain as campus landmarks. ▪

Georgia Burleson Hall

74a. Carroll Science Hall
74b. Carroll Chapel and Library (Carroll Library)

Baylor University / 1429 S. Fifth Street / 1901, 1923

Messer and Smith, architects, 1901

Birch D. Easterwood, architect, 1923 (interior of library)

When Rufus Burleson was named President Emeritus in 1897 and Oscar Henry Cooper was named as new president, Baylor officials began to plan the next growth spurt, and these two buildings were the result. The university hired a pair of English émigré architects from Fort Worth, Howard Messer and S. Wemyss-Smith, to design the buildings. Smith visited a number of college campuses with new science buildings, including the University of Chicago and Washington University in St. Louis, in the company of President Cooper and E. R. Nash, the treasurer of what was then known as the Board of Trustees. (Nash would later serve on the Building Committee for the First Baptist Church.) The university characterized both buildings as "classical with a touch of French Renaissance."

In 1901 it was announced that George W. Carroll of Beaumont, a prosperous lumberman whose wealth was supplemented by oil royalties from Spindletop, would pay for construction of a new science hall: $60,000 for the building and another $15,000 to equip it. Carroll Science Hall was constructed in the traditional manner: load-bearing limestone walls for the basement and first floor, with beaded mortar joints for a higher finish, and then brick walls above. The building faced south toward Speight, and the main entrance was marked by four Ionic columns. The overall style was consistent with Beaux-Arts classicism, as promoted by the French national school of architecture, but the mansard roofs looked back to an even earlier form of French classicism.

The main exterior materials were all shipped in by railroad. The university expressed an interest in using Lueders stone, a grayish limestone found in Jones County north of Abilene. The town of Lueders had been connected to the Central Texas Railroad only in 1900. The brick came from even farther away. It was St. Louis pressed brick, a new type of machine-made brick formed by hydraulic pressure, resulting in a more dense, heavy, and durable product. The buff color of Carroll Science and Carroll Library is typical of such brick.

Amazingly, this building housed all of the science departments of Baylor and then some. Immediately inside the front door were a new office for the president on the right and the registrar's office to the left. Immediately ahead was an impressive staircase, and behind this was a semicircular lecture room. The first floor also included classrooms and laboratories for the physical sciences. The second floor housed the chemistry department, and on the third floor were geology, mineralogy, astronomy, and biology. In the center of the fourth floor was a conservatory, forty by fifty feet, with a roof entirely of glass.

George Carroll's son, F. L. Carroll of Dallas, made a donation of $50,000 to erect a matching building that would house a larger chapel and the library. Again, Messer and Smith were the architects, and they used limestone, St. Louis pressed brick, a heavy copper cornice, and a slate roof. Rising above all was a dome, which lit an interior dome of

Carroll Science Hall

art glass in the chapel. The building was situated at the corner of Fifth and Speight, thus facing Carroll Science, which was across a plaza to the north. Although there was a door on the north side of Carroll Chapel and Library, the main entrance faced Fifth Street. That door was marked by two Ionic columns twenty-two feet high. The rest of the building had pilasters created out of pressed brick, with every eighth rows of brick recessed to create the appearance of stone blocks, a feature found in the French classical tradition.

The entrance led into a marble stair hall, which rose to the chapel on the second floor. Straight ahead was the library. This one floor contained the main reading room, the stacks for books, an office for the librarian and an adjoining vault for rare books and documents, and separate rooms for the Browning Collection, the J. B. Tidwell Bible Collection, and the nascent collection of historical materials on Texas. Upstairs was the chapel, which also doubled as an auditorium. The stage was at the west end, opposite the entrance. The seats were inclined and bowled—that is, rising toward the back and curving around the stage—to provide excellent acoustics. A series of marble columns supported the art-glass skylight, which was the principal ornament of the room. The sons of F. L. Carroll chipped in $5,000 to procure a first-rate organ. The works were produced by Ed Pfeifer and Son of Austin; the case was designed by architect Smith.

These two buildings were the only works of S. Wemyss-Smith on campus, but he designed several other libraries in Texas, including the Carnegie Libraries in Belton (1904, now the Bell County Museum) and in Cleburne (1905, now the Layland Museum). In 1907 Smith moved to Oklahoma City and joined the practice of Solomon A. Layton. In 1910 Layton and Smith designed the Oklahoma State Capitol, built 1914–17.

Alas, a fire on February 11, 1922, destroyed the interior of the chapel. The building was reworked solely as a library, to be known as Carroll Library. Birch D. Easterwood, who had recently designed Brooks Dormitory, designed the new interiors, which had a reinforced-concrete frame, and Waco contractor J. E. Johnson built them. The project was completed by 1924. Baylor remained without a large space for a chapel until the construction of Waco Hall in 1929–30.

Carroll Science was renovated in 1982; the renovation was designed by Page Southerland Page of Austin. A hailstorm in 1992, which damaged some of the windows, led to a remodeling in 1993–94, designed by F&S Partners of Dallas. The work on both buildings removed all of the original windows and replaced them with large single panes of smoked glass, which seriously compromised the historic character of the buildings. Otherwise the exteriors are quite intact, but very little original fabric remains in either interior. ◼

Carroll Chapel and Library (Carroll Library)

815 Columbus Avenue / 1910–13, 1915, 1921, 1924, 1929
Waller and Field (Fort Worth), architects, with Scott and Pearson associated, 1910–13
Milton W. Scott, architect for additions of 1915, 1921, and gymnasium of 1924
T. Brooks Pearson, architect for north wing, 1929

The fine old Waco High School was built over a period of nearly thirty years. The project was initiated by a school board of heavy hitters, including Edward Rotan, Kenneth H. Aynesworth, W. E. Darden, and W. B. Brazelton. The building is usually attributed to Milton W. Scott, but a glance at the gray granite cornerstone tells a much more complicated story. The front section, built between 1910 and 1913, was designed by Waller and Field of Fort Worth in conjunction with Scott and Pearson of Waco. The contractor was J. E. Johnson of Waco, a Waco native who had already built the First Baptist Church and the Columbus Avenue Baptist Church and whose firm later built the Hilton Hotel, the Penland house, and Waco Hall.

Waller and Field was a relatively new firm, but senior partner Marion L. Waller had already designed eleven school buildings in Fort Worth and had won the contract for the original buildings of the West Texas Normal School in Canyon (now West Texas A&M University). Scott and Pearson were also busy designing the Smith-Parker-Migel and Shear-Callan houses farther up Columbus Avenue. Waller and Field sent one of their engineers, Maurice J. Sullivan, to work on the project out of the office of Scott and Pearson. (After the original phase of the high school was finished, Sullivan moved to Houston and became a prominent architect there.) The most striking feature of the building is the portico facing Columbus Avenue, with two-story fluted columns in the Roman Ionic order. The design was very similar to Waller's design for the original Fort Worth High School (later Paschal) south of downtown, also begun in 1910.

T. Brooks Pearson left the firm to practice on his own, and Milton W. Scott continued to work on most of the numerous additions to the building. The wing facing Eighth Street came next, in 1916. A matching wing facing Ninth Street and an auditorium were added in 1921. The north addition in 1929 completed the building. The drawings for this were produced not in the office of Milton W. Scott but by his former partner, T. Brooks Pearson. Local contractor James S. Harrison built it. The entire structure—floors, frame, and roof—was built of concrete and covered over with brick. The trim work for most of the later additions was made of Waco Art Stone. The combination auditorium and gymnasium, a freestanding structure to the northwest of the main building, was built in 1924 at a cost of $60,000. It had brick walls and a steel truss roof. All of the additions followed the style of the neoclassical original building except for the gymnasium, which featured Tudor Revival ornament, newly popular in the 1920s.

The high school closed in 1971, and the building was put to a number of different uses, among them serving as the home of the Ollie Mae Moen Discovery Center before it moved to its permanent home in the new Mayborn Museum Complex in 2004. The

Waco High School (later Historic Lofts at Waco High)

Waco Independent School District put the building up for sale in 1995, but a buyer was not forthcoming for more than a decade. Finally, in 2009-10, the old high school was converted into 104 units of affordable housing, a notable Waco success in adapting a historic building to a new purpose. ◼

<h1 align="center">76. First District School, Colored
(later the Helen Marie Taylor Museum)</h1>

701 Jefferson Avenue / 1918

This building is a testament to the policy of segregated schools that was in in effect in Waco (and the rest of the American South) from the end of Reconstruction until the slow implementation of *Brown v. Board of Education of Topeka, Kansas* of 1954. Later, it became the home of a private museum devoted to the history of Waco and the United States. But it has also been acknowledged as a place frequented by the Waco Indians before they left the area.

A gray granite Texas historical marker, placed in front of the building in 1936, the year of the centennial of Texas' independence from Mexico, states that this was the site of the village of the Waco Indians. It is unclear why this precise site was identified as the site of the village, but it was along what was later known as Barron's Creek, and it does sit in a grove of ancient live oak trees.

The earliest educational institution for African Americans in Waco seems to have been Paul Quinn College, which was founded in Austin in 1872 and moved to Waco in 1877. In the mid-1880s the City of Waco was planning to build a central high school at the northeast corner of South Fourth and Webster (now a parking lot) and apparently felt pressured to build something for the African American young people who would not be allowed to attend the new school. It was decided to build two frame buildings, one for students who lived north of Austin Avenue and one for students who lived south of the avenue. (The new central high school was two stories and brick.) The Second District School was a one-story frame building on South First Street between Jackson and Webster. On the Sanborn Map of 1899 the building was flanked by small frame houses marked as "Negro Tenements." The First District School was a two-story frame building with a four-story tower at the northwest corner. Both of these buildings were in use by the 1886–87 school year.

The original First District School building lasted for more than three decades and was replaced with the current building by 1918, perhaps because an impressive new high school for white children had been built nearby in 1910–11 and perhaps with some sense of guilt about the 1916 lynching of Jesse Washington, which had horrified a great many people across the country. The new building was an improvement, but in no way equal to the impressive neoclassical structure for white students. The building faced east, with entrances at the north and south ends. The basic color of brick was red, but door and window openings were outlined with dark brown bricks.

Both entrances led to a long north-south hallway lit by the windows at the north and south ends. There were two classrooms on the east side and three on the west side. All the classrooms had tall ceilings—sixteen feet high on the first floor and twelve feet on the second floor. However, there were no restrooms in the building (some were later added on the west side), and there was no lunchroom. (Later a small frame building was built for a lunchroom just north of the building.) In 1950 the building was still heated by stoves. Separate but equal it was not.

First District School, Colored (later Helen Marie Taylor Museum)

Among the many African Americans who studied at this school was Vivienne Lucille Malone, the daughter of Pizarro and Vera Estelle Allen Malone. She went on to Fisk University in Nashville, then taught at Paul Quinn College for seven years. She became one of the first African Americans to earn a doctorate in mathematics and became the first black professor at Baylor University.

The integration of Waco schools led to the closing of both the Waco High School on Columbus and this school, and it sat empty for a number of years. (All students, black and white, were to attend the new Waco High, formerly known as Richfield High.) When Helen Marie Taylor, a Waco native who was then living in Richmond, Virginia, came back home to attend the dedication of the McCulloch House as a historic house museum, she noticed the old school building and saw its potential. She bought the building in 1986 and opened it as a museum in 1993 with the assistance of Calvin Smith, director the Strecker Museum and chair of the Department of Museum Studies at Baylor. A lack of local support led to the closing of the museum in 1998, and it has been open only sporadically since then. ■

Paul Quinn College / 1020 Elm Avenue / 1922–23
William Sidney Pittman (Dallas), architect

In 1872 the American Methodist Episcopal Church founded a college for freed slaves and the children of freed slaves in Austin. The college moved to Waco in 1877 and to East Waco in 1881. At that time it was named for William Paul Quinn, a Methodist missionary. In 1881 East Waco was still predominantly industrial, but the site of the college was beyond all that, virtually on the edge of town.

In 1899 the campus consisted of two brick buildings and a number of one-story frame buildings. One brick building was two stories and had recitation rooms on the first floor and a women's dormitory on the second; the other was a one-story men's dormitory. The frame buildings included the chapel, kitchen, laundry, music room, printing office and carpenter's shops, and two small houses.

The one-story brick building, built in the mid- to late 1880s, has at various times been a women's dorm, a men's dorm, a science lab, and an administration building. It is the oldest surviving building on campus. Its segmental windows, a feature of the French Second Empire style, echoed those of the Main Building and Burleson Hall at Baylor, built just a few years before. Two early, or perhaps even original, chimneys survive. However, beneath the pronounced segmental window hoods the upper third of the window is blocked off to cover a modern dropped ceiling inside.

In December 1901 the two-story brick building burned. The cornerstone for a new building was laid at commencement the next year on June 12, 1902. This was a much more ambitious building, three stories tall, brick with stone trim. It was L-shaped, and where the two wings met, a shorter wing projected forward, fronted by a pair of octagonal towers framing the front door. The two wings had stepped gables, giving it something of a Dutch Colonial look. The first two floors were devoted to classrooms and administrative offices; the third floor was a new women's dorm. This building was destroyed in the early 1950s.

The college was ready to expand again in 1921, when Bishop Joshua Jones purchased land to the northeast of the campus, which allowed for the construction of William Decker Johnson Hall. (It was named for the current bishop of the African Methodist Episcopal Church.) The new building was designed by a prominent African American architect, William Sidney Pittman. Born in Montgomery, Alabama, in 1875, Pittman studied at the Tuskegee Institute with Robert R. Taylor, the first black graduate of the Massachusetts Institute of Technology and the architect of most of the buildings on the Tuskegee campus. After attending the Drexel Institute in Philadelphia, Pittman became Taylor's right-hand man and also married Portia Washington, the daughter of Tuskegee founder Booker T. Washington. They came to Texas in 1913 and settled in Dallas.

Pitmann brought a new level of professionalism to design for the campus; he produced a full set of working drawings and written specifications, which could be consulted by potential contractors in Waco, Dallas, and Houston. His designs for a new women's dormitory for Paul Quinn were ready for examination by January 1921. The building was to

William Decker Johnson Hall

bring a new level of technological sophistication to campus as well: the structure was concrete reinforced with steel and with curtain walls of pressed brick made not far away in Mexia.

A very cost-conscious architect, Pittman used virtually no applied ornament. Instead, he used brick in a variety of shades and outlined each window with brick of a darker shade. The principal facade had a one-story porch with two staircases and six square posts supporting a second-story gallery. The brickwork at the cornice is corbeled, adding another subtle element of interest. It was three stories with a raised basement. The estimated cost was $150,000, though it turned out to be closer to $165,000. The building was expected to be much larger, and it is clear from the south end of the building, which has only a door but no windows for each floor, that at the minimum a wing to match the one at the north was planned, if not much more. Although initially planned as a women's dormitory, when opened, the building had the library and chapel on the first floor, a dormitory for men on the second and third floors, and a dining room and laundry in the basement. In 1950 the basement housed the science department. As of this writing, it has been abandoned for many years but still has the potential for restoration. ◼

Baylor University / 1929
Birch D. Easterwood, architect
Harry L. Spicer, consulting engineer

When Samuel Palmer Brooks became president of Baylor in 1902, he inherited a campus with a main building, a women's dorm, a library/chapel, and a science building. There were 783 students. One glaring absence was a men's dormitory, which had been planned by Larmour and Herbert to match Georgia Burleson Hall but was never built. Male students were placed in ad hoc dormitories or found their own rooms in boarding houses near the campus. Fund-raising proved to be a challenge, and it was not until the conclusion of World War I that Brooks sensed the time had come to build a men's dorm.

President Brooks chose a young Waco architect, Birch D. Easterwood, to design this new dormitory and, he hoped, many other future buildings. Easterwood was no college boy himself but combined correspondence school study with hours behind the drafting table of Milton W. Scott. By 1916 he was practicing on his own. Brooks had received a master's degree from Yale University and hoped that new Baylor buildings would reflect the best practices of Eastern schools. Apparently Brooks was particularly impressed with the later American Colonial style now thought of as Georgian, which was not a strength of the Yale campus but was starting a surge of popularity that would last well into the 1920s.

One did not have to go to the East Coast to find important examples of the Colonial Revival. The very first building of Southern Methodist University (SMU), Dallas Hall, was designed by Shepley, Rutan and Coolidge of Boston and built from 1912 to 1915. Dallas Hall was very consciously modeled on the Rotunda at the University of Virginia (UVA), designed by former president Thomas Jefferson. The other buildings that Jefferson designed for UVA were brick pavilions (with classrooms and homes of the professors) and dormitories; in them Jefferson explored different models of ancient classicism. At SMU subsequent buildings continued to be built with red brick, white trim, and classical details but were more generically Colonial Revival than specifically based on Jefferson's campus.

Baylor trustees (now known as regents) approved preliminary design work in the fall of 1919, and Easterwood quickly produced a complete set of plans. In February 1920 the contract was awarded to J. S. Harrison and Sons of Waco. James S. Harrison was a Waco native and evolved from brick mason to general contractor; in the first decade of the century he had built the First Baptist Church, the Columbus Avenue Baptist Church, and the Seventh and James Baptist Church. Work on the dorm proceeded apace until June 1921, when the university ran out of money. Work was stopped with no roof on the building. W. G. Lacy, a Waco civic leader, was named chairman of a committee to sell bonds to complete the building. Within weeks construction was under way again, and the building was essentially completed by the end of 1921.

Women's Memorial Dormitory

The building charted a new course for the Baylor campus that would be followed for more than two decades. Brooks was the first Baylor building to face downtown Waco. It was U-shaped, with the U opening toward campus. The ground floor was faced with stone; three floors above were faced with red brick. This was specifically "tapestry brick," which had a rough, striated surface that gave it more texture; it was popular with prominent northeastern architects and was immensely popular in Waco (and elsewhere) in the 1920s. The stone for Brooks Hall was from New Bedford, Massachusetts, and the slate roof was from Bangor, Maine.

In 1924 fund-raising began for a women's dormitory of the quality of the men's dorm, to cost a similar amount, $350,000. Fund-raising, however, was sluggish, and by May 1927 only $158,518 had been raised. President Brooks insisted that before work would begin on the new dorm, the entire sum would have to be pledged and half of it paid. At this point the Texas Baptist Women's Missionary Union entered the scene. They promised to fund the construction of the dormitory—though it is unclear how this related to the $158,518 already pledged.

As planning for the building ramped up, Mattie Brooks, wife of President Brooks, formed a committee of women to oversee the project. In addition to Mattie Brooks, local members included Kate Spencer, a prominent member of Columbus Avenue Baptist Church whose husband, R. B., was a Waco lumberman; Irene Marschall, a Baylor grad and dean of women whose half sister, Cornelia Marschall, was to become a legendary Baylor biology professor; and Claude Johnson, matron of one of the Baylor women's dorms and wife of

Charles D. Johnson, the head of the Department of Commerce and Business Administration at Baylor.

In October 1928 this committee traveled with architect Birch D. Easterwood to see women's dorms at Southwestern University in Georgetown and the University of Texas at Austin (UT). At the latter they visited the Alice Littlefield Dormitory, in the Spanish Colonial style, and the Scottish Rite Dormitory, just north of the UT campus, which was a refined expression of the Colonial Revival style. Both of these dorms were designed by Herbert M. Greene of Dallas, who was simultaneously university architect and engaged in private practice; wearing the latter hat he had recently designed the Grand Karem Shrine in Waco. The Baylor women seem to have been especially impressed with the Colonial Revival dorm for the Scottish Rite.

The official groundbreaking took place in October 1928, but Easterwood was working on the plans well into 1929. For this project Easterwood was associated with Harry L. Spicer as consulting engineer, perhaps because the building was to have a concrete frame rather than the hollow tile block walls used for Brooks Dormitory. (Spicer was also associated with Lang and Witchell on Waco Hall.) The expected cost was $350,000—roughly the same as Brooks's estimate—but in June the winning bid, by S. B. Swigert, was for $246,000. This savings must have been a relief to Baylor officials, as Waco Hall was going up at exactly the same time. That building was funded by large donations from the citizens of Waco, and the donation from the Women's Missionary Union was substantial enough that Easterwood's plans had to be approved not by Baylor's trustees but by the women's committee.

The building was dedicated on October 15, 1930. The school newspaper, the *Lariat*, hailed it as "the South's finest Dormitory." Like Brooks Dorm it was U-shaped, with the courtyard to the rear, and built with a veneer of red tapestry brick. Unlike Brooks, which also used actual stone, Women's Memorial used concrete formed to look like stone columns and other neoclassical trim, which was probably another source of savings. The pediments on the portico and on both of the pavilions at each end were higher than on a typical Georgian or neoclassical buildings; this awkwardness was caused by the fact that an entire fourth floor was crammed underneath the roof. The pediments had higher peaks because they aligned with the higher roof.

The first floor contained the dining room, a drawing room and three smaller living rooms, a club room that could be used by any women's organization, and a suite for the dean of women. Somehow the first floor also contained the university bakery, dressing rooms and showers for the dorm staff, and even some regular dorm rooms. Above this the building was mostly dormitory rooms, but with a chapel on the third floor and, in the attic, a space for sleepovers called the "Hilarium." This was also the first Baylor dorm to have a telephone in every dorm room. ▪

79. Waco Hall

Baylor University / 1929–30
Lang and Witchell (Dallas), architects
Harry L. Spicer, associate architect

The impetus for Waco Hall was the fire that gutted Carroll Chapel and Library in 1922. By the time that Birch D. Easterwood had designed the new interior, the university administrators had decided not to rebuild the chapel on the upper floor or the dome above it, dedicating it solely as the library instead. A proposal to move Baylor to Dallas led the citizens of Waco to pledge that they would raise $1 million for the new auditorium. (The auditorium was also to take the place of the chapel in old Carroll; Baylor's chapel still meets in the building at this writing.) In addition to serving as an auditorium, the building contained a lecture hall and several smaller classrooms.

At this time the chief designer for Lang and Witchell was Dudley S. Green, who had succeeded Charles Erwin Barglebaugh. Green was from England and came to the United States in 1900 at age sixteen. He worked in the office of Waco architect Sam Herbert and ended up marrying Herbert's daughter Emma. Lang and Witchell's early use of the Prairie style gave way to a modernized classicism (sometimes termed "Greco-Deco") that had been pioneered by the architect Bertram Grosvenor Goodhue and the sculptor Lee Lawrie. The associate architect, Harry L. Spicer, had first shown up in Waco in 1913 as a draftsman for Roy E. Lane; by 1917 he was practicing on his own as an architect and structural engineer. In 1929 he was consulting with Birch Easterwood on Women's Memorial Dormitory and designing Waco's City Hall, another modern take on classicism.

Waco Hall is distinctive for several reasons. First, it reflected a deep study of the Nebraska State Capitol (designed 1920, built 1922–32) and the Los Angeles Public Library (1925–26), both by Goodhue Moreover, the massing of the building was very sophisticated, with units clearly marking the double-height lobby, with lower wings holding an assembly room on the east and two levels of classrooms on the west. Beyond the lobby the auditorium and the stage were clearly expressed on the exterior as well. The frame was a combination of steel and concrete but covered with a veneer of stone at each entrance and cream-colored brick almost everywhere else. The coping at the roofline was made of terra-cotta, as were the sills beneath the windows and the perforated window grilles for the toilet rooms beneath the stairs. The terra cotta was supplied by the Atlantic Terra Cotta Company of New York City, who also provided ornament elements for the Hilton Hotel and other Waco buildings.

On the main front, which faced north toward campus, but also on the east and west sides were three doors, above which were three large round-arched windows with steel frames. Both ends of this composition were concluded with buttresses, out of which grew human figures looking toward each other. Such "buttress sculptures" had been used with great effect at the Nebraska State Capitol and the Los Angeles Public Library. On these two buildings the figures were carved out of stone and were attempts to portray specific ancient lawgivers or thinkers; in the Waco building they were formed out of terra-cotta and depicted more generically ancient authorities. Some impish draftsman in the office of Lang and Witchell marked the two figures keeping watch over the main entrance of Waco Hall as "Mother" and "Dad."

The contractor was J. E. Johnson of Waco. John E. Johnson was a native of Norway who immigrated to the United States in 1886 and was in Waco by 1892. He worked as a carpenter and then as a general contractor; an important early project was phase 1 of the Waco High School on Columbus, designed by Waller and Field of Fort Worth. More recently he had built the Hilton Hotel by Lang and Witchell and its expansion by Milton W. Scott. He had already worked with Scott on the Penland house near Cameron Park and on the McDermott Motor Company on Washington Avenue. By 1930 he had handed the reins of the business over to his thirty-two-year-old son, Edwin, and the senior Johnson died March 9, 1930, just as work was finishing up on Waco Hall. It was dedicated on May 27, 1930, which was Baylor's commencement.

In 1939 Samuel Gideon, a professor of architecture at the University of Texas, praised Waco Hall in the architectural section of the *WPA Guide to Texas*, commenting that the "cream-colored brick walls and modern treatment contrast pleasantly with the dull red tone and the design of the other buildings." ■

Waco Hall

Baylor University / 1938–40
Birch D. Easterwood and Son, architects

As the university continued to grow, it was decided that a new building could house administrative offices, academic space for the departments of education and languages, and space for the Texas Collection and the Baylor Museum. (The Texas Collection had been founded in 1923 with the donation of more than a thousand volumes on Texas history and culture from Kenneth Aynesworth; the Baylor Museum had its roots in the natural history collection started when the university was in Independence, but in Waco was curated by John K. Strecker from 1903 to 1933.) The building was supposed to cost $150,000, though over time that low number crept up to a more realistic $250,000. The architects were Easterwood and Son and contractor was S. B. Swigert; this was the team that had designed and built Women's Memorial Dormitory.

The expectation was for the building to be in the Colonial Revival style. The building was not to have a central dome, probably because that might seem to be imitating Dallas Hall at SMU. On the other hand, a cupola would be too diminutive a feature. Easterwood's solution was to make the central block four stories, which would serve as a base for a Renaissance-inspired dome with round-arched windows and a cupola above. The dome was so tall that Baylor president Pat Neff called it a "tower," and it rose above any of the pinnacles of Old Main or Burleson Hall. The dome was somewhat along the lines of Independence Hall in Philadelphia, an icon of the American Colonial style.

The new Baylor building had three-story wings that terminated in pavilions with hipped roofs. Both the north elevation facing downtown Waco and the south elevation facing Waco Hall had central porticoes with four Corinthian columns. Neoclassical ornaments such as festoons were liberally applied to the pediments and elsewhere on the exterior. The building was certainly the most ornate of any of the Colonial Revival buildings on campus. Yet, between all the Colonial trim was a thoroughly modern structure: a concrete frame, floors, and roofs, making it fireproof except for the wood frame of the roof.

As the building was nearing completion in fall 1939 the trustees decided to name it Pat Neff Hall in honor of the Baylor president who was also a former governor of Texas. According to the newspapers the trustees did this over the objections of Governor Neff. Perhaps this honor for Neff inspired the trustees to rename the newly relocated museum as the Strecker Museum.

In one respect the dome of Pat Neff Hall was thoroughly modern: it was made of stainless steel. President Neff admired this feature very much, calling it "the only stainless-steel tower west of the Empire State building." In fact, he became concerned that rambunctious Baylor students would try to paint their class number on the tower, which was a stunt sometimes pulled on Old Main. During chapel in October 1940 he specifically warned the class of 1944 not to try it and suggested that painting class numbers on Old Main should

Pat Neff Hall

also be explicitly forbidden. Sixty years later Baylor covered the stainless-steel dome with gold leaf so that it would match the cupola on twenty-year-old Draper Hall.

To the southwest of Pat Neff was a second women's dormitory, Catherine Alexander Hall. This was built simultaneously with Pat Neff Hall and designed by the same architectural firm. Unlike Brooks and Women's Memorial, it was not U-shaped, though the central entry and pavilions at each end were clearly marked. The columns were perhaps the most classically correct of any of the Colonial Revival buildings, thanks to the fact that the ground-floor entrance served as the base for the columns of the portico above. If Pat Neff Hall is the most distinguished of Baylor's Colonial Revival buildings, Alexander is a close second. ■

Catherine Alexander Hall

1030 Live Oak Street / 1939–40
Birch D. Easterwood and Son, architects

Although Milton W. Scott had forged a close relationship with the Waco school district, starting with the Sanger Avenue School and continuing with Waco High School and many others, Scott passed away in June 1933. During the 1920s Birch Easterwood had forged an equally close relationship with Baylor University, starting with Brooks Hall, so the design of a new junior high for East Waco in 1939 went to Birch D. Easterwood and Son.

It might seem peculiar for Waco to be building a nice new school in the middle of the Great Depression. It was built because it was funded by the Federal Works Agency, a part of the Public Works Administration, which was in turn part of President Franklin D. Roosevelt's New Deal. The contractor was C. C. Ramsey, who had previously built the Ike Kestner house in Castle Heights. An open house at the completed building was held on September 6, 1940.

In 1939 this site was close to the northeastern edge of town. The site of the school was between Live Oak Avenue and St. Charles Avenue (the latter street was incorporated into Waco Drive). The main block of the school was placed on top of what had been part of Astrid Street. Built of brick-faced tile, the construction was considered fireproof. The shingles on the roof were wood, but they were supported by steel trusses. The building had a five-part plan, and the front walls of the outer wings had windows clustered in threes. In addition to the classrooms and associated rooms, the building had an auditorium with a stage at the east end.

Though the building was only a single story, Birch and Kenneth Easterwood did their best to make it a Baylor-worthy example of the Colonial Revival. The redbrick walls contrasted nicely with the stone (or, in some cases, Waco Art Stone) trim. The portico with its four Doric columns was so grandly scaled that it might have been comfortable on a taller building. Where the portico met the main roof sat an octagonal cupola with eight round-arched windows and topped with a colonial-looking weather vane. The main double doors had a large semicircular fanlight above and was framed with pilasters supporting a triangular pediment. The windows were also generously scaled—sixteen panes over eight—and above each window in the main block were Art Stone panels of a neoclassical urn flanked with festoons. Georgian-era quoins framed each corner. ◼

East Waco Junior High School

82. Bill Daniel Student Center

Baylor University / 1940–42, 1946–47
Robert Leon White, architect
C. H. Page and Son, associate architects

In England student union referred to student government, but in the United States it became associated with a building where students could congregate, whether they lived on or off campus, whether in a dormitory, a fraternity or sorority house, in a boarding house, or at home. The first student union building was constructed by the University of Pennsylvania in 1896. By the 1920s there were still only a dozen or so. The most important precedent in Texas was at the University of Texas, where the union building was designed by Paul Philippe Cret in 1931–32.

A native of France, Cret trained at the École des Beaux-Arts in Paris, the fountainhead of academic classicism in the late nineteenth and early twentieth centuries. Cret moved to the United States and taught at the University of Pennsylvania while maintaining a private practice. The UT Student Union was sited at the West Mall and Guadalupe Street. It was L-shaped and three stories. A tower at the southwest corner led into a double-height sky-lit lobby, which prefaced a large ballroom. On the ground floor beneath this space was a cafeteria. The wing to the east contained smaller meeting rooms and offices.

In 1940 Baylor retained Robert Leon White of Austin as architect for the new Student Union Building. White was a native Texan and received two degrees in architecture from UT. More important for this commission was that White worked as supervising architect at UT from 1926 to 1934 and 1937 to 1958. As supervising architect he was responsible for carrying out the designs of Cret, including those for the Texas Union. Associated with him on the Baylor project was the firm of C. H. Page and Son. Charles Henry Page Sr. and his brother Louis Charles Page designed the Littlefield Building at Sixth and Congress in Austin (1910, 1915) and the Travis County Courthouse (1930).

Though work on Baylor's building was suspended for the duration of World War II, it was completed in 1947. The Student Union Building merged the Colonial Revival style that was virtually mandatory at Baylor with a subtle analysis of the spaces needed in such a building. Where the UT building was studiously asymmetrical, the Baylor building was rigorously symmetrical, at least as originally designed. The central section, marked by a colonnade, balustrade, and urns, included a large banquet and assembly room on the main floor and a cafeteria on the ground floor.

The Texas Union featured a grand external staircase to the lobby of the ballroom but shunted the entrance to the ground floor off to one side. The Baylor Union has a splendid staircase but also two entrances to the ground floor, one to each side of the staircase. The grand staircase led to a triple-height Great Hall, which led into the banquet and assembly room, now known as the Barfield Drawing Room. Unlike the Cret building, where the ballroom was lit by windows on the west but had a loggia on the east, the Baylor building has loggias on both sides, preserving classical symmetry.

Chapter 6

Bill Daniel Student Center

On the ground floor beneath the Great Hall were support spaces, including a barber-shop, a beauty shop, and restrooms. Beyond this were the cafeteria and the serving room. Echoing the loggias above were passages that also could serve as smaller areas for dining or meeting. At the western end of the south loggia was a tearoom. And on the other side of the south wall was a stage for a natural amphitheater, which still exists at this writing. Opposite this, just to the north of the building, was a terrace, which was later sacrificed for an expansion to the building.

While the central part of the building was for large, communal spaces, the wings contained a variety of smaller spaces. The south wing on the ground floor was set aside for the Baylor Bookstore; on the north were a lounge, recreation rooms, and men's and women's locker rooms. On the first floor both wings had large and impressive rooms at the end. On the south was a Faculty Men's Lounge and on the north a Faculty Women's Lounge. The hallways leading to these rooms included more offices and restrooms but also a lounge for male students on the south and for female students on the north. The rooms for faculty were emphatically acknowledged on the exterior by framing pilasters and a heavily ornamented window.

Like all Baylor buildings since Women's Memorial the Student Union Building had a concrete frame and floors. However, the modern feature most likely to be appreciated by students was that it was one of the first Baylor buildings to be air-conditioned as part of its original design.

Across Fifth Street from the Student Union was Rena Marrs McLean Gym, designed by Easterwood and Easterwood in 1937 but built after World War II. This was first Baylor building on the east side of Fifth Street. ◾

83. Armstrong Browning Library

Baylor University / 710 Speight Avenue / 1948–51
Wyatt C. Hedrick (Fort Worth), with Eggers
and Higgins (New York), architects
Morris Architects, Inc. (Houston), architects,
1994–95 (renovations and porte cochere)

A. J. Armstrong, the longtime chair of the English Department at Baylor, also founded the largest collection of books, papers, paintings, furniture, and other artifacts related to the poets Robert Browning and Elizabeth Barrett Browning and saw that it was housed in one of the jewels of the campus. He was a man obsessed with quality—albeit of a rather traditional bent—who even brought the prominent African American contralto Marian Anderson to Baylor for a performance in Waco Hall at a time when she was not allowed to perform at Constitution Hall in Washington (see *Historic Homes*, 51).

Armstrong began collecting material about the Brownings in 1912, the same year he was appointed chair. He donated his collection to Baylor six years later, and a special room was created in Carroll Chapel and Library to house it. When the building burned in 1922, the entire Browning Collection was saved. The university decided to remodel the interior to house only the library—Birch D. Easterwood served as architect—and a new room was created, which housed the collection from 1924 to 1951.

An extremely well-traveled man, Armstrong hoped to create a stand-alone building that would speak to the richness of European culture. In the 1930s he began conversations with John Russell Pope, an architect who had studied at Columbia University, then the American Academy in Rome, and the École des Beaux-Arts in Paris, the French national school of architecture. Pope designed the National Archives Building, the National Gallery of Art, and the Jefferson Memorial, all in Washington, DC. But before he could design anything for Armstrong, Pope died of cancer in 1937. Otto R. Eggers and Daniel Paul Higgins, who had worked with Pope since 1907 and had been partners in his firm since 1922, completed the design work for the National Gallery and the Jefferson Memorial, renaming the firm Eggers and Higgins.

In working with Eggers and Higgins Armstrong had no lack of European sources on which to model his library in Waco. In particular he dreamed of an outer foyer that would be modeled on the gilded staircase of the Burgos Cathedral in Spain, a 1520–27 Renaissance addition to the thirteenth-century Gothic church. Armstrong also hoped for a Foyer of Meditation that would be based on the Arab Hall (which he called the Oriental Room) of Leighton House, the home of the Victorian painter Frederic Leighton in London. The house was begun in 1866 but expanded in 1877–79 to display the collection of tiles that Leighton had acquired in Persia.

Armstrong was also planning to commission a great deal of stained glass for the building. Around 1936 he began planning these windows with Charles J. Connick, who had opened a stained-glass studio in the Back Bay of Boston in 1913. Armstrong may have been impressed that Connick had designed the rose windows of both St. Patrick's Cathedral and

St. John the Divine in New York and the chapels of Princeton University and the University of Pittsburgh. Or he may have been impressed that Connick had known the poetry of Browning since he heard it in Sunday School or that he was friends with the living poet Robert Frost. Connick never saw the windows installed or even completed, as he died in 1945 at age seventy. Orin E. Skinner became president of the studio and completed the commission.

The earliest drawing for the building showed a somewhat more conventionally classical building. The entrance hall was to be the same height as the rooms that flanked it, and as a result the hipped roof of the Foyer of Meditation was quite visible on the exterior. Four pairs of pilasters marked the entrance, and a single pilaster marked both corners of the central section. The upper floor was set back from the front elevation and seems to have contained only a few rooms. The numerous square panes of glass in the windows indicate that stained-glass windows were yet to enter the picture.

By the fall of 1944 Eggers and Higgins and Armstrong had developed a schematic version of the plan. The ground floor was to house the English Department. There were six classrooms, but the three larger ones had movable partitions so that up to nine classes could be held at once. This was a building that very definitely had a *piano nobile*, a floor of greatest importance: from the start it contained Armstrong's grand entrance hall, Foyer of Meditation, and two other rooms: a Treasure Room for the most important artifacts in the collection and a study hall. On the exterior the entry hall had been increased in height, though not to the same height as the Foyer of Meditation. The upper floor now contained two more classrooms, offices (including a large one for Armstrong), and workrooms. On the exterior the pilasters were no longer paired, and they were spread out more evenly along the center of the facade. It is clear that the front wall of the outer foyer would curve forward, and at this point the door was reached by a pair of curving stairs. (There were also plans for terraces on the east and west sides.) But it is also clear that stained-glass windows would be used in many of the rooms.

In 1945 Armstrong was far enough along in fund-raising to give the go-ahead to the architects for a full set of plans and specifications. At this point a new architect entered the scene: Wyatt C. Hedrick of Fort Worth. A native of Virginia, Hedrick was an architect and engineer who opened his own construction company in Dallas in 1914; he was the builder and presumably the designer of the Miller Cotton Mill in Waco, later known as the L. L. Sams and Sons complex. In 1921 his firm merged with Sanguinet and Staats (the architects of the ALICO Building), and he eventually bought out his partners. He had worked with architect William Ward Watkin of Houston on the Administration Building (1925) and Chemistry Building (1928) at Texas Tech University in Lubbock. Apparently, Eggers and Higgins were not going to be able to supervise the work or Armstrong found their fee for the drawings too steep.

The 1945 blueprints were essentially a much more detailed version of the Eggers and Higgins design. The main difference was that the Foyer of Meditation was now square, where previously clipped corners had made it an octagon. Perhaps most tellingly, the Treasure Room on the main floor was now the Hankamer Treasure Room.

Armstrong Browning Library

Earl C. Hankamer and his wife of Houston became critical funders of the project, even presenting Armstrong with a silver trowel for the laying of the cornerstone. Although World War II was over and drawings were in hand, work on the building did not begin. Apparently the cost of the building exceeded what Armstrong had raised.

In deciding what to cut, the architects soon focused attention on what was now being called the Reception Foyer. Inspired by the Golden Staircase at Burgos Cathedral, the stairs would begin in the middle of the room, rise to a landing about twelve steps up, then break to both sides before returning to the entrance to the upper floor. This would open into the narrow corridor connecting the east and west parts of the upper floor, but a door opposite this entrance would provide a dramatic view into the Foyer of Meditation. The architects planned to use marble throughout the Reception Foyer, for the stair railings and balusters, the steps and risers, the pilasters on the walls, and arches above the doors. In summer 1948 Armstrong had to say good-bye to this lavish dream and substitute a rather utilitarian staircase tucked between this room and the Foyer of Meditation.

Also cut were the two side terraces, and the curving exterior staircase became a rectilinear (and much less flashy) approach to the building. An addition to the 1948 plans was a room dedicated to Elizabeth Barrett Browning. This did not involve much new expense; rather, it was created from a classroom and workroom at the northwest corner of the upper floor.

In structure the building was very modern, with a concrete frame and floors, except for the Foyer of Meditation, which had a steel frame. (The building was also air-conditioned, then a rarity at Baylor.) The exterior was much simplified from earlier versions. The outer veneer was Indiana limestone with a base of Texas red granite. The window spandrels, however, were aluminum, another modern touch that recalled Hedrick's work at Texas Tech. Over the various iterations of the plan the number of pilasters had decreased from ten to eight to four. Indeed, the exterior was so plain that it looked like the Depression-era style for public buildings known as "stripped classicism."

Only the doors predict the richness inside. They were of bronze, with five panels in each leaf, with images drawn from a passage in one of Browning's poems. These bas-relief panels were sculpted by Robert A Weinman. Inside this door the Reception Foyer in its diminished state was fairly nondescript except for the large stained-glass windows. The walls were mainly St. Clair marble, found in Oklahoma, Arkansas, and Missouri, which was a limestone that polished to a marble-like sheen.

The three principal rooms were based on the country where the Brownings lived and work for many years—Italy—and specifically based on the Italian Renaissance. In addition, an emphasis was placed on using the finest materials. The Hankamer Treasure Room had a wainscot of walnut, above which were antique plaster walls. The fireplace was made of Indiana limestone, and the hood above featured the Browning coat of arms. The floors were of oak, while the coffered ceiling was richly painted. The Jones Research Hall, sponsored by John Leddy and Erin Bain Jones, dispensed with the antique plaster of the Treasure Room in favor of solid walnut walls, though the ceiling was plastered, framed by a single row of wooden coffers. On the inner wall of this room was an alcove, with the stained-glass window of the Pied Piper of Hamlin, which had been commissioned years before for the Browning Room in Carroll Library and moved to this new and prominent location.

Though Armstrong had been struck by the exotic richness of the Arab Room at Leighton House, that exoticism was toned down for the Foyer of Meditation. The lower ceilings of the other two rooms gave way to a soaring domed space. There were two entrances from the Reception Foyer, with an alcove centered between them. In the center of each of the other three walls was a large arched window with gold and amber glass. These windows were not as rich as those in the other rooms, but they made the room lighter yet played off the walnut of the walls. Each of the windows and the alcove were framed by a pair of columns set within the walls. Each column was a single piece of Red Levanto marble (quarried in Turkey) with capitals and bases of St. Clair marble. The alcove on the north was several steps above the marble floor and contained the bronze of the clasped hands of Robert and Elizabeth, sculpted by the American artist Harriet Hosmer in 1853. Above the alcove was a small balcony that allowed a splendid view of the room from the upper floor. Though the room was not named for them, Verna and Marrs McLean made the room possible by a generous donation. ◼

Chapter 6

84. Tidwell Bible Building

Baylor University / 1949–54
Birch D. Easterwood and Son, architects

After Baylor's Bible Department became a seminary in 1905 and moved to Fort Worth in 1910—becoming the Southwestern Baptist Theological Seminary—the university had to create a new Bible Department. President Brooks tasked Josiah Blake Tidwell, a charismatic and very conservative Baptist minister, to create a department with an academic rather than professional focus. Tidwell became a fixture on the Baylor campus, teaching until his death in 1946 at age seventy-six.

Plans for a new Bible building named in his honor were surfacing even while he was alive. The earliest known proposal is a sketch by Birch D. Easterwood, which was published in the *Lariat* on May 31, 1937. That and another Easterwood proposal were in the Colonial Revival style. Easterwood had inaugurated that style at Baylor with Brooks Dormitory, followed by Women's Memorial Dormitory. The plans for Tidwell went nowhere, perhaps because Easterwood's Pat Neff Hall and Alexander Dorm were ahead in line, and by the time those buildings were finished, World War II resulted in a postponement of all new construction.

In November 1944 it was announced that fund-raising for the new building would commence, led by Baylor trustee H. L. Kokernot Sr. It would be built on the south side of Speight, between Waco Hall and the Baylor Theater. It was also announced that the architect would be Guy A. Carlander, a "prominent Amarillo architect." Carlander was a native of Kansas and had worked for the design department of the Santa Fe Railroad before becoming an architect in Amarillo in 1920. In 1923 he designed the Garza County Courthouse in the Panhandle town of Post, and in 1929 the First Baptist Church in Amarillo. His most important Waco connection was that he was the husband of Mary Lile, the stepdaughter of J. B. Tidwell. (Her mother, Alma, had become Tidwell's third wife in 1926.) Since Tidwell was still alive in 1944, this selection must have had his approval if not his encouragement.

Carlander produced two designs for Tidwell. The first, published the year after the namesake's death, featured a central tower flanked by low wings. With echoes of the Louisiana State Capitol, which had been completed in 1931, Carlander was attempting to extend the "stripped classicism" of the previous decade. By 1950 Baylor had a new president, W. R. White, who succeeded Pat Neff in 1948, and also a new plan for Tidwell. This new scheme was for a ten-story tower, narrow in front and wider on the sides. In fact, the front would consist of a vertical tier of windows, which would form "a solid shaft of light." On each side were six vertical elements that Carlander certainly meant to be read as medieval buttresses; these elements rose above the tenth floor to engage with the windowless tower, thus becoming flying buttresses, as seen on many Gothic cathedrals. At the same time the design was closely attuned to the streamlined industrial design of the 1930s.

Tidwell Bible Building

Fund-raising, however, stalled. The university had told Carlander that the building should cost $600,000; when bids were requested from contractors, the only estimate that came back was for $1.5 million. When Carlander was unable to produce a design at the lower cost, he was fired. (A lawsuit ensued.) In 1952 Baylor turned to Birch D. Easterwood and his son Kenneth, who had a long track record of designing buildings for Baylor that were handsome and traditional and came in more or less on budget. However, the design for Tidwell that they completed in early 1953 cast aside their go-to Colonial Revival style for a modernistic sort of classicism.

The hipped-roof tower was the primary focus, but to each side the facade gradually stepped down to two-story wings. The tower had a large number of windows, though not the "solid shaft of light" of which Carlander had dreamed. Four brick piers frame three shafts; between the second and fifth floors the glass was set within classical window frames, with a triangular pediment on the second, a broken scroll pediment on the third, and a flat pediment on the fourth, all with stone spandrels with neoclassical festoons. In both wings brick piers were given classical ornament, though only first-floor windows had triangular pediments.

The base of the building was Carthage limestone from southwestern Missouri; all detailing was also stone, but the rest of the building was a beige-colored common brick. On the south side of the building was the Miller Chapel. This was a large double-height space with typical Colonial Revival detailing. Viewed from the front the wings seemed perfectly symmetrical, but on closer inspection the east wing had rooms only on the north side of the corridor because the Baylor Theater, though set back from Speight, came very close to the building. The theater was later replaced by Bobo Spiritual Life Center.

Construction finally began in April 1953, and the building was dedicated on October 22, 1954, which was Baylor homecoming. The cost was $600,000. At first the building was large enough to house the departments of religion, history, sociology, philosophy, sacred music, and German. In 2020 it housed only the first two.

The final touches to the building, the stone panels depicting scenes from the Bible, were not completed until 1960. The Old Testament panels were at the top of the tower, while the New Testament scenes were placed on the sides of the tower between the third and fourth floors. The sculptors were Ira Correll and his son Ross Correll of Austin. A native of Indiana, the elder Correll had produced architectural sculpture for the Hall of State at Fair Park in Dallas and the San Jacinto Monument near Houston. When creating the panels for Tidwell, he was eighty-eight years old; he died in 1964 at age ninety-one.

Paul Quinn College / 1020 Elm Avenue / 1952
J. Scribner Dunne, architect

In the 1950s Paul Quinn College experienced another growth spurt. Two new structures were built in the Colonial Revival style, echoing the style of Baylor's Pat Neff Hall and many other buildings on the Baylor campus. However, the Bishop Joseph Gomez Administration Building (1952) and the (Bishop) Abraham Grant Building (1954) were both built of Austin limestone, with a portico in the center and two dormer windows on the hipped roofs. (The Administration Building also had a small tower or cupola, which rang out chimes on the quarter hour.) The Administration Building was two stories and contained offices and classrooms; Grant Hall was two stories on top of a raised basement and had a refectory (or dining hall) in the basement, a women's dormitory on the two main floors, and offices for counselors and rooms for guests on the first floor. The designer was apparently J. Scribner Dunne, a draftsman for the Mailander Company, which produced display cases for stores. A drawing of Grant Hall in the newspaper was sign "J. S. Dunne."

Paul Quinn College moved to Dallas in 1990, taking over the former campus of Bishop College in hopes of attracting more students to a campus in a larger city. It transitioned from a campus of 22 acres to one of 132 acres. In that same year, a nonprofit organization was incorporated dedicated to using the old Quinn campus for educational and community purposes. A public charter school, the Rapoport Academy, now occupies several of the buildings. In 2014 and 2015, Rapoport Academy spent $3 million to renovate the Administration Building and enlarge it to the west, adding seven thousand square feet to the original thousand. The exterior wall beneath the portico was carefully cleaned, creating a contrast with the rest of the wall, and the architects created a compatible hipped-roof addition that matched the new stone to the original Austin limestone. ◼

Bishop Joseph Gomez Administration Building

Masonic Buildings and Museums

86. Masonic Lodge #92

724 Washington Avenue / 1913–14
Milton W. Scott, architect

This is the oldest of the three Masonic buildings in Waco and the only one designed by a local architect. Milton W. Scott had partnered with Glenn Allen and then T. Brooks Pearson but by 1912 was on his own. In 1912 a perspective drawing was published in a promotional booklet titled *Waco—the Hub of Texas*. The gray granite cornerstone at the northeast corner of the building indicted that the stone was laid in 5913—which combined the 1,913 years after the birth of Christ with the 4,000 years that it was calculated had preceded his birth.

Scott designed a Greek temple at the corner of Washington Avenue and Eighth Street with a single wing to the east. Essentially the first floor was the base of the temple, and the upper two floors were the temple proper. The front of the temple was on the Washington Avenue side. The columns, which were attached to the wall, were of the Greek Doric order. One of the things that made it Greek Doric rather than Roman was that the columns did not have a base. The four engaged columns were framed by Doric piers, which were encased in brick. On the upper floors along the Eighth Street side pilasters (flat representations of columns) continued the temple form.

The building was close to complete by the end of 1913, but the dedication had to wait until the new year. The expectation was that Masons from around the state would come to Waco for the event. The building ended up costing $60,000, and the Masons anticipated spending another $3,500 for furnishings for their meeting room on the third floor. The *Waco Daily Times-Herald* reported that the "building is modern and up to date in every particular"—they were especially impressed by the elevator service (in a three-story building!) and the steam heating.

Beneath the temple were three rental spaces fronting on Eighth Street. Underneath the wing to the east was the entrance flanked by a commercial space to each side. Scott's drawing indicates that there were mezzanine windows above the display windows. Scott did not anticipate the use of awnings, but they were added at an early date. The two spaces on Washington were slow to rent. They were both still vacant in 1916; by 1923 one space

Masonic Lodge #92

was occupied by a plumbing company and the other by offices for the Masonic lodge. At the corner was the New Temple Drug Store; next to that was a grocery store; the space nearest the alley was a flower shop in 1916 and a wallpaper store in the 1920s.

The upper floor of the exterior is much as it was originally built. At some time the mezzanine windows were covered in a crude fashion. Even more crude were the door and siding recently installed on the Eighth Street facade.

For the house of the secretary of all Masonic bodies in Waco, see 3024 Novice in the Karem Park Addition (*Historic Homes*, 105); for the proprietor of the drugstore, see 2316 Gorman Avenue (*More Historic Homes*, 180). ▨

87. Grand Karem Shrine Building

701 Washington Avenue / 1927–28
Herbert M. Greene Co. (Dallas), architects, with Roy E. Lane, associated
J. S. Harrison Construction Company, general contractor

This is one of three historic Masonic buildings in Waco and the only one that is not still owned by the organization. The Masonic Lodge #92 is down the street to the west, and the Grand Masonic Lodge of Texas is one block to the north. Previously on this site there had been the Waller S. Baker house, a two-story frame Victorian house designed by W. W. Larmour for Baker, the law partner of Shapley P. Ross. After Baker's death in 1913 it had become the home of a traveling salesman, James T. Scott, and then a boarding house operated by his widow, Clara. Since 1923 the members of the Karem Temple had been dreaming of a six-story building on this corner that would cost $300,000 or more. By 1925 they were working on plans with Victor G. Koch, who was the city engineer, but the project was now estimated at $350,000.

In 1927 they hired prominent Dallas architect Herbert M. Greene to design a building that would be only three stories and cost $150,000. Greene, a native of Pennsylvania, received a degree in architecture from the University of Illinois and was practicing in Dallas by 1897. His Dallas designs included the Dallas News building, two Presbyterian churches, a Jewish synagogue, and stores for Titche-Goettinger, Volk's, and Neiman-Marcus.

Greene was a Mason and designed Scottish Rite Temples in Dallas, El Paso, San Antonio, and Joplin, Missouri, and the Scottish Rite Dormitory for Girls in Austin, just north of the University of Texas campus. The latter commission led to Greene being named university architect in 1922, and he designed many UT buildings, including Garrison, Waggener, Biology, Chemistry, and Gregory Gymnasium. He was sufficiently busy that he associated with Roy E. Lane for supervision of this Waco building. Bids were opened in December 1927, and J. S. Harrison Construction Company won the contract.

The Grand Karem Shrine Building was thoroughly modern in construction, with concrete frame, floors, and roof. Red tiles on the roof gave the building a Mediterranean feel, while the entrance, made of Waco Art Stone or some other concrete composite imitating real stone, was Moorish in style. The roof of the western part of the building was higher than the eastern part, to allow for a grand ballroom on the third floor. The first floor was largely rental space for stores and offices. Near the back of the building was a small penthouse, with a prominent chimney rising at the northwest corner. The building was dedicated in November 1928 with elaborate ceremonies; it ended up costing $175,000.

In 1995 the Shriners sold the building to McLennan County when the group moved to a suburban location. For more than twenty years the building was underutilized but remained largely intact; the most egregious alteration was the insertion of darkly smoked plate-glass windows on the two principal facades, which is completely inappropriate for a 1928 building. Most original windows do survive on the west and north facades, thereby

Grand Karem Shrine Building

providing a model for anyone hoping to restore the windows facing the street. In 2018 the building was purchased by Chip and Joanna Gaines, with plans to turn it into a downtown hotel.

88. Masonic Grand Lodge Memorial Temple of Texas

715 Columbus Avenue / 1947–49

Broad and Nelson (Dallas) and Robert Leon White (Austin), architects

Walter Cocke Jr., resident architect

A. J. Rife Construction Company, contractor

The earliest Masonic temple in Texas was in Houston; the cornerstone was laid June 13, 1867. When that first temple was built, most of the state's population was in East and Central Texas, but by the turn of the century it was clear that Waco was much more centrally located. The temple moved to Waco in 1904, when a three-story white brick building was erected at the northeast corner of Franklin Avenue and South Sixth Street. The architect was James E. Flanders of Dallas, who had been a Mason since 1895. The cornerstone did not mention Flanders, but it did name all the members of the Building Committee, which included Waco mover and shaker Edward Rotan. (For his houses, see *Historic Homes*, 12 and 58.) When the present building was constructed, the Masons sold the old temple to the state of Texas for $225,000. It was used as a National Guard Armory, though the auditorium on the upper floor was to be made available for civic meetings.

The Building Committee for the present building included two more recent Waco luminaries: Pat M. Neff, who had been governor of Texas from 1921 to 1925 and then president of Baylor University from 1932 to 1947, and Lee Lockwood, a Waco businessman and leading Mason. The building cost approximately $2 million. Ground was broken on December 23, 1947, and the building was dedicated December 7, 1949.

The temple was designed by the Dallas architectural firm of Broad and Nelson. Donald Nelson was a Chicago native whose architectural degree was from MIT; he followed this with several years of study in France. Returning to Chicago, he joined the firm of Bennett, Parsons and Frost and helped design the Chicago Century of Progress Exposition in 1933. This experience recommended him for work on the Texas Centennial Exposition in Dallas, and after the fair he remained in Dallas. After a stint in the US Army Air Forces during World War II, he partnered with Thomas D. Broad, a native of Paris, Texas, who studied at the University of Texas and Harvard. He designed the original Administration Building at Love Field and the Masonic Temple in Dallas.

Associated with Broad and Nelson on this project was Robert Leon White, who had been involved for many years in the design and construction of buildings on the University of Texas campus and had recently designed the Student Union Building on the Baylor campus. Waco architect Walter Cocke Jr., who had grown up next door at 617 Columbus, served as resident architect. He was responsible for visiting the construction site on a regular basis and ensuring that the plans of the architects were being followed. The contractor for the building was A. J. Rife Construction Company of Dallas. This company had previously built the Fine Arts Museum at Fair Park in Dallas, which later became the Dallas Museum of Fine Arts.

The new temple was situated on an entire city block. Earlier, the southwestern corner of this block was the site of the two-story brick house of Gregor and Portia McGregor.

Masonic Grand Lodge Memorial Temple of Texas

McGregor had been a physician while living in Wesley, Texas, near Brenham but focused on real estate investments after moving to Waco in the early 1870s. The lot was 329 feet wide and 265 feet deep. The temple itself was 236 feet wide and 218 feet 8 inches deep.

Though steeped in Masonic tradition, the structure was quite modern. The first floor was framed in concrete; above this was a steel frame. The exterior walls were concrete blocks with a veneer of granite from West Chelmsford, Massachusetts. Much of the entrance was built with marble from Knoxville, Tennessee, and the stone for the two huge columns came from Bedford, Indiana. The interior walls were also made of concrete blocks. In total the structure required 720 tons of steel, 5,500 cubic yards of concrete, and 30,000 cubic feet of granite and other stones.

The central part of the facade consisted of two towers, which were seventy-seven feet in height; between them were the entrance and a large stained-glass window, surrounded by Masonic symbols. Lower wings were on each side. The door was approached by three sets of steps and a pair of easy winding ramps, making the building wheelchair accessible long before it was required by the Americans with Disabilities Act of 1990. In front of the ramp on the right side were cornerstones from two previous grand Masonic temples: the marble cornerstone from the original temple in Houston and the gray granite one from the earlier Waco temple. An awareness that Texans were likely to approach the building in their automobiles led to the creation of a secondary entrance from the west on Eighth Street, with a canopy that was cantilevered out from the wall.

In front of the towers were two massive columns, which supported a pair of globes. These were designed in collaboration with Past Grand Master Jewel P. Lightfoot. They were intended to recall the pillars Jachin and Boaz in the temple of King Solomon in Jerusalem. All dimensions were to Masonic specifications. Each of the globes was carved from a single stone: on the left was a terrestrial globe; and on the right, a celestial globe.

Over the entrance was a huge stained-glass window, thirty-three feet high and fourteen and one-third feet wide, which represented the Masonic Charter Oak. Roger McIntosh and his wife, Georgia Jensen McIntosh, designed it, and Henry Lee Willett Studios executed it. Roger and Georgia were stained-glass artisans in Dallas; Willett, a native of Philadelphia, was a second-generation stained-glass artist who led the firm to national and even international prominence.

A bas-relief sculpture, *The Construction of the Temple of Solomon*, stretched across the facade and was framed by the wings to each side. The sculpture was designed by Raoul Josset, a Frenchman who studied with the prominent sculptor Antoine Bourdelle in Paris before moving to the United States in 1932. His classicizing style was very compatible with art deco buildings and monuments, of which he did several in Texas in the late 1930s, including *The Spirit of the Centennial* for the Administration Building at Fair Park in Dallas, the statue of George Childress at Washington-on-the-Brazos State Park, the winged angel at Monument Hill near La Grange, and the Fannin Memorial in Goliad. While Josset designed the work and was listed in large letters as the sculptor, the piece was actually carved by Harry Liva, who got second billing.

The main hallway inside, known as the concourse, was not laid out in a straight line but instead curved to the side and rear. This created a crescent shape, appropriate for a Masonic building. To the left were various Masonic offices; to the right were the Grand Lodge Library and Museum and the grand secretary's office. The most impressive space was the auditorium, known as the Lodge Room. There were 1,600 seats on the main floor and another 2,100 in the balcony; additional seating on the stage brought the total to 3,740.

A special section of the *Tribune-Herald* at the time of the temple's dedication noted that Masons approaching it for the first time uttered "exclamations of amazement." It further noted that "even Wacoans who have become familiar with the Temple during its construction period were surprised at its imposing appearance." The local Masonic community was sufficiently pleased with the building that the firm was brought back to Waco in 1968 to design the Scottish Rite Library and Museum, now known as the Lee Lockwood Library on Waco Drive. ▨

2801 W. Waco Drive / 1968–69
Donald Nelson of Broad and Nelson (Dallas), architect

The Ancient and Accepted Scottish Rite of Freemasonry—generally known simply as the Scottish Rite—is a part of Freemasonry that allows for further exploration of Masonic principles. It was founded in Charleston, South Carolina, in 1801 and was established in Texas in 1867. This library and museum were created to mark the hundredth anniversary of the Scottish Rite in Texas. Waco businessman Lee Lockwood was the sovereign grand inspector general of Sottish Rite Masons in Texas, and he was the driving force behind the project. The library and museum were to focus on the history and government of the United States and, of course, on Freemasonry.

Lee Lockwood Library and Museum

Waco had been the home of the Masonic Grand Lodge of Texas since 1904, and a very impressive Grand Lodge Memorial Temple had been built on Columbus Avenue only twenty years before. The Scottish Rite Foundation of Texas hired Donald Nelson, the architect of the Grand Lodge, to design the Lee Lockwood Library. (The consulting architect on the Grand Lodge, Robert Leon White of Austin, had passed away in 1964.) The budget for the Lockwood Library was $1 million exclusive of furnishings and landscaping, which was a substantial amount, but only half the budget for the Grand Lodge. Nelson was working on the design in 1967; the cornerstone was leveled May 4, 1968, and the building was completed the next year.

Unlike the Grand Lodge the new building had a very limited budget for exterior ornamentation. As a result the Masonic symbolism was muted; the most noteworthy feature was the pair of sphinxes flanking the main entrance. These were close copies of the sphinxes at the House of the Temple at 1733 Sixteenth Street NW in Washington, DC, headquarters of the Southern Jurisdiction of the Scottish Rite. This building, based on the Mausoleum of Halicarnassus in Turkey, was built from 1911 to 1915 to the designs of John Russell Pope, who had been A. J. Armstrong's first choice to design a Browning Library at Baylor.

The Lee Lockwood Library was a large rectangular box with a veneer of Indiana limestone—no towers, no columns, no stained glass. The focal point was four square piers clad in limestone, which formed something of a portico, but behind this the door was part of a wall of glass, which seems to be an echo of Philip Johnson's design for the Amon Carter Museum in Fort Worth, though that portico stretched across the entire facade.

Inside the front door was a fifty-eight-hundred-square-foot lobby and concourse, which was two stories high. Paneling was hand-rubbed walnut, and the floors were Italian travertine. Straight ahead was a 350-seat auditorium with opera seats covered in gold. (On the floor above was a similar meeting room for local lodges upholstered in blue.) At the west end of the building was the library, which had floors of domestic marble. (Elsewhere in the building the floors were covered in institutional vinyl.) Above the library was the office of Sovereign Grand Inspector General Lee Lockwood. Opposite this on the east end were offices that were to be rented to the Waco Scottish Rite bodies. The museum occupied much of the basement level.

The building occupied the two city blocks between Twenty-Seventh and Twenty-Ninth Streets, which meant that the center of the building aligned with Twenty-Eighth Street across Waco Drive. That throughway, which allowed Texans to hurtle through Waco in their automobiles, had been built less than two decades earlier. The Lockwood Library assumed that all visitors would be arriving by car and allowed for ample parking on both sides of the building, holding 250 cars.

90. Texas Ranger Hall of Fame and Museum

100 Texas Ranger Trail / 1967–68, 1970, 1973–76 and after
David Carnahan, architect

The sprawling complex that is the current Texas Ranger Hall of Fame and Museum started as a small building, which is, amazingly, still the front door of the institution. The initial plan was to have it look like a rustic 1840s fort, but with air-conditioning. However, the image that architect David Carnahan created seemed more out of western movies than early Texas history. Nevertheless, the institution has grown at a steady pace and stuck with the original style, which has essentially become a style all its own: Texas Ranger Rustic.

The Texas Rangers were first organized in 1823 by Stephen F. Austin to provide law and order on the frontier. During the Mexican-American War the Rangers fought alongside the US Army, but in these early years their mission was not well defined. In 1874 the Democratic state legislature, the first since Reconstruction, authorized the Rangers as a military unit. They found themselves fighting Indians and cattle rustlers along the border. The latter brought them into conflict with Mexicans and Hispanics living in Texas, which increased in the tumultuous years after the Mexican Revolution in 1910. Historians estimate that Rangers killed some five thousand Hispanics between 1914 and 1919. Their reputation was in tatters, but in 1938 the Rangers were placed under the Texas Department of Public Safety. Their new director, Colonel Homer Garrison, burnished their reputation as the premier state law-enforcement agency, using the latest scientific methods to fight crime.

The idea for such an institution was first floated in 1963. Roger Conger, who was mayor of Waco at the time, recalled that Jimmy LeBlond, who worked locally in public relations, had come up with the original idea. Promoters suggested using the part of the old First Street Cemetery nearest the river. This was already public land and adjacent to where Interstate 35 was to be built. Originally it was to be called Fort Fisher Museum and was to include one large room for the museum, a tourist information center, and the regional headquarters of the Texas Rangers. The museum was named the Homer Garrison Museum for the man who had overseen the Texas Rangers since 1938. Beyond this would be campgrounds with views of the river.

The notion of placing such a museum in Waco was based on a three-week stay by Rangers in 1837. The visit was instigated by a Comanche attack on Fort Parker, near present-day Groesbeck. William S. Fisher, secretary of war of the Republic Texas, tasked Captain Thomas H. Barron and forty-four soldiers/rangers with creating a road from the falls of the Brazos (in Falls County just below the present town of Marlin) to the Waco Indian village situated along the banks of the Brazos in what is now downtown Waco. Initially Secretary of War Fisher ordered them to build a fort, but three weeks later he ordered them to depart. For three weeks they had been living in brush shelters—precise location unknown—and certainly had no time to construct any sort of permanent fort, much less one built of stone. Indeed, it is said that the soldiers gave their location the name Fort Fisher as they were leaving, which suggests that it was more sarcastic than honorific.

The "reconstructed" Fort Fisher had a front gallery with rustic posts, random limestone walls and chimneys, and modern windows covered with rustic wrought-iron grills. To the rear was an ell of boards and battens. Rustic it was, but the design was highly imaginative and in no way related to any building in 1840s Texas. Virtually all buildings in 1830s and 1840s Texas were wood—brick and stone emerged as alternatives in the 1850s. When the US Army began building forts in western Texas after the Civil War, they were large, permanent, and federally funded. Some forts, such as Fort Concho in San Angelo, were built by German stonemasons from Fredericksburg, who would have been appalled by the rough piles of stone on the modern Fort Fisher.

The Fort Fisher Museum was design by David Carnahan, a Waco native and graduate of Texas A&M University, who was to become a partner in the architectural firm of Bennett, Carnahan, Hearn and Thomas. Barsh Construction took the contract to build it for $98,642. Ground was broken in December 1967, with Colonel Homer Garrison turning the first spade of dirt himself. In remarks at the groundbreaking Garrison defended the work of the Rangers in the Rio Grande Valley. He claimed that the accusations of brutality came from "misguided liberals" and that the charges were "absurd." (Garrison died the next year, before the museum was completed.) The building was dedicated on October 25, 1968, as part of Baylor homecoming. (The next day Baylor beat Texas A&M by a score of 10-9.)

The curator of the Homer Garrison Museum was Gaines de Graffenried, a banker, rancher, and leading gun collector. The Waco City Council (which owns and operates the museum) appointed a committee to help screen gifts to the museum, which consisted of local historian Roger Conger; Strecker Museum director, Bryce Brown; architect David Carnahan; owner of Texian Press, Robert Davis; and head of the Texas Ranger unit in Waco, Captain Clint Peeples. Curator de Graffenried donated much of his collection to the museum, and as a result the focus of the museum in its early years was on firearms.

At first the museum was open only on Sunday afternoons, but by 1970 it was open seven days a week. The new museum was sufficiently popular that within two years additions to the complex began. A separate building was erected for the tourist information center, which gave additional room for the museum in the original building. Next door to the information center a hamburger stand was built, which would have been an amenity for museum visitors and also nearby campers. These were both completed in 1970. David Carnahan designed both these structures, and they were variants on the style of the original building. The burger stand had stone ends, with board-and-batten front and back walls. Like the original building it had rustic porch posts, and though the museum now has more finished posts, the rustic ones remain on what is now the office of the Texas Ranger Association Foundation. (This group supports active and retired Texas Rangers and their immediate families.) The visitor information center was a more modern take on the rustic style, utilizing plate glass in addition to rock and wood.

Texas Ranger Hall of Fame and Museum

In its earliest years the museum was essentially local, but Gaines de Graffenried and Roger Conger hoped to enlarge the museum and increase its profile by making it a Texas Ranger Hall of Fame. In 1973 they devised a celebration of the Rangers' 150th anniversary and parlayed that into the creation of a Hall of Fame. David Carnahan returned to design an additional twelve-thousand-square-foot structure to stand between the original building and the river. The building was to be of native stone and cedar; a central theater would be surrounded by exhibition galleries. The style of the original building and the new wing was now said to be "Texas frontier style." Hooker Construction of Waco agreed to build it for $349,200. By the time it was dedicated in February 1976 the bill had risen to $725,000.

The institution has continued to grow, with each addition a variation on the theme of Texas Ranger Rustic, and most designed by Bennett, Carnahan, Hearn and Thomas. (David Carnahan died in 2001.) These include a large meeting space, John Knox Hall, which was planned for various uses, including for art shows, coin shows, and gun shows. Between 2007 and 2010 a Texas Ranger Education Center and a new Texas Ranger Company F Headquarters were built on part of the former campgrounds. In 2011 the Tobin and Anne Armstrong Ranger Research Center quadrupled the size of the museum's archive and library. This $1.1 million facility was designed by James A. McBride of Houston, who donated his services. The new center was at a right angle to the original building, and this west facade concludes with a round tower, providing an additional focal point to the overall complex. ▪

Architects of Waco's Historic Buildings

Local Architects

W. W. Larmour

15. Columbus Avenue Baptist Church
1300 Columbus Avenue / 1906–7

W. W. Larmour with Samuel P. Herbert

73a. Old Main
Baylor University / 1886–87

73b. Georgia Burleson Hall
Baylor University / 1887–88

Milton W. Scott

44. McLendon Hardware Company (later River Square Center)
213 Mary Avenue / Circa 1908; severely damaged 1953; renovated 1995–97

86. Masonic Lodge #92
724 Washington Avenue / 1913–14

5. First Lutheran Church (later Grace Church)
1008 Jefferson Avenue / 1916–17

9. First Church of Christ, Scientist (later Olive Branch Christian Fellowship)
1101 Columbus Avenue / 1924

27. Central Motor Company (Dodge dealership)
904, 906, and 908 Austin Avenue / 1924–25

32. McDermott Motor Company (Buick dealership)
1125 Washington Avenue / 1928–29

60. Hilton Hotel / Roosevelt Hotel / Roosevelt Tower
400 Austin Avenue / expansion of 1929

Milton W. Scott with Glen Allen (as Allen and Scott)

2. First Baptist Church
500 Webster Avenue / 1906

43. Artesian Manufacturing and Bottling Co. (Dr Pepper Museum and Free Enterprise Institute)
300 S. Fifth Street / 1906

Milton W. Scott with T. Brooks Pearson (as Pearson and Scott)

52. Waco Drug Company (later Insurors of Texas Building)
225 S. Fifth Street / 1910–11 (enlargement by E. McIver Ross, 1922–23)

Milton W. Scott with Waller and Field and T. Scott Pearson (as Pearson and Scott)

75. Waco High School (later Historic Lofts at Waco High)
815 Columbus Avenue / 1910–13, 1915, 1921, 1924, and 1929
Waller and Field (Fort Worth) and Scott and Pearson / 1910–13
Milton W. Scott for additions of 1915, 1921, and gymnasium of 1924; T. Brooks Pearson for north wing, 1929

T. Brooks Pearson

68. Central Fire Station and Drill Tower
1010 and 1016 Columbus Avenue / 1931–32

E. McIver Ross
52. Waco Drug Company (later Insurors of Texas
    Building)
225 S. Fifth Street / enlargement of 1922–23

Ross and Cason
E. McIver Ross and Herman F. Cason
49. Texas Telephone Company Exchange
119 N. Ninth Street / 1915–16

Cason Brothers
Herman F. Cason and Harry Cason
6. St. John's Methodist Church (later Greater New Light
    Missionary Baptist Church)
925 N. Eighteenth Street / 1921–22

Herman F. Cason
31. Commercial Building
1023, 1025, and 1027 Austin Avenue (originally 1017,
    1019, and 1021 Austin Avenue) / 1927

39. Elite Café (later Magnolia Table)
2132 S. Valley Mills Drive / 1941, 2018

Birch D. Easterwood
58. Liberty National Bank Building (later One Liberty
    Place)
601 Austin Avenue / 100 N. Sixth Street / 1922–23

25. Commercial Building
625 Franklin / 1923

74a and 74b. Carroll Science Hall and Carroll Chapel
    and Library (Carroll Library), Baylor University
1429 S. Fifth Street / rebuilt 1923

15. Columbus Avenue Baptist Church Sunday School
    Annex
1300 Columbus Avenue / 1924

11. Waco Central Christian Church (later the
    Mighty Wind Worship Center)
1100 Washington Avenue / 1924–25

78. Women's Memorial Dormitory
Baylor University / 1929

13. Herring Avenue Methodist Church (later St. Paul
    African Methodist Episcopal Church)
1302 Herring Avenue / 1932

Birch D. Easterwood and Son
80a. Pat Neff Hall
Baylor University / 1938–40

81. East Waco Junior High School
1030 Live Oak Street / 1939–40

84. Tidwell Bible Building
Baylor University / 1949–54

Roy E. Lane
12. St. Francis on the Brazos Catholic Church
315 Jefferson / 1928–31

Harry L. Spicer
59. Stratton Building
800 Austin Avenue / 1922–23

29. Citizens National Bank
514 Austin Avenue / 1926–27

30. Commercial Building (later Simply Irresistible)
1018 Austin Avenue / 1927–28

35. Sleeper Building
826–828 Austin Avenue / 1928

36. Clemens Building
701 Austin Avenue / 1929

67. Waco City Hall
300 Austin Avenue / 1929–30

Walter Cocke Jr.
14. St. Mary of the Assumption Catholic Church
Washington Avenue at Fourteenth Street / 1942

15. Columbus Avenue Baptist Church
1300 Columbus Avenue / Remodeled 1949–51

16. St. Alban's Episcopal Church
305 N. Thirtieth Street / 1949–50, 1952–53

Walter Cocke Jr. and Robert S. Bennett
62b. First National Bank Office Building
801 Washington Avenue / 1963–64

J. Scribner Dunne
38. Losavio Grocery Store
1528 Austin / 1938–39

85. Bishop Joseph Gomez Administration
    Building, Paul Quinn College
1020 Elm Avenue / 1952

N. E. Wiedemann
17. Congregation Agudath Jacob (later Sul Ross
    Senior Center)
1414 Jefferson Avenue (originally 405 N. Fifteenth
    Street) / 1950

Wiedemann and Salmond
Newell E. Wiedemann and Don E. Salmond
5. First Lutheran Church (later Grace Church)
1008 Jefferson Avenue / enlargement of 1956–58

Harris H. Roberts and Associates
40. Sachs Austin Avenue (later Sironia)
1509 Austin Avenue / 1953–54

J. W. Bush and James D. Witt
71. Waco-McLennan County Library
1717 Austin Avenue / 1961

J. W. Bush and John Dudley (as Bush and Dudley)
19. First Methodist Church
4901 Cobbs / 1967, 1975–76

72. Bledsoe-Miller Recreation Community Center
300 N. Martin Luther King Jr. Boulevard / 1971–72

David Carnahan
90. Texas Ranger Hall of Fame and Museum
100 Texas Ranger Trail / 1967–68, 1970, 1973–76

Out-of-Town Architects

Thomas M. Griffith (New York)
63. Waco Suspension Bridge
University-Parks Drive between Franklin Avenue
    and Washington Avenue / 1870

William Pitt Wentworth (Boston)
1. St. Paul's Episcopal Church
515 Columbus Avenue / 1878–79

J. Riely Gordon (San Antonio)
65. McLennan County Courthouse
501 Washington Avenue / 1900–1902

Messer and Smith (Fort Worth)
74a and 74b. Carroll Science Hall and Carroll Chapel
    and Library (Carroll Library), Baylor University
1429 S. Fifth Street / 1901

Waller and Field (Fort Worth)
75. Waco High School (later Historic Lofts at
    Waco High)
815 Columbus Avenue / 1910–13

Sanguinet and Staats (Fort Worth)
55. Amicable Life Insurance Company Building (ALICO)
425 Austin Avenue / 1910–11

25. Bankers Trust Building
526–528 Austin Avenue / 1915–16

Lang and Witchell (Dallas)
56. Riggins Hotel (later the Raleigh Hotel, now an
    office building)
801–807 Austin Avenue / 1912–14

37. The Waco Hippodrome
724 Austin Avenue / 1913; rebuilt to the design of
    other architects, 1929
60. Hilton Hotel / Roosevelt Hotel / Roosevelt Tower
400 Austin Avenue / 1927–28

79. Waco Hall
Baylor University / 1929–30

**F. M. Mann (Urbana, Illinois) with Scott,
Pearson and Dean (Waco)**
3. First Presbyterian Church
1100 Austin Avenue / 1911–12

C. W. Bulger and Son (Dallas)
57. The Praetorian Building
601 Franklin Avenue / 1913–15

**Missouri Valley Bridge and Iron Co.
(Leavenworth, Kansas)**
63. Waco Suspension Bridge
University Parks Drive between Franklin Avenue
    and Washington Avenue / 1914

William Sidney Pittman (Dallas)
77. William Decker Johnson Hall, Paul Quinn College
1020 Elm Avenue / 1922–23

Adams and Adams (San Antonio)
8. St. James United Methodist Church
600 S. Second Street / 1924

R. H. Hunt Co. (Dallas)
10. Austin Avenue United Methodist Church
    (later First Methodist Church Downtown)
1300 Austin Avenue / 1924–25

Wyatt C. Hedrick (Fort Worth)
51. Miller Cotton Mill (later L. L. Sams and Sons
    Manufacturing Company, now L. L. Sams
    Historic Lofts)
2000 S. First Street / 1919–20, 1946

83. Armstrong Browning Library, Baylor University
710 Speight Avenue / 1948–51

62a. First National Bank Building
811 Washington Avenue / 1954–55

J. N. MacCammon (Dallas)
61. Medical Arts Building (later National Lloyd's Building)
900 Austin Avenue / 1927–29

Herbert M. Greene Co. (Dallas)
87. Grand Karem Shrine Building
701 Washington Avenue / 1927–28

Henry T. Phelps (San Antonio)
56. Riggins Hotel (later the Raleigh Hotel, now an
    office building)
801–807 Austin Avenue / remodeled 1929

W. H. Schimmelpfennig (Washington, DC)
70. United States Courthouse
800 Franklin Avenue / 1935–37

Robert V. Derrah (Los Angeles)
53. Coca-Cola Bottling Company
1201 Austin Avenue / 1938

Robert Leon White (Austin)
82. Bill Daniel Student Center
Baylor University / 1940–42, 1946–47

**Broad and Nelson (Dallas) with
Robert Leon White (Austin)**
88. Masonic Grand Lodge Memorial Temple of Texas
715 Columbus Avenue / 1947–49

Donald Nelson of Broad and Nelson (Dallas)
89. Lee Lockwood Library and Museum
2801 W. Waco Drive / 1968–69

E. H. Hezner (Chicago)
41. Pioneer Savings Association
823 Washington Avenue / 1955

**A. C. Lenander (Columbus, Ohio) with Spicer,
Bush and Witt**
42. First Federal Savings and Loan (later Guaranty Bank)
1226 Austin Avenue / 1958–60

McKee and Kamrath (Houston) with Bush and Witt
18. Temple Rodef Sholom
1717 N. Forty-First Street / 1961

Steinbomer and Duffin (San Antonio)
19. First Methodist Church
4901 Cobbs / 1962–63

Jay Frank Powell (Midland)
55. Amicable Life Insurance Company Building (ALICO)
425 Austin Avenue / remodeled 1964–66

Maps of Building Locations

Maps by Eric Ames

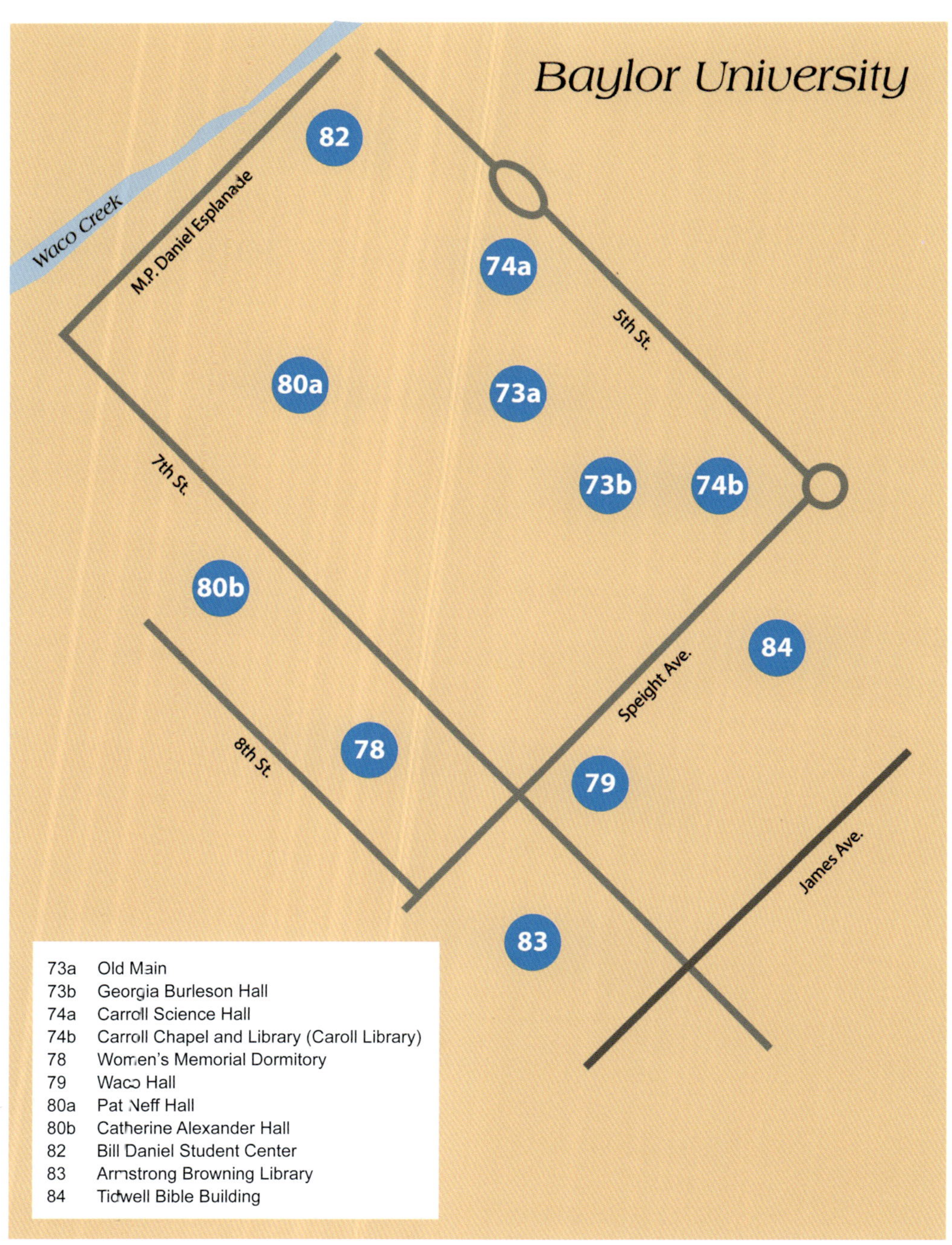

73a   Old Main
73b   Georgia Burleson Hall
74a   Carroll Science Hall
74b   Carroll Chapel and Library (Caroll Library)
78   Women's Memorial Dormitory
79   Waco Hall
80a   Pat Neff Hall
80b   Catherine Alexander Hall
82   Bill Daniel Student Center
83   Armstrong Browning Library
84   Tidwell Bible Building

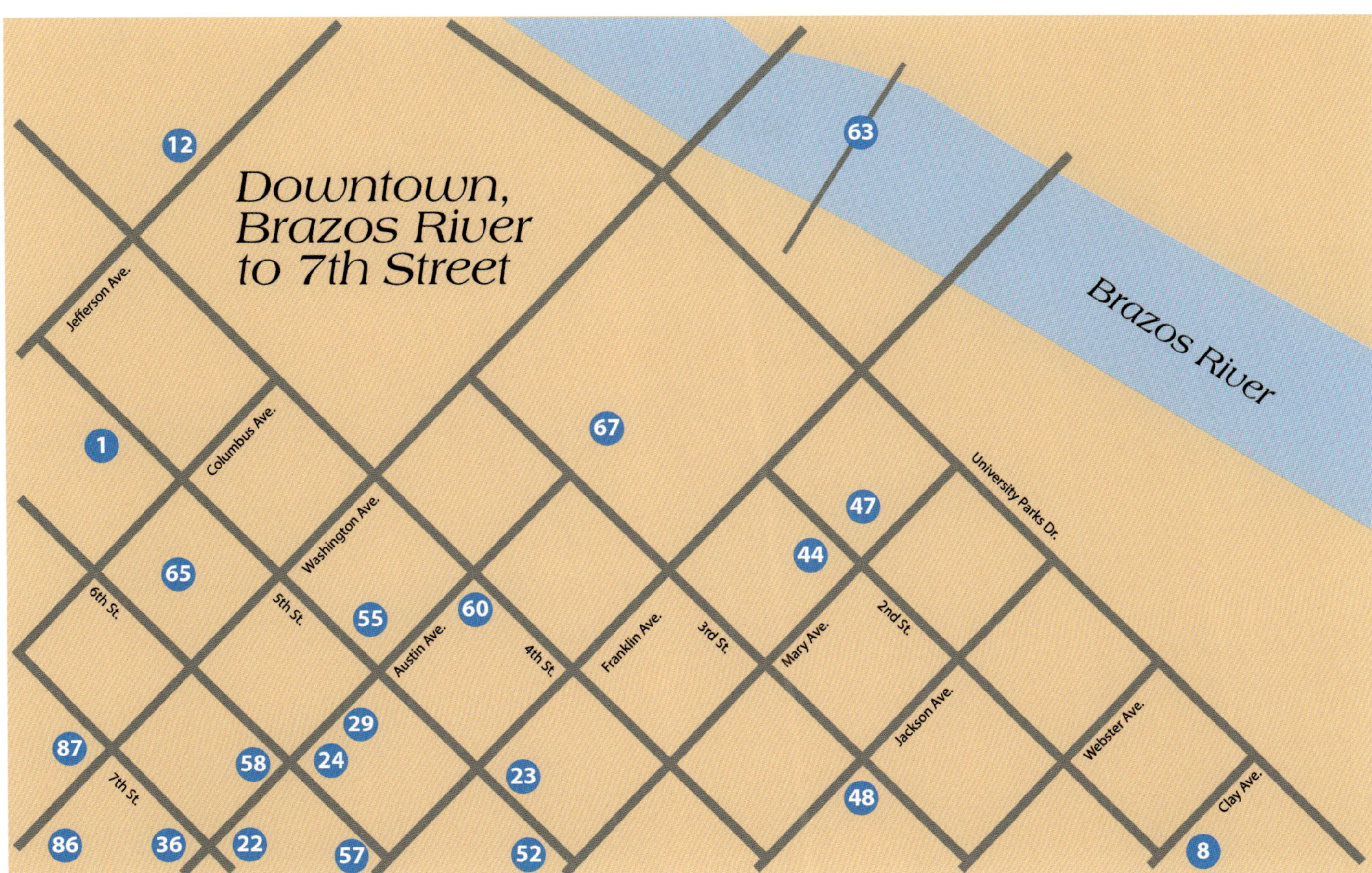

1	St. Paul's Episcopal Church	36	Clemens Building	58	Liberty National Bank Building
8	St. James Methodist Episcopal Church	44	McLendon Hardware Company	60	Hilton Hotel/Roosevelt Tower
12	St. Francis on the Brazos Catholic Church	47	Hanna-James-Taylor Building	63	Waco Suspension Bridge
22	The Cameron Building	48	Commercial Building	65	McLennan County Courthouse
23	Commercial Building	52	Waco Drug Company	67	Waco City Hall
24	Bankers Trust Building	55	Amicable Life Insurance Company Building	86	Masonic Lodge #92
29	Citizens National Bank	57	The Praetorian Building	87	Grand Karem Shrine Building

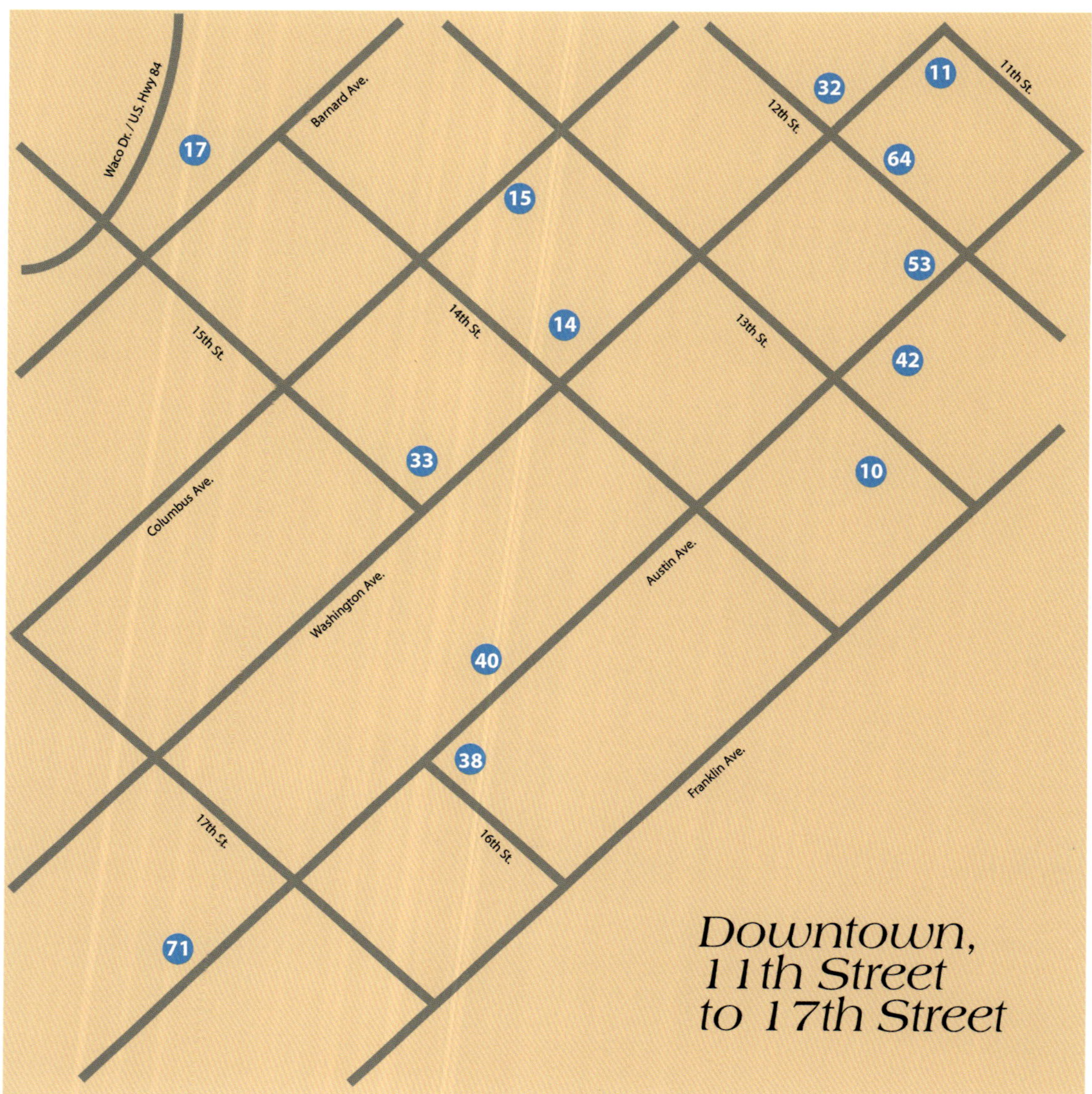

10	Austin Avenue Methodist Church	38	Losavio Grocery Store
11	Waco Central Christian Church	40	Sachs Austin Avenue (later Sironia)
14	St. Mary of the Assumption Catholic Church	42	First Federal Savings and Loan
15	Columbus Avenue Baptist Church	53	Coca-Cola Bottling Company
17	Congregation Agudath Jacob	64	West End Fire Station
32	McDermott Motor Company	71	Waco-McLennan County Library
33	Gulf Filling Station		

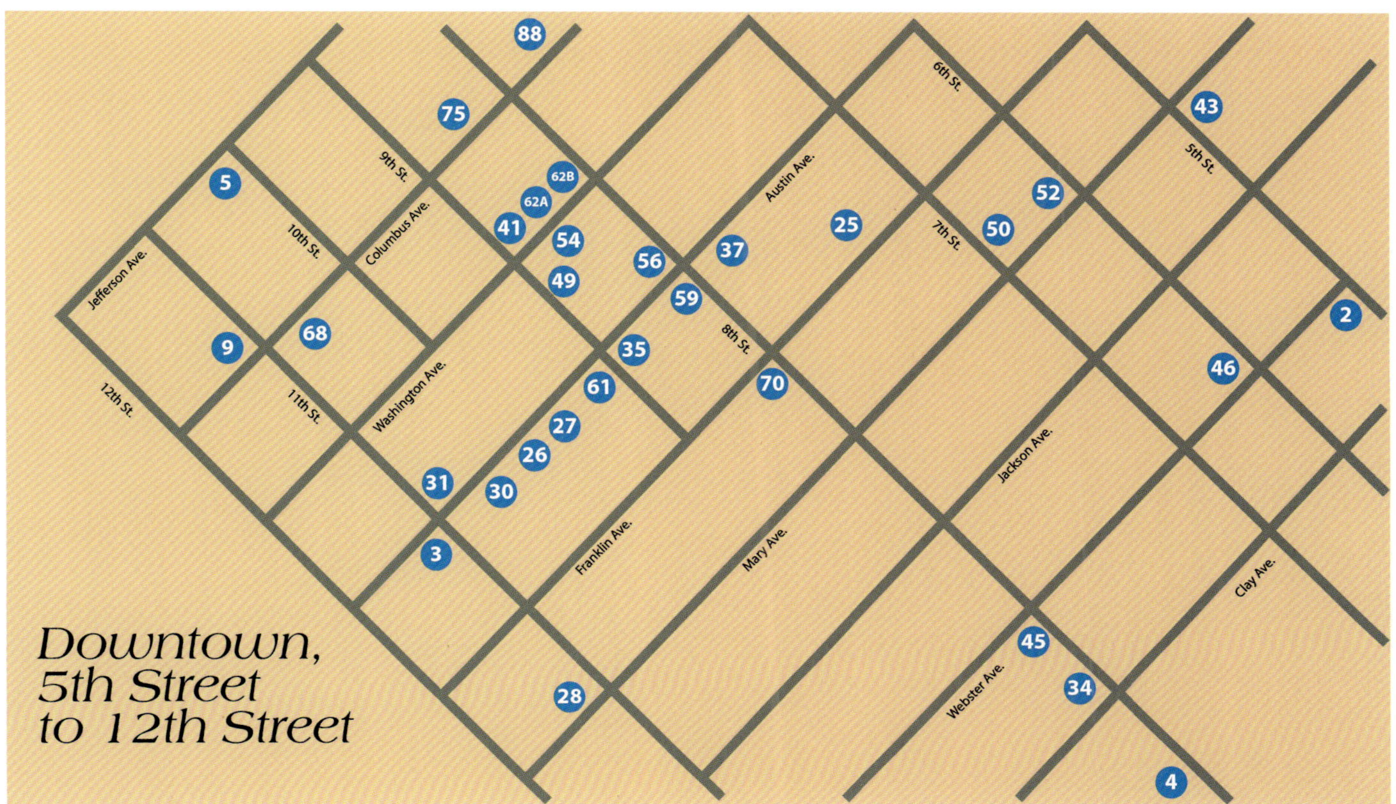

Downtown, 5th Street to 12th Street

2	First Baptist Church	34	Magnolia Filling Station	56	Riggins Hotel
3	First Presbyterian Church	35	Sleeper Building	59	Stratton Building
4	Deutsche Evangelische Zions-Kirche	37	The Waco Hippodrome	61	Medical Arts Building
5	First Lutheran Church	41	Pioneer Savings Association	62a	First National Bank Building
9	First Church of Christ, Scientist	43	Artesian Manufacturing and Bottling Co.	62b	First National Bank Office Building
25	Commercial Building	45	Merrick Medicine Company	68	Central Fire Station and Drill Tower
26	The Cruger Company Building	46	Brazos Valley Cotton Oil Mill	70	United States Courthouse
27	Central Motor Company	49	Texas Telephone Company Exchange	75	Waco High School
28	Texas Fireproof Storage Company	50	Williams Dry Goods Company	88	Masonic Grand Lodge Memorial Temple of Texas
30	Commercial Building	52	Waco Drug Company		
31	Commercial Building	54	Southern Bell Telephone Company		

Digital Resources

Waco City Directories from 1876 to 1923–24 are digitized and available online via the Baylor University Libraries
Digital Collections at https://digitalcollections-baylor.quartexcollections.com.
Sanborn Fire Insurance Maps are available at the Library of Congress at https://www.loc.gov/collections/sanborn-map
s/?fa=location:texas%7Clocation:mclennan+county%7Clocation:waco.
Many Texas Sanborn Fire Insurance Maps in the Perry-Castañeda Library Map Collection at the University of Texas
are available online at https://legacy.lib.utexas.edu/maps/sanborn/texas.html.
Many Waco (and Texas) newspapers are digitized and available on the Portal to Texas History at https://texashistory.
unt.edu/.
United States Census Records up to 1940 have been digitized and are accessible through HeritageQuest Online, as
part of Ancestry.com.

Sources for the historical information in the text are listed by building. Frequently cited sources have been shortened
as indicated below:

Greaves and Walker, *Milton W. Scott's Waco*	B. J. Greaves and Mildred G. Walker, *Milton W. Scott's Waco* (Waco: Dr Pepper Museum and Free Enterprise Institute, 1998).
Henry, *Architecture in Texas*	Jay Henry, *Architecture in Texas: 1895–1945* (Austin: University of Texas Press, 1993).
Larmour, *Architectural Waco*	W. W. Larmour, *Architectural Waco: Showing Principal Buildings Erected by W. W. Larmour, Architect* (Waco: Brooks and Wallace, n.d. [circa 1896]); reprinted in *Waco Heritage and History* 4, no. 3 (Fall 1973): 1–22.
Moorhead, *Buildings of Texas*	Gerald Moorhead, with James W. Steely, W. Dwayne Jones, Anna Mod, John C. Ferguson, Cheryl Caldwell Ferguson, Mario L. Sánchez, and Stephen Fox, *Buildings of Texas: Central, South, and Gulf Coast* (Charlottesville: University of Virginia Press, 2013).
Robinson, *The People's Architecture*	Willard B. Robinson, *The People's Architecture: Texas Courthouses, Jails, and Municipal Buildings* (Austin: Texas State Historical Association, 1983).
Robinson, *Reflections of Faith*	Willard B. Robinson, with Jean M. Robinson, *Reflections of Faith: Houses of Worship in the Lone Star State* (Waco: Baylor University Press, 1994).

Scardino and Turner, *Clayton's Galveston* — Barrie Scardino and Drexel Turner, *Clayton's Galveston: The Architecture of Nicholas J. Clayton and His Contemporaries* (College Station: Texas A&M University Press, 2000).

TGCAMB — *Texas General Contractors Association Monthly Bulletin* [accessed at the Metropolitan Research Center, Houston Public Library].

WCCN — "Beautiful Waco—a Home and Garden Number," *Waco Chamber of Commerce News*, April–May 1926; reprinted in *Waco Heritage and History* 1, no. 1 (Spring 1970): 26–48.

The WPA Guide to Texas — Writers Program of the Works Project Administration in the State of Texas, *Texas: A Guide to the Lone Star State* (New York: Hastings House, 1940); reprinted, with a new introduction by Don Graham, as *The WPA Guide to Texas: The Federal Writers Project Guide to Texas* (Austin: Texas Monthly Press, 1986).

Chapter One: Houses of Worship

1. St. Paul's Episcopal Church

Sanborn Maps, 1889, sheet 14; 1893, sheet 10; 1899, sheet 16; 1926, sheet 2

Larmour, *Architectural Waco*, 18

WCCN, 39

St. Paul's Episcopal Church: A History in Photographs (Waco: St. Paul's Episcopal Church, 2009)

2. First Baptist Church

Sanborn Maps, 1885, sheet 7; 1889, sheets 4 (church) and 12 (new site); 1893, sheet 8; 1899, sheet 8 (Larmour church); 1926, sheet 29 (Allen and Scott church)

Larmour, *Architectural Waco*, 13

"Cornerstone of First Baptist Church Laid with Impressive Ceremonies," *Waco Daily Times-Herald*, February 4, 1906, 5.

1908 Yearbook, First Baptist Church, Waco, Texas (Waco: First Baptist Church, 1908), 8, 11, 13

Waco Tribune-Herald, June 4, 1950, 27

Waco News-Tribune, August 12, 1950, 1

Robinson, *Reflections of Faith*, 172

Greaves and Walker, *Milton W. Scott's Waco*, 28–29

Moorhead, *Buildings of Texas*, 125

3. First Presbyterian Church

"Cornerstone of First Presbyterian Church Laid This Morning," newspaper clipping dated September 27, 1911, in [*Minutes & Record of Congregational Meetings of the First Presbyterian Church of Waco*], 1891/1937, https://texashistory.unt.edu/ark:/67531/metapth1221003/

Waco Morning News, October 20, 1911, 5

Sanborn Maps, 1885, sheet 8 (church Second and Jackson); 1899, sheet 9 (church at 812 Austin); 1926, sheet 19 (present church)

William J. Battle, "Art in Texas: An Outline," *Southwest Review* 14, no. 1 (1928): 56

Amanda Sawyer, "First Presbyterian Church," *Waco History*, accessed December 30, 2018, https://wacohistory.org/items/show/84

4. Deutsche Evangelische Zions-Kirche (German Evangelical Zion's Church; later New Branch Worship Center)

Waco City Directories, 1910–16

Sanborn Maps, 1899, sheet 26 (old church); 1926, sheet 34 (new church)

Zion United Church of Christ—100th Anniversary, October 25, 1981

5. First Lutheran Church (later Grace Church)

Sanborn Map, 1926, sheet 204

Waco News-Tribune, May 13, 1954, 1 (Reed contract for dormitory); December 13, 1955, 9 (Moody Liberal Arts Building)

Gynter Quill, "A New Church Plant for 75th Anniversary," *Waco Tribune-Herald*, May 3, 1959, 29

Greaves and Walker, *Milton W. Scott's Waco*, 30

6. St. John's Methodist Church (later Greater New Light Missionary Baptist Church)

Waco City Directories, 1900–1901 to 1923–24 (Cason family)

Waco News-Tribune, September 26, 1921, 2; December 10, 1921, 10; May 30, 1922, 5; October 22, 1922, 32; March 18, 1929, 3 (J. F. Cason obituary)

Sanborn Maps, 1926, sheet 215; 1926/1950, sheet 215

7. New Hope Baptist Church

Proverbs 29:18

Waco News-Tribune, January 1, 1922, 10; January 3, 1922, 9 (groundbreaking); May 20, 1923, 27 (completion)

Sanborn Map, 1926, sheet 211 (old New Hope); sheet 221 (new New Hope)

TGCAMB, June 1923, 29

Paul Fisher and Prisca Bird, "New Hope Baptist Church," 2021, http://www.wacohistory.org/items/show/27

8. St. James Methodist Episcopal Church

Waco City Directories, 1878–79 to 1923–24

Sanborn Maps, 1885, sheet 4 and 1889, sheet 3 (first frame building); 1893, sheet 5 and 1899, sheet 5 (first brick church); 1926, sheet 31

Texas Trade Review and Industrial Record 25 (1920): 28–29

Christopher Long, "Adams, Carleton W.," *Handbook of Texas Online*, accessed June 12, 2018, http://www.tshaonline.org/handbook/online/articles/fad25

J. B. Smith, "Dwindling Flock of St. James Methodist Church Looks to Sell Downtown Waco Landmark," *Waco Tribune-Herald*, December 12, 2015

J. B. Smith, "Buyers of Landmark St. James Methodist Building Hope to Preserve History," *Waco Tribune-Herald*, September 24, 2016

9. First Church of Christ, Scientist (later Olive Branch Christian Fellowship)

Waco News-Tribune, June 10, 1921, 12

Sanborn Maps, 1926, sheet 204; 1926/1950, sheet 204

Greaves and Walker, *Milton W. Scott's Waco*, 27

Personal conversation with Henry W. Wright, July 29, 2020

10. Austin Avenue United Methodist Church (later First Methodist Church Downtown)

Sanborn Map, 1926, sheet 17

TCGAMB, June 1924, 27

Ellis A. Davis and Edwin H. Grobe, eds. and comps., *Encyclopedia of Texas* (Dallas: Texas Development Bureau, 1922), 1:307–8, https://texashistory.unt.edu/ark:/67531/metapth41244/m1/349/

Waco Times-Herald, November 13, 1954, 1

T. Bradford Willis, *A Brief History of the Austin Avenue Methodist Church of Waco, Texas*, 1991, http://files.usgwarchives.net/tx/mclennan/history/1991/abriefhi/abriefhi77nms.txtRobinson, *Reflections of Faith*, 204

Atlantic Terra Cotta Company records, Alexander Architectural Archives, University of Texas Libraries, University of Texas at Austin

11. Waco Central Christian Church (later the Mighty Wind Worship Center)

TGCAMB, July 1924, 28; September 1924, 19

WCCN, 39

12. St. Francis on the Brazos Catholic Church

TGCAMB, November 1928, 25; December 1928, 25; February 1929, 24

Roy E. Lane drawings, Roy E. Lane Papers, Texas Collection, Baylor University

Sanborn Map, 1926/1950, sheet 212

The WPA Guide to Texas, 358

Robinson, *Reflections of Faith*, 147–48

Henry, *Architecture in Texas*, 171

Moorhead, *Buildings of Texas*, 122

13. Herring Avenue Methodist Church (later St. Paul African Methodist Episcopal Church)

Waco News-Tribune, April 29, 1929

TGCAMB, December 1931 (Birch D. Easterwood); January 1932, 18 (N. A. Palmer)

Sanborn Maps, 1926, sheet 271 (1911 church building); 1926/1950, sheet 271 (1932 church building and educational building)

Terri Jo Ryan, "Brazos Past: Waco Methodists Raised a Sanctuary in 1 Day," *Waco Tribune-Herald*, January 8, 2011

14. St. Mary of the Assumption Catholic Church

Sanborn Maps, 1885, sheet 8; 1889, sheet 15; 1893, sheet 11; 1899, sheet 24; 1926, sheet 1; 1926/1950, sheets 1, 202, and 203

Larmour, *Architectural Waco*, 21 (Academy of the Sacred Heart claimed by Larmour)

Bird's Eye Views of Waco, 1873, 1886, and 1892, "Texas Bird's Eye Views," Texas Collection, Baylor University

Waco News-Tribune, July 3, 1940, 12 (Cocke named
    architect); December 10, 1947, 1, 18 (St. Mary's
    School); May 2, 1950, 3 (St. Joseph's Bellmead)
"Church Dedicated at Waco, Texas," *Southern Messenger*,
    March 10, 1910
"$135,000 Catholic Church Is Planned," *Clifton Record*,
    February 28, 1941, 4
Jean L. Berres, "History of St. Mary's Catholic Church
    of the Assumption," 1997, https://stmarys-waco.org/
    history-of-our-parish
 "From the Archives," accessed July 8, 2018, https://
    stmarys-waco.org/photoalbums/from-the-archives
    (historic photos of the church and parish life)
Scardino and Turner, *Clayton's Galveston*, 216–17

15. Columbus Avenue Baptist Church

Waco Daily Times-Herald, August 27, 1906, 5; September
    15, 1906, 4; May 7, 1907, 5; June 10, 1907, 5
Sanborn Maps, 1926, sheet 203; 1926/1950, sheet 203
Jack Winton Gunn, *History of Columbus Avenue Baptist
    Church, Waco, Texas* (Waco: Texian Press, 1970),
    29–32, 45, 74–75, 80
Robinson, *Reflections of Faith*, 226–27

16. St. Alban's Episcopal Church

Waco News-Tribune, January 21, 1950, 10; February 16,
    1952, 10; November 16, 1952, 30
I Chronicles 22:5

**17. Congregation Agudath Jacob (later Sul Ross Senior
Center)**

Sanborn Maps, 1889, sheet 14 (not there); 1893, sheet
    11 (still not there); 1899, sheet 24 (one-story frame
    "school house"); 1926, sheet 2 (there); 1926/1950—
    from plans; 1926/1950, sheet 202 (new building)
"Synagogue and Memorial Center," *Waco News-Tribune*,
    April 15, 1950, 3
Waco Tribune-Herald, September 21, 1969, 12; October 31,
    1971, 11
Terri Jo Ryan, "Congregation Agudath Jacob Marks 120th
    Anniversary," *Waco Tribune-Herald*, March 15, 2008

18. Temple Rodef Sholom

Larmour, *Architectural Waco*, 19
Greaves and Walker, *Milton W. Scott's Waco*, 25
Sanborn Maps, 1889, sheet 9; 1893, sheet 17 (Larmour
    building); 1926, sheet 20 (Scott building)
"Temple Rodef Sholom Dedicated," *Jewish Herald*

(Houston), September 30, 1910, https://texashistory
    .unt.edu/ark:/67531/metapth69019/?q=Waco
Exodus 25, especially 31–37, and Exodus 37, especially
    17–22
Gerald Moorhead, "Wright Face: The Work of MacKie &
    Kamrath," *Cite* (Fall 1988): 19–20, http://offcite.org/
    wp-content/uploads/sites/3/2010/03/WrightFace_
    Moorhead_Cite21.pdf
Robinson, *Reflections of Faith*, 128
Prisca Bird, "Temple Rodef Sholom," *Waco History*,
    accessed July 13, 2018, http://wacohistory.org/items/
    show/17

19. First Methodist Church

Henry J. Steinbomer (1902–64) Drawings, 1940–64,
    Church Architecture in Central Texas, Alexander
    Architectural Archives, University of Texas Libraries,
    University of Texas at Austin (drawings of church
    dated 1962)
Waco Tribune-Herald, September 10, 1961, 1, 10; April
    22, 1962, 1; March 24, 1963, 31; November 23, 1963, 10;
    May 13, 1967, 10; May 11, 1973, 19; August 24, 1975, 17
Waco News-Tribune, September 1, 1962, 6; February 10,
    1968, 10
Waco Citizen, October 30, 1969, 1
San Antonio Express, July 11, 1964, 9-A (Steinbomer
    obituary)

Chapter Two: Commercial Buildings

20. Cornish Building (later Kestner's Dry Goods Store)

Waco City Directories, 1884–85 to 1916
Sanborn Maps, 1893, sheet 24 (frame house); 1899, sheet
    50 (original building); 1926, sheet 72 (remodeled
    building)
Waco Morning News, November 3, 1913, 7 (building
    auctioned)
J. B. Smith, "Slipping Away: In Search of Waco's Most
    Endangered Historic Buildings," *Waco Tribune-
    Herald*, April 19, 2015

21. S. H. Clinton Grocery and Feed Store

Waco City Directories, 1896–97 to 1923–24
Sanborn Maps, 1899, sheet 50 (frame buildings); 1926,
    sheet 73 (brick building)
J. B. Smith, "Slipping Away: In Search of Waco's Most
    Endangered Historic Buildings," *Waco Tribune-
    Herald*, April 19, 2015

22. The Cameron Building

Waco City Directories, 1911–12 to 1951

Sanborn Maps, 1899, sheet 9 (previous building); 1926, sheet 5; 1926/1950, sheet 5

Waco Morning News, January 2, 1913, 8; October 24, 1913, 7

23. Commercial Building

Sanborn Maps, 1889, sheet 8; 1926, sheet 10

Waco City Directories, 1911–12 to 1932–33

24. Bankers Trust Building

Texas Trade Review and Industrial Record (Dallas) 21 (June 15, 1916): 6

Waco City Directories, 1913 to 1923–24

Waco Morning News, October 13, 1915, 27, 55; October 23, 1915, 18; November 22, 1915, 6; January 16, 1916, 2; January 20, 1916, 8

Sanborn Maps, 1926, sheet 6; 1926/1950, sheet 6

Atlantic Terra Cotta Company records, Alexander Architectural Archives, University of Texas Libraries, University of Texas at Austin

Waco Semi-Weekly Tribune, June 5, 1915, p. 2

25. Commercial Building

TGCAMB, March 1923, 28; May 1923, 32; July 1923, 33; December 1923, 34

Sanborn Maps, 1899, sheet 9; 1926, sheet 5; 1926/1950, sheet 5

26. The Cruger Company Building

Waco News-Tribune, January 9, 1923, 3; April 1, 1923, 5; April 5, 1923, 12; June 3, 1923, 14; June 10, 1923, 8 (old location); June 24, 1923, 13 (new location)

Sanborn Maps, 1893, sheet 17; 1899, sheet 30; 1926, sheet 20; 1926/1950, sheet 20

Henry, *Architecture in Texas*, 19–20

Greaves and Walker, *Milton W. Scott's Waco*, 17

27. Central Motor Company

Sanborn Maps, 1893, sheet 17; 1926, sheet 20; 1926/1950, sheet 20

Waco News-Tribune, December 10, 1924, 1

Greaves and Walker, *Milton W. Scott's Waco*, 17

Henry, *Architecture in Texas*, 67–68

Moorhead, *Buildings of Texas*, 124

28. Texas Fireproof Storage Company (later Balcones Distillery)

Waco City Directories, 1921–22, 1923–24

TGCAMB, October 1922, 20; November 1922, 23

Waco News-Tribune, April 1, 1923, 9; April 16, 1923, 3; April 22, 1923, 16

Sanborn Maps, 1926, sheet 21; 1926/1950, sheet 21

29. Citizens National Bank

Waco News-Tribune, July 14, 1926, 8; October 1, 1926, 7; April 5, 1927, 7; August 26, 1927, 12; September 14, 1927, 2; October 23, 1927, 1 (Cameron), 2 (Barnes); April 8, 1928, 11

TGCAMB, December 1926, 25

Sanborn Map, 1926/1950, sheet 6

30. Commercial Building (later Simply Irresistible)

Larmour, *Architectural Waco*, 20 (Higginson house)

TGCAMB, September 1927, 33

Waco Tribune-Herald, September 4, 1927, 2

Waco News-Tribune, October 23, 1927, 1

Sanborn Maps, 1926, sheet 19 (Higginson house); 1950, sheet 19

Chester H. Liebs, *Main Street to Miracle Mile: American Roadside Architecture* (Boston: Little, Brown for the New York Graphic Society, 1985), 10–13 (taxpayers)

31. Commercial Building

TGCAMB, May 1927, 33

Waco News-Tribune, May 18, 1927, 8

Sanborn Maps, 1889, sheet 9; 1893, sheet 17; 1899, sheet 30; 1926, sheet 19 (McMullen house); 1926/1950, sheet 19

32. McDermott Motor Company

TGCAMB, June 1928, 25; September 1928, 25

Sanborn Maps, 1899, sheet 16 (Goldstein and Migel houses); 1926/1950, sheet 204

Greaves and Walker, *Milton W. Scott's Waco*, 23

33. Gulf Filling Station

Sanborn Map, 1926/1950, sheet 202

Waco City Directories, 1930–31

J. B. Smith, "Car-Crazy Brothers Restore Vintage Gulf Station Downtown," *Waco Tribune-Herald*, September 29, 2014

34. Magnolia Filling Station (later Mama and Papa B's Bar-B-Que)

Sanborn Maps, 1926, sheet 28; 1926/1950, sheet 28

W. Dwayne Jones, *A Field Guide to Gas Stations in Texas*, October 2003, http://www.thc.texas.gov/public/upload/preserve/survey/survey/Guide%20Gas%20Stations.pdf

35. Sleeper Building

Waco News-Tribune, April 29, 1928, 16; July 6, 1928, 2; September 2, 1928, 5; September 19, 1928, 9

Sanborn Map, 1926/1950, sheet 20

36. Clemens Building

TGCAMB, December 1928, 15; February 1929, 33

Sanborn Map, 1926/1950, sheet 5

Waco News-Tribune, June 17, 1929

Waco City Directories, 1928, 1930–31

37. The Waco Hippodrome

Waco Morning News, June 25, 1913, 7; June 27, 1913, 2; July 11, 1913, 10; February 8, 1929, 10

Waco Times-Herald, February 7, 1929, 1, 3

Waco Tribune-Herald, September 1, 1929, 23

The Western Architect: A National Journal of Architecture and Allied Arts 20, no. 7 (July 1914): 76 (Hippodrome in Dallas)

Sanborn Maps (Dallas), 1921, sheet 4 (Hippodrome in Dallas); (Waco), 1926, sheet 5; 1926/1950, sheet 5

Yearbook: Texas State Association of Architects, Published by the Convention Committee of the Tenth Annual Convention held at Waco, Texas (Waco, 1917), 31 (copy at the Texas Collection, Baylor University)

Moorhead, *Buildings of Texas*, 124

38. Losavio Grocery Store

US Census, 1910–40

Waco City Directories, 1907–8 to 1936

Sanborn Maps, 1899, sheet 7 (old store); 1926/1950, sheet 314

Waco Tribune-Herald, February 26, 1938, 8; August 28, 1938, 10

Waco News-Tribune, November 2, 1942, 5

39. Elite Café (later Magnolia Table)

"Oral Memoirs of George Nicholas Colias," interview by Vicki Klaras, January 13. 1987, Baylor University Institute for Oral History, transcript, 27–28, https://digitalcollections-baylor.quartexcollections.com/Documents/Detail/oral-memoirs-of-george-nicholas-colias-transcript/1570682

Waco Tribune-Herald, October 12, 1942, 8

40. Sachs Austin Avenue (later Sironia)

Waco News-Tribune, October 14, 1953, 5

Waco Tribune-Herald, October 25, 1953, 14; July 11, 1954, 34

US Census, 1920–40

Historic postcards, https://picclick.com/Sachs-Austin-Avenue-Fashion-Shop-Waco-Texas-TX-330972655187.html; https://business.facebook.com/sironia.waco/

41. Pioneer Savings Association

Waco Tribune-Herald, March 7, 1954, 1, 12; January 1, 1955, 5; January 5, 1955, 16; March 20, 1955, 33; April 28, 1955, 4; July 25, 1955, 2; November 13, 1955, 32; November 20, 1955, 3; November 22, 1955, 24; November 27, 1955, 6

42. First Federal Savings and Loan (later Guaranty Bank)

Waco News-Tribune, March 12, 1959, 2

Waco Tribune-Herald, February 22, 1959, 101; November 8, 1959, 10; June 3, 1960, 56, 58, 61

Mike Copeland, "Old Guaranty Bank Building Bought, to Be Renovated for Downtown Waco Office Space," *Waco Tribune-Herald*, February 22, 2017

Chapter Three: Wholesale and Manufacturing

43. Artesian Manufacturing and Bottling Co. (Dr Pepper Museum and Free Enterprise Institute)

Sanborn Maps, 1899, sheet 8 (Rotan Grocery); 1926, sheet 10

"Contract Let for Big Business Building," *Waco Daily Times-Herald*, February 12, 1906, 8

"The Elgin Press Brick Company," *The Clay-Worker* 45–46, no. 2 (August 1906): 141

The Southern Carbonator and Bottler, September 1906, 39–41

Greaves and Walker, *Milton W. Scott's Waco*, 5, 19

Henry, *Architecture in Texas*, 19–20

Moorhead, *Buildings of Texas*, 124–25

44. McLendon Hardware Company (later River Square Center)

Historic postcards, Texas Collection, Baylor University

Sanborn Maps, 1926, sheet 11; 1926/1950, sheet 11

Greaves and Walker, *Milton W. Scott's Waco*, 21

45. Merrick Medicine Company (later the Findery)

Waco City Directories, 1904–5 to 1916

Sanborn Maps, 1899, sheet 25 (Victorian house); 1926, sheet 28 (current building)

Terri Jo Ryan, "Waco Company Still Producing Medicine Dating to Early 20th Century," *Waco Tribune-Herald*, January 30, 2010

46. Brazos Valley Cotton Oil Mill (later Magnolia Market at the Silos)

Sanborn Maps, 1889, sheet 12; 1893, sheets 13 and 14; 1899, sheet 25; 1926, sheet 29; 1926/1950, sheet 29

J. B. Smith, "HGTV 'Fixer Upper' Stars Planning Move to Downtown Waco with Magnolia Market," *Waco Tribune-Herald*, October 4, 2014

J. B. Smith, "HGTV Stars Get TIF Funds for Magnolia Market, as Does Doris Miller Memorial," *Waco Tribune-Herald*, November 18, 2014

Mike Copeland, "HGTV 'Fixer Upper' Stars See Downtown Waco Silo Project Take Shape," *Waco Tribune-Herald*, April 6, 2015

Mike Copeland, "Magnolia Market Contractor Wins State Award," *Waco Tribune-Herald*, September 9, 2016

47. Hanna-James-Taylor Building (later Holiday Hammond Lofts)

Waco City Directories, 1911–12 to 1951

Sanborn Maps, 1926, sheet 12; 1926/1950, sheet 12

48. Commercial Building

Waco City Directories, 1910 to 1923–24

Sanborn Maps, 1899, sheet 17 (frame houses); 1926, sheet 30; 1926/1950, sheets 9 and 30

Waco News-Tribune, January 11, 1923, 2 (ad for Mason Transfer and Storage Co. at 401 S. Third)

Austin American-Statesman, February 22, 1924, 7 (charter for Crawford-Austin)

Boys' Life, May 1928, 56

Daily Sun (Goose Creek, Texas), July 24, 1940, 4

San Antonio Register, October 9, 1942, 1

49. Texas Telephone Company Exchange

Waco Morning News, October 31, 1915, 91

Telephony 71, no. 16 (October 14, 1916): 20–23

Sanborn Map, 1926, sheet 20

50. Williams Dry Goods Company (later Waco Dry Goods, later Altura Luxury Lofts)

Waco City Directories, 1916 to 1923–24

Sanborn Map, 1926, sheet 10

"The Mercantile Trust Company of St. Louis Transacts Business in Texas," *El Paso Herald*, October 30, 1919, 7

"Williams Dry Goods Company Occupies 75,000 Square Feet of Floor Space—but That's Not All," *Waco News-Tribune*, April 2, 1922 16

Waco News-Tribune, February 11, 1923, 14; October 24, 1926, 1

J. B. Smith, "98-Year-Old Downtown Waco Warehouse to Become Lofts with Prime Views," *Waco Tribune-Herald*, August 10, 2015

51. Miller Cotton Mill (later L. L. Sams and Sons Manufacturing Company, now L. L. Sams Historic Lofts)

Waco News Tribune, October 28, 1919, 15; November 1, 1919, 11; November 5, 1919, 3; November 25, 1919, 9; November 27, 1919, 11; June 4, 1920, 12; May 21, 1921, 3; January 17, 1922, 7

Christopher Long, "Hedrick, Wyatt Cephas," *Handbook of Texas Online*, accessed June 22, 2021, https://www.tshaonline.org/handbook/entries/hedrick-wyatt-cephas

Amanda Sawyer, "L. L. Sams and Sons," *Waco History*, accessed June 22, 2021, https://wacohistory.org/items/show/77

Geoff Hunt, "Texas Buildings over Time: Miller Cotton Mills (L. L. Sams Building) at 100 Years, 1920–2020, Waco Texas," posted January 15, 2020, https://blogs.baylor.edu/texascollection/2020/01/15/miller-cotton-mills-ll-sams-building/

52. Waco Drug Company (later Insurors of Texas Building)

Waco City Directories, 1910 to 1926

"Waco Is Building Up-to-Date Structures," *Waco Semi-Weekly Tribune*, May 20, 1911, 4

"The Mercantile Trust Company of St. Louis Transacts Business in Texas," *El Paso Herald*, October 30, 1919, 7

"Waco Has It," *Waco News-Tribune*, April 2, 1922, 6

"If You Doubt Revival of Business and Activity of Central Texas Trade Visit the Waco Drug Company," *Waco News-Tribune*, February 11, 1923, 11

Waco News-Tribune, April 1, 1923, 9

TGCAMB, December 1922, 21

Sanborn Map, 1926, sheet 10

Margaret Swett Henson and Deolece Parmelee, *The Cartwrights of San Augustine: Three Generations of Agricultural Entrepreneurs in Nineteenth-Century Texas* (Austin: Texas State Historical Association, 1993), 297–99, 310–11
Greaves and Walker, *Milton W. Scott's Waco*, 22

53. Coca-Cola Bottling Company
Sanborn Map, 1926/1950, sheet 17
Larmour, *Architectural Waco*, 15
Cornerstone (Derrah and Pearson)
Waco Tribune-Herald, June 26, 1938, 33
Sarah Miller, "William Cameron House," *Waco History*, accessed December 29, 2018, https://wacohistory.org/items/show/151

54. Southwestern Bell Telephone Company (later McLennan County Archives)
Waco News-Tribune, June 3, 1947, 14; August 26, 1947, 1; October 26, 1947, 33; June 25, 1954, 30
Sanborn Map, 1926/1950, sheet 20

Chapter Four: Skyscrapers

55. Amicable Life Insurance Company Building (ALICO)
Original drawings of the building, "Sanguinet, Staats and Hedrick Collection," Alexander Architectural Archive, University of Texas at Austin
Sanborn Map, 1926, sheet 6
Waco Tribune-Herald, September 20, 1964, 2; December 6, 1964, 1, 19; May 16, 1965, 112; October 28, 1965, 52
Waco News-Tribune, October 15, 1965, 1
Henry, *Architecture in Texas*, 133–34
Judith Singer Cohen, *Cowtown Moderne: Art Deco Architecture of Fort Worth, Texas* (College Station: Texas A&M University Press, 1988), 22, 53–59, 70–73, 77–83, 122–35, 156–60 (Koeppe), and 39–46 (Finn)
Moorhead, *Buildings of Texas*, 122
John S. Wilson and Geoff Hunt, *Gildersleeve: Waco's Photographer* (Waco: 1845 Books, 2019), 284–91

56. Riggins Hotel (later the Raleigh Hotel, now an office building)
Sanborn Map, 1926, sheet 20
The Tradesman 70 (September 10, 1913): 36
Hotel Monthly 47 (February 1916): 80, 89; (March 1916): 46
TGCAMB, December 1928, 25

Historic postcards, https://www.amazon.com/Riggins-Fireproof-Original-Vintage-Postcard/dp/B00S9CEUD4; https://www.ebay.com/itm/402517242495; and https://blogs.baylor.edu/texascollection/2018/05/22/texas-over-time-raleigh-building-waco-t https://blogs.baylor.edu/texascollection/2018/05/22/texas-over-time-raleigh-building-waco-tx/
Henry, *Architecture in Texas*, 50–52
Moorhead, *Buildings of Texas*, 124

57. The Praetorian Building
Waco City Directories, 1916 and 1917–18
Sanborn Maps, 1926, sheet 5; 1926/1950, sheet 5

58. Liberty National Bank Building (later One Liberty Place)
Waco News-Tribune, April 1, 1923, 9; April 18, 1923, 8 (Easterwood and King offices); May 19, 1923, 1, 3, and 7 (grand opening); May 25, 1924, 29 ("Some Easterwood Landmarks")
Sanborn Map, 1926, sheet 5
Bankers Monthly (September 1922), 108
Geoff Hunt, "A Disastrous Season in Waco: The Liberty Building Explosion, Fall 1936," posted July 10, 2014, http://blogs.baylor.edu/texascollection/2014/07/10/a-disastrous-season-in-waco-the-liberty-building-explosion-fall-1936/

59. Stratton Building
Waco News-Tribune, September 20, 1922, 7; December 24, 1922, 18; March 18, 1923, 12; June 30, 1923, 10
TGCAMB, October 1922, 20; November 1922, 19; December 1922, 21
Sanborn Map, 1926, sheet 20

60. Hilton Hotel / Roosevelt Hotel / Roosevelt Tower
TGCAMB, June 1927, 26; August 1927, 33; February 1929, 24; March 1929, 23; May 1929, 32
Sanborn Map, 1926/1950, sheet 6
Amanda Sawyer, "Roosevelt Hotel," *Waco History*, accessed January 6, 2018, http://www.wacohistory.org/items/show/41
Moorhead, *Buildings of Texas*, 122
Atlantic Terra Cotta Company records, Alexander Architectural Archives, University of Texas Libraries, University of Texas at Austin

61. Medical Arts Building (later National Lloyd's Building)

TGCAMB, September 1927, 27; October 1927, 25; January 1928, 26

Waco News-Tribune, September 20, 1927, 1; September 21, 1927, 1; November 17, 1927, 14; April 1, 1928, 24; May 5, 1928, 9; May 12, 1928, 3; May 21, 1928, 5; September 12, 1928, 1; September 13, 1928, 7; September 17, 1928, 8; October 17, 1928, 5; October 25, 1928, 10; November 11, 1928, 49; November 18, 1928, 6; January 5, 1929, 12; January 6, 1929, 25; February 17, 1929, 5; March 1, 1929, 5; March 6, 1929, 8; April 5, 1929, 5; June 16, 1929, 22

Sanborn Map, 1926/1950, sheet 20

Moorhead, *Buildings of Texas*, 124

62. First National Bank Building

Larmour, *Architectural Waco*, 21

Scardino and Turner, *Clayton's Galveston*, 216–17

Southern Messenger, March 10, 1910

Waco News-Tribune, August 24, 1954, 1, 15; August 25, 1954, 1, 16; October 1, 1954, 5

Sanguinet, Staats and Hedrick, Drawings, photographs and archival records, 1910–69, 1981, Alexander Architectural Archives, University of Texas Libraries, University of Texas at Austin (drawings for First National Bank by Hedrick, 1955)

Carl Hoover, "1950s Mural to Remain out of Sight, but Hopes Remain for Future Display," *Waco Tribune-Herald*, August 7, 2010

Katie Robinson Edwards, *Midcentury Modern Art in Texas* (Austin: University of Texas Press, 2014), 153–59 (Stanley Fogel)

Waco News-Citizen, February 22, 1962, 1 (tower)

Waco News-Tribune, March 16, 1963, 22; April 1, 1963, 1; November 13, 1963, 15 (tower)

Waco Tribune-Herald, November 29, 1964, 19 (tower)

Chapter Five: Public Buildings

63. Waco Suspension Bridge

Sanborn Maps, 1885, sheets 2 and 3; 1889, sheets 2 and 18; 1893, sheets 3 and 23; 1899, sheets 2 and 51

The WPA Guide to Texas, 357–58

Moorhead, *Buildings of Texas*, 125

64. West End Fire Station

Waco City Directories, 1890–91 to 1951

Sanborn Maps, 1926, sheet 19; 1926/1950, sheet 19

65. McLennan County Courthouse

Sanborn Maps, 1899, sheets 2 (old courthouse), 16 (site of new courthouse), and 7 (across from new courthouse); 1926, sheet 2 (new courthouse)

Robinson, *The People's Architecture*, 200–207

Chris Meister, *James Riely Gordon: His Courthouses and Other Public Architecture* (Lubbock: Texas Tech University Press, 2011), 185–90

Moorhead, *Buildings of Texas*, 122

66. Waco Water Pumping Station

Waco City Directories, 1898–99 to 1923–24, especially 1904–5, 2, 35

Sanborn Maps, 1889, sheet 8; 1893, sheet 16; 1899, sheet 4; 1926, sheet 92; 1926/1950, sheet 92

W. M. Sleeper, "History of the Water Plant at Waco under a Water Commission," *Fire Engineering*, May 17, 1916, https://www.fireengineering.com/leadership/history-of-the-water-plant-at-waco-under-a-water-commission/#gref

J. B. Smith, "Slipping Away: In Search of Waco's Most Endangered Historic Buildings," *Waco Tribune-Herald*, April 19, 2015

67. Waco City Hall

Sanborn Maps, 1926, sheet 7 (old City Hall); 1926/1950, sheet 7 (new City Hall)

TGCAMB, December 1930, 20; October 1931, 16; November 1931, 21; March 1932, 14

"Fire Station to Be Erected at Waco," *Dallas Morning News*, November 9, 1931, sec. 2, 6

"Meers Builds Fire Department into Smooth Machine," *Waco Tribune-Herald*, June 25, 1939, copy in vertical file at Texas Collection, Baylor University

68. Central Fire Station and Drill Tower

Sanborn Maps, 1893, sheet 10 (old Central Station); 1926/1950, sheet 204 (new Central Station)

TGCAMB, June 1928, 25; February 1929, 24; June 1929, 26; July 1929, 24; August 1929, 17

Larmour, *Architectural Waco*, 13

Robinson, *The People's Architecture*, 292–93

69. Waco Veterans Administration Hospital (Doris Miller Department of Veterans Affairs Medical Center)

TGCAMB, June 1930, 26; February 1931, 11

The WPA Guide to Texas, 362

Cynthia Field, *The Nation Builds for Those Who Served: An Introduction to the Architectural Heritage of the Veterans Administration* (Washington, DC: The Veterans Administration and the National Building Museum, 1980), 23

Michael C. Quinn (with research by Peter Flagg Maxson), National Register nomination for "Veterans Administration Hospital Historic District," February 7, 1994

Waco City Directories, 1932–33

70. United States Courthouse

TGCAMB, February 1933, 10; April 1933, 8

Waco News-Tribune, February 13, 1933, 1; May 29, 1935, 2; September 4, 1935, 1, 6; October 31, 1935, 1; December 3, 1935, 10

Waco Tribune-Herald, October 6, 1935, 13; November 10, 1935, 1; November 24, 1935, 21; March 21, 1937, 23

Sanborn Map, 1926/1950, sheet 22

Greaves and Walker, *Milton W. Scott's Waco*, 44–45

Philip Parisi, *The Texas Post Office Murals: Art for the People* (College Station: Texas A&M University Press, 2004), 102, 144, 161

71. Waco-McLennan County Library

Sanborn Maps, 1926, sheet 19 (Carnegie library); 1926/1950, sheet 13 (Cameron house)

Original plans by Roy E. Lane for Cameron house, Texas Collection, Baylor University

Plans for 1961 building by Bush and Witt, Waco-McLennan County Public Library

Waco News-Citizen, February 20, 1962, 14

Robert Darden, *An Austin Avenue Legacy: 100 Years with the Waco-McLennan County Library* (Waco: Waco-McLennan County Library, 1997)

Terri Jo Ryan, "Waco Past," *Waco Tribune-Herald*, July 30, 2008

Don Bolding, "Renovated Waco Central Library Reopens to Awe, Fanfare," *Waco Tribune-Herald*, February 24, 2013

72. Bledsoe-Miller Recreation Community Center

Waco Tribune-Herald, September 8, 1946, 10; February 2, 1947, 37

Waco News-Tribune, June 11, 1947, 5; January 20, 1971, 1, 20; May 15, 1973, 3

Waco Citizen, January 21, 1971, 1; June 3, 1971, 8; August 19, 1971, 23; November 25, 1971, 7; September 7, 1972, 7

Chapter Six: Education

73. Old Main and Georgia Burleson Hall, Baylor University

Fort Worth Gazette, June 19, 1886, 3

Sanborn Maps, 1889, sheets 12 (old Baylor) and 17 (new Baylor); 1893, sheet 22; 1899, sheet 40; 1926, sheet 56

Larmour, *Architectural Waco*, 3

The WPA Guide to Texas, 361

Willard B. Robinson and Todd Webb, *Texas Public Buildings of the 19th Century* (Austin: University of Texas Press for the Amon Carter Museum of Western Art, 1974), 145, 186

Kenneth Hafertepe, *Abner Cook: Master Builder on the Texas Frontier* (Austin: Texas State Historical Association, 1992), 163–65 (Agricultural and Mechanical College)

Moorhead, *Buildings of Texas*, 126

74. Carroll Science Hall and Carroll Chapel and Library (Carroll Library), Baylor University

The Lariat, May 4, 1901, 1; August 17, 1901, 1; September 7, 1901, 7; November 9, 1901, 1, 3; August 9, 1902, 1

Joseph Bradfield Thoburn, *A Standard History of Oklahoma* (Chicago: American Historical Society, 1916), 4:1537 (biography of S. Wemyss-Smith)

TGCAMB, August 1922, 21; October 1922, 20; November 1922, 23; December 1922, 11

Waco News-Tribune, April 1, 1923, 9

Sanborn Map, 1926, sheet 56

75. Waco High School (later Historic Lofts at Waco High)

B. B. Paddock, *A History of Central and Western Texas* (Chicago: Lewis Publishing, 1911), 1:287–88

TGCAMB, July 1924, 28; October 1928, 24; November 1928, 33

Waco News-Tribune, June 17, 1929

Sanborn Maps, 1926, sheet 1; 1926/1950, sheet 1

Greaves and Walker, *Milton W. Scott's Waco*

Moorhead, *Buildings of Texas*, 124

76. First District School, Colored (later the Helen Marie Taylor Museum)

Sanborn Maps, 1889, sheet 13 (Second District School); 1899, sheet 23 (First District School); 1926, sheet 211; 1926/1950, sheet 211

Bruce Glasrud and Merline Pitre, *Black Women in Texas History* (College Station: Texas A&M University Press, 2008), 85

77. William Decker Johnson Hall, Paul Quinn College

Sanborn Maps, 1899, sheet 53; 1926, sheet 75; 1926/1950, sheet 75

Dallas Express, January 8, 1921, 5; March 12, 1921, 3; May 7, 1921, 3; December 16, 1922, 5; June 16, 1923, 1; December 29, 1923, 1; September 20, 1924, 3; October 4, 1924, 3

Houston Informer, November 10, 1923, 4

The WPA Guide to Texas, 360

Moorhead, *Buildings of Texas*, 127

J. B. Smith, "Slipping Away: In Search of Waco's Most Endangered Historic Buildings," *Waco Tribune-Herald*, April 19, 2015

78. Women's Memorial Dormitory, Baylor University

Blueprints, in Baylor University Archive, Architecture Collection

Daily Lariat, May 31, 1927, 2; October 11, 1928, 1, 2, 4; October 24, 1928, 1; May 23, 1929, 1; October 15, 1930, 1

Waco News-Tribune, October 9, 1928, 1–2; October 25, 1928, 5; December 20, 1928, 7

Corsicana Daily Sun, May 7, 1929, 16

Brownsville Herald, May 27, 1929, 5

TGCAMB, March 1929, 23; June 1929, 26, 33

The WPA Guide to Texas, 361

Sanborn Map, 1926/1950, sheet 56

Atlantic Terra Cotta Company records, Alexander Architectural Archives, University of Texas Libraries, University of Texas at Austin

79. Waco Hall, Baylor University

Blueprints, Baylor University Archive, Architecture Collection

The WPA Guide to Texas, 361

Sanborn Map, 1926/1950, sheet 59

Henry, *Architecture in Texas*, 201–2

Atlantic Terra Cotta Company records, Alexander Architectural Archives, University of Texas Libraries, University of Texas at Austin

80a. Pat Neff Hall, Baylor University

Blueprints, Baylor University Archive, Architecture Collection

Waco News-Tribune, July 17, 1938, 15; August 10, 1938, 1; October 16, 1940, 5

Clifton Record, September 1, 1939, 1

Graham Leader, January 11, 1940, 9

Shamrock Texan, February 1, 1940, 7

Waco Tribune-Herald, January 12, 2001, 1C

The WPA Guide to Texas, 361

Sanborn Map, 1926/1950, sheet 56

Henry, *Architecture in Texas*, 100–101

Moorhead, *Buildings of Texas*, 126

81. East Waco Junior High School

Sanborn Maps, 1926, sheet 88; 1926/1950, sheet 88

Plaque on front of building

Waco News-Tribune, September 5, 1940, 3

82. Bill Daniel Student Center, Baylor University

Waco News-Tribune, May 31, 1947, 10

Sanborn Map, 1926/1950, sheet 56

Carol McMichael, *Paul Cret at Texas: Architectural Drawing and the Image of the University in the 1930s* (Austin: Archer M. Huntington Art Gallery, University of Texas at Austin, 1983), 76–81, 172–77

Hank Todd Smith, ed., *Austin: Its Architects and Architecture (1836–1986)* (Austin: Austin Chapter, American Institute of Architects and Heritage Society of Austin, 1986), 10, 41, 72–73

83. Armstrong Browning Library, Baylor University

A. Joseph Armstrong, "The New Browning Library," *Baylor Bulletin* 47, no. 3 (September 1944): 3–56

Blueprints, Baylor University Archive, Architecture Collection

Waco News-Tribune, July 29, 1948, 1; January 4, 1950, 16; September 12, 1950, 1; May 25, 1951, 1; November 9, 1951, 2; November 30, 1951, 14; December 5, 1951, 13

Waco Tribune-Herald, October 30, 1949, sec. III, 20; September 10, 1950, 51; January 7, 1951, 32; December 2, 1951, 37

Daily Lariat, February 24, 1950, 1, 9; November 30, 1951, 1

Sanborn Map, 1926/1950, sheet 59

Roy E. Mayes, "Marble at Its Best," *Stone* 73, no. 3 (March 1952)

Orin E. Skinner, "Connick in Retrospect," *Stained Glass* (Spring 1975): 16–19

84. Tidwell Bible Building, Baylor University

Blueprints, Baylor University Archive, Architecture Collection

Baylor Lariat, May 31, 1937; November 24, 1944, 1; April 4, 1947, 5; October 14, 1954, 1; July 21, 1960

Waco Tribune-Herald, February 23, 1947, 12; October 17, 1954, 1

Waco News-Tribune, April 13, 1948, 15; January 2, 1950, 1; August 3, 1952, 1; October 23, 1954, 2

E. R. Buckley and H. A. Buehler, *Quarrying Industry of Missouri*, vol. 2 (Jefferson City, MO: Tribune Printing, 1904), chapter 8 and plates 18 and 19, https://quarriesandbeyond.org/states/mo/mo-quarrying_indust_mo_1904_3a.html#chapter_6

Corpus Christi Times, January 5, 1964 (Ira Correll obituary)

Austin American, July 13, 1952, 16

Sanborn Map, 1926/1950, sheet 59

Henry, *Architecture in Texas*, 72–73, 106–7

85. Bishop Joseph Gomez Administration Building, Paul Quinn College

Sanborn Maps, 1899, sheet 53; 1926, sheet 75; 1926/1950, sheet 75

The WPA Guide to Texas, 360

Moorhead, *Buildings of Texas*, 127

Brandice Nelson, "Paul Quinn College," *Waco History*, accessed June 3, 2018, http://wacohistory.org/items/show/79

J. B. Smith, "Slipping Away: In Search of Waco's Most Endangered Historic Buildings," *Waco Tribune-Herald*, April 19, 2015

Chapter Seven: Masonic Buildings and Museums

86. Masonic Lodge #92

Sanborn Maps, 1889, sheet 6 (corner of lot empty); 1893, sheet 12 (small-frame meat market on corner); 1899, sheet 9 (one-story brick store); 1926, sheet 5

"Masonic Temple" (unsigned architectural rendering), in *Waco—the Hub of Texas* (Waco: Young Men's Business League, 1912)

"Will Soon Dedicate Masonic Building," *Waco Daily Times-Herald*, December 21, 1913

Greaves and Walker, *Milton W. Scott's Waco*, 26, 44

87. Grand Karem Shrine Building

TGCAMB, December 1923; September 1925, 25; November 1927, 24; December 1927, 26; January 1928, 33

Sanborn Maps, 1885, sheet 8; 1889, sheet 15; 1893, sheet 11; 1899, sheet 24; 1926, sheet 1 (Baker house); 1926/1950, sheet 1 (Grand Karem Shrine)

Larmour, *Architectural Waco*, 20 (Waller Baker house, as Walter S. Baker house)

Waco City Directories, 1896–97 to 1923–24

Dallas Morning News, February 5, 1928, 4; September 16, 1928, 8

Christopher Long, "Greene, Herbert Miller," *Handbook of Texas Online*, accessed July 4, 2018, http://www.tshaonline.org/handbook/online/articles/fgr94

J. B. Smith, "Grand Karem Shrine Building Downtown Could Become Joint County-City Project," *Waco Tribune-Herald*, March 1, 2016

Cassie L. Smith, "No Offers to Buy Downtown Grand Karem Shrine Building," *Waco Tribune-Herald*, May 15, 2018

Mike Copeland, "Waco's Power Couple to Turn Former Grand Karem Shrine Building into Hotel," *Waco Tribune-Herald*, October 3, 2019

88. Masonic Grand Lodge Memorial Temple of Texas

Sanborn Maps, 1889, sheet 15; 1893, sheet 11; 1926, sheet 6 (Temple on Franklin); 1926/1950, sheet 1

The WPA Guide to Texas, 360 (Flanders)

"James Edward Flanders: Dallas' First Architect," accessed July 5 2018, http://jameseflanders.homestead.com/JEFChapter7.html

"Administrative History of Broad and Nelson," an inventory of Donald S. Nelson's architectural records, drawing, and photographs, Alexander Architectural Archives, University of Texas Libraries, University of Texas at Austin, https://legacy.lib.utexas.edu/taro/utaaa/00042/aaa-00042.html

"Masonic Section," *Waco Tribune-Herald*, December 6, 1949, especially 4, 6, 10

Waco Tribune-Herald, September 27, 1969, 36

Moorhead, *Buildings of Texas*, 122

Jack Sheridan, obituary of Raoul Josset, *Lubbock Avalanche-Journal*, undated but reproduced as part of an inventory of his records and photographs, Alexander Architectural Archives, University of Texas Libraries, University of Texas at Austin, https://legacy.lib.utexas.edu/taro/utaaa/00026/aaa-00026.html

François Lagarde, "Raoul Josset and the 1936 Texas Centennial," in *The French in Texas: History, Migration, Culture*, ed. François Lagarde (Austin: University of Texas Press, 2003), 287–92

89. Lee Lockwood Library and Museum

Waco Tribune-Herald, March 10, 1968, 20; September 27, 1969, 36

Waco Citizen, February 27, 1969, 49

Dayton Kelley, ed., *The Handbook of Waco and McLennan County, Texas* (Waco: Texian Press, 1972), 159

90. Texas Ranger Hall of Fame and Museum

Waco News-Tribune, October 25, 1967, 2; November 14, 1967, 11; November 15, 1967, 1; December 5, 1967, 2; December 13, 1967, 1; October 21, 1968, 4; May 24, 1973, 16

Waco Tribune-Herald, January 31, 1968, 16; March 24, 1968, 19; August 3, 1974, 1; September 4, 1974, 16; January 8, 1976, 1

J. B. Smith, "Texas Ranger Hall of Fame and Museum Expansion to Open Up Scholarly Research," *Waco Tribune-Herald*, August 11, 2011

Waco Citizen, August 10, 1972, 20; June 28, 1973, 4; March 7, 1974, 10; July 3, 1981, 1; August 28, 1981, 18; July 27, 1982, 1; August 24, 1982, 2; July 5, 1985, 1; September 29, 1989, 9; November 13, 1981, 1; December 20, 1988, 1

West News (West, Texas), April 10, 1970, 7

Roger N. Conger, "Fort Fisher: The Texas Ranger Museum at Waco," in *Antique Arms Annual*, 1971, reprinted in *Waco's Champion: Selections from the Papers of Roger Norman Conger*, ed. and bibliographer Marion Travis (Waco: Historic Waco Foundation, 1990), 195–98